NECESSITY AND LANGUAGE

NECESSITY AND LANGUAGE

MORRIS LAZEROWITZ AND ALICE AMBROSE

ST. MARTIN'S PRESS
New York

Library of Congress Cataloging in Publication Data

Lazerowitz, Morris, 1909–
    Necessity and language.

    Includes index.
    1. Philosophy—addresses, essays, lectures.
2. Necessity (philosophy)—addresses, essays, lectures.
3. Analysis (philosophy)—addresses, essays, lectures.
4. Mathematics—philosophy—addresses, essays, lectures.
I. Ambrose, Alice, 1906–   II. Title.
B29.L32   1985   149'.943   85-22201

ISBN 0-312-56259-4

Printed in Great Britain

CONTENTS

ACKNOWLEDGEMENTS

Those papers in this volume which have been previously published originally appeared as follows

1. Necessity and Language in *Ludwig Wittgenstein. Philosophy and Language* (Allen & Unwin, London, 1972). Reprinted by permission of the publisher.
2. Factual, Mathematical and Metaphysical Inventories in *Essays in Analysis* (Allen & Unwin, London, 1966). Reprinted by permission of the publisher.
3. A Priori Truths and Empirical Confirmation in *Critica*, Vol. XV, no. 44 (1983), published by permission of the editor.
4. Assuming the Logically Impossible in *Metaphilosophy*, vol. 15 (1984), published by permission of the editor.
5. Invention and Discovery in *Essays in Analysis* (Allen & Unwin, London, 1966). Reprinted by permission of the publisher.
6. Mathematical Generality in *Ludwig Wittgenstein. Philosophy and Language* (Allen & Unwin, London, 1966). Reprinted by permission of the publisher.
7. The Infinite in Mathematics in *The Language of Philosophy* (D. Reidel Pub. Co., 1977). Reprinted by permission of the publisher.
8. The Metaphysical Concept of Space in *Studies in Metaphilosophy* (Routledge & Kegan Paul, 1964). Reprinted by permission of the publisher.
9. The Passing of an Illusion in *The Language of Philosophy* (D. Reidel Pub. Co., 1977). Reprinted by permission of the publisher.

EDITOR'S INTRODUCTION

It is no easy task to introduce a seminal work in philosophy. One's immediate impulse is to try to survey and if possible summarise the myriad of crucial insights contained in the work in question. But such an inclination is plainly too ambitious; a folly born from the lingering belief that the solution — or rather, dissolution — of philosophical problems can somehow be simplified or foreshortened. There are a host of penetrating arguments contained in these papers which, when they have finally been fully understood and digested, will have a major impact on the development of analytic philosophy and the philosophy of mathematics; indeed, on philosophy *simpliciter*. The most that I can hope to accomplish in this brief introduction is to provide a starting point from which to approach this book by crystallising what is perhaps the principal theme of this particular volume of Lazerowitz and Ambrose's writings.

The problem of necessity remains one of the most pressing issues in modern philosophy. While philosophers have vainly struggled to elucidate the nature of necessity by investigating the manner in which we recognise necessary truths, or by identifying the source of necessity, Alice Ambrose and Morris Lazerowitz have elucidated and developed Wittgenstein's radical and somewhat schematic approach to the problem in a manner which has dramatic implications, not only for our understanding of the nature of necessity, but for the very practice of resolving a philosophical problem. By focusing on the logical grammar of necessary propositions, the authors have demonstrated that even before we can make sense of the putatively 'epistemological' or 'ontological' dimensions of the problem of necessity, we must first clarify what it is for a proposition to be necessary; and this is entirely a question of logical grammar. But then, once we have clarified this logical matter, no so-called 'twofold problem of necessity' remains to trouble us; we have already said all that can or need be said about what constitutes a necessary truth: about what constitutes the necessity of those propositions which are 'unshakeably certain'.

It cannot be stressed too highly how significant this argument is, not merely for the clarification of so major a philosophical issue, but, even more importantly, for our understanding of the nature of a philosophical question *per se*, and hence of the manner in which such problems are to be resolved. It is not — as the authors have so categorically established — via the construction of a philosophical *theory*. Rather, the route to enlightenment lies in the patient and meticulous clarification of the logical grammar of the expressions which have generated our puzzlement. Propositions such as '2 + 2 = 4' or 'Nothing can be red and green all over simultaneously' have long been the source of profound philosophical perplexity, from whence have issued the elaborate metaphysical systems which have proliferated throughout the history of philosophy. In the following essays the authors rigorously elucidate the manner in which philosophy must clarify why it is that such seemingly innocuous expressions give rise to spurious metaphysical, ontological or epistemological worries; and thence, to clarify why the theories built up in response to the confusions generated by such propositions transgress the bounds of logical grammar.

In those cases given above, our puzzlement arises chiefly from the failure to grasp that the expressions involved are grammatical conventions, not empirical propositions, which are used as norms of representation which fix the use of concepts, not ordinary descriptions that are (contingently) true or false. It is precisely by treating them as empirical propositions, however, that we are led into the traditional metaphysical or sceptical muddles which have for so long plagued philosophy. For, when viewed in such a light it seems only natural to search for the source of our knowledge or the grounds of our certainty that such a fact is true. But such incoherent questions only set us off on the abortive tasks of trying to transcend the bounds of sense or of seeking to discount doubts which are not irrefutable but are rather unintelligible. What the authors ultimately bring us to see is essentially that the solution to such typical philosophical dilemmas lies, not in the construction of transcendental arguments or the quest for the supra-sensible foundations of our knowledge, but rather in the precise clarification of the logical grammar of the expressions which have given rise to confusion.

The consequence of such a *philosophical* investigation is that the supposedly metaphysical 'truth' involved turns out to be nothing more than a 'shadow of a rule of grammar'. That is, it is by disclosing the linguistic conventions which underpin such propositions that we dispel the metaphysical shadows cast by grammar. The misguided attempt to transcend the bounds of sense will abruptly cease when the philosopher recognises that he has been trying to formulate answers to nonsensical 'questions'. Likewise, apparently unresolvable sceptical dilemmas will only vanish once it has been understood that we are dealing with grammatical conventions: autonomous expressions which stand in no need of justification because they are antecedent to truth. For the rules of grammar determine what makes sense, they cannot themselves be true or false. There is no such thing as justifying grammar by reference to reality, therefore, because any description of reality presupposes grammatical rules, and thus cannot be employed to justify those rules.

The significance of this argument — for both analytic philosophy and the philosophy of mathematics — is still far from having been fully absorbed. This collection of Lazerowitz and Ambrose's major essays on the fundamental issues involved will go a long way towards correcting this situation. Gathered here in a single volume are some of their most influential essays on the problem of necessity, together with stimulating new material in which the authors continue to break important fresh ground. This collection will thus quickly establish itself as one of the classics of contemporary philosophy, the fruits of two of our most gifted and influential philosophers.

S. G. SHANKER
CHRIST CHURCH, OXFORD

1 NECESSITY AND LANGUAGE

Wann man sich von der Wahrheit fürchtet (wie ich
jetzt), so ahnt man nie die *volle* Wahrheit.

(Wittgenstein)

Underlying much of Wittgenstein's later thinking was the wish to
reach a correct understanding of the nature of philosophical utterances, and this wish is also discernible in his *Tractatus*.[1] His later
investigations led him to some iconoclastic ideas about what a philosophical theory is and what a philosopher does who supports his
theory with an argument. Wittgenstein saw more deeply into philosophy than anyone before him, but, for the most part, he seemed to
prefer to express his perceptions in metaphorical language rather
than in the language of straightforward reportage. Part of the reason
for this may have been the wish to soften the hard things he saw.
Remarks like 'philosophical problems arise when language *goes on
holiday*'[2] and philosophical language is 'like an engine idling, not
when it is doing work'[3] give expression to disturbing perceptions into
the nature of technical philosophy, but use a form of the mechanism
of *sotto voce* to deflect them. Where their translations into prosaic
language would tend to stir up anxiety, these words can be accepted
as colourful jibes which need not be taken seriously.

It is important to notice that he stated in a number of places that
philosophical propositions are not empirical. This insight into the
nature of philosophical propositions (and into the modes of investigation employed in philosophy) made it fundamentally important
for him to understand the logical difference between empirical statements and statements which have *a priori* necessity, and especially
to understand the nature of necessity, to obtain, so to speak, an
inside look at it. He appears to have emerged with a conventionalist
view, which on the surface at least he seems never to have given up.
This is the view, generally speaking, that necessary propositions are
about the literal use of terminology in a language. A number of
writers have described him as a conventionalist, and it must be
allowed that there is considerable justification for this description.
One of his frequently cited expressions, 'rule of grammar', which he
used to characterise necessary propositions, unquestionably lends

some substance to the claim that he took one of the traditional positions about logical necessitation. On one occasion G. E. Moore, who was puzzled by the term 'rule of grammar', remarked to me that he thought Wittgenstein meant by it what is meant by the more familiar term 'necessary proposition'. My impression at the time was that Moore thought Wittgenstein was so using 'rule of grammar' that in his use of the term a rule of grammar was *not* verbal. Moore's line of reasoning was perhaps the following: a rule of grammar in Wittgenstein's sense is a necessary proposition, and since a necessary proposition says nothing about usage, a rule of grammar says nothing about usage. There can be no doubt, however, that Wittgenstein wished by his special use of the word 'grammar' to say that *in some way* necessary propositions are verbal.

I

Conventionalism is open to a number of obvious objections which Wittgenstein must have known. It is worth remarking that conventionalists who are aware of these objections are not moved to give up their position. This is mystifying and certainly calls for an examination, for if conventionalism is taken at face value as making a factual claim about the nature of necessary propositions, the objections are as conclusive as any objections could possibly be. One frequently repeated criticism is that to suppose a necessary proposition to be one which makes a declaration about verbal usage, or one which 'records usage', is to imply that a necessary proposition is not necessary. The negation of a true verbal proposition is a false verbal proposition, but not a proposition which could not, in principle, be true. Put roughly, the negation of a true verbal proposition is not a self-contradiction, and precisely the same kind of investigation which establishes the truth of a verbal proposition, such as recourse to dictionaries and the like, could theoretically establish its denial. To use an expression of Wittgenstein's, we know what it would be like for a verbal proposition, which happens to be true, to be false, and for one which is false to be true. By contrast, we do not know what it would be like for a false arithmetical *proposition* to be true — for example, for 4 + 3 to be less than 7. Taken literally, the *philosophical* claim that necessary propositions are about usage is refuted with complete finality by the objection that the view that they are implies that they are not necessary.

Another well-known objection is that a necessary proposition does not say anything about terminology, because it says nothing about what language it is expressed in or about any words occurring in it. The two sentences 'Red is a colour' and 'Rot ist eine Farbe' have the same meaning, which would not be the case if the propositions expressed in the English sentence made a declaration about words occurring in the sentence, and the proposition expressed in the German sentence made a declaration about words occurring in it. Wittgenstein certainly was aware of these objections, and there is reason to think that his conventionalism, which undoubtedly was the usual philosophical article at first, was transformed by his growing insight into the way language works.

Verbal usage and logical necessity are in the same way bound up with each other, and it is not going too far to think that part of Wittgenstein's investigation into language and necessity was directed to bringing to the surface in what way they are bound up. Thus, in more than one place Wittgenstein remarks that a philosopher rejects a notation under the illusion that he is upsetting a proposition about things.[4] This observation shows a recognition of the difference between an explicitly verbal statement and its semantic counterpart formulated in a different idiom; an idiom which easily gives rise to the illusion that the statement is about things. The difference between a verbal proposition and a necessary proposition may only be a difference in the form of speech in which they are expressed. But the difference in the form of speech may be of great importance, and seeing this difference can lead to an understanding of the way in which language and necessity are connected. To put the matter more concretely, seeking the unlikeness, without losing sight of the likeness, between, say, the proposition that being an uncle entails being male and the proposition that being male is part of the meaning of the *word* 'uncle' can lead to a correct understanding of how the *sentence* which expresses the entailment proposition is related to the proposition it expresses.

Consider for a moment the following sentences:

(1) A camel is a herbivore.
(2) Ein Kamel ist ein Pflanzenfresser.
(3) A camel is an animal.
(4) Ein Kamel ist ein Tier.
(5) The word 'animal' applies, as a matter of usage, to whatever 'camel' applies to.

(6) The word 'Tier' applies, as a matter of usage, to whatever 'Kamel' applies to.

Having a clear notion of necessity requires seeing how (3) and (5) are related to each other, i.e. in what way 'A camel is an animal' is like 'The word "animal" applies as a matter of usage, to whatever "camel" applies to'; and in what way they are unlike. To see this it is necessary to see also what (1), 'A camel is a herbivore', has in common with (3), and in what way it is different from (3). Furthermore, it is important to see how the fact that (1) and (2) have the same meaning is both like and unlike the fact that (3) and (4) have the same meaning. A clear grasp of these features of likeness and unlikeness requires seeing how (3) is related to (5), and (4) to (6).

Getting a proper view of these matters will help us understand what it is about the *philosophical* view that necessary propositions are verbal, or that they state facts of usage, which makes it possible for a philosopher to hold it despite being aware of conclusive objections to it. Seeing what makes this possible will help dispel the mystery surrounding a long-standing dispute in which able philosophers with a well-preserved sense of reality can, to all appearances, debate the truth-value of a view which is known to be false without having strange ideas about each others' psychology.

Some philosophers, for one reason or another, have denied that there is a difference between logically necessary and empirical propositions, a direct consequence of which is that there is no difference in kind between the propositions expressed by 'A camel is a herbivore' and 'A camel is an animal'. Without going into the reasons for the philosophical claim that there is no difference, it can be seen that the mode of verification relevant to the proposition expressed by the first sentence is different from the mode of verification relevant to the proposition expressed by the second: observation is relevant to the first but not to the second.[5] Both sentences, equally, can be expressed as general statements of the form 'All a's are b's', i.e. as 'All camels are herbivores' and 'All camels are animals', which makes it tempting to think that both are generalisations. Their grammatical similarity appears to blind some philosophers to an important semantic difference between them. The proposition expressed by the first sentence, unlike the proposition expressed by the second, does not, to use Kant's phrase, have 'strict universality'. The first is an inductive generalisation from observed instances and could in principle be upset by future instances: no number of confirming cases, however large, removes the theoretical possibility of there being a camel that is not a herbivore. By contrast, the second proposition has strict universality, which is to say that, unlike the first, it does not carry with it the theoretical possibility of being upset by a counter-instance. This means that it is not an inductive generalisation.

C. I. Lewis has stated that a logically necessary proposition might, in addition to having an *a priori* demonstration, be established by 'generalisation from observed instances',[6] that is, be established in the way in which a law of nature is established in science. Undoubtedly what Lewis was impressed by — and perhaps wished to highlight — is the similarity between the sentences expressing the two. But putting aside considerations of this sort, it will be clear that taken at face value his claim implies both that a logically necessary proposition of the form 'All a's are b's' has an associated theoretical disconfirming instance and that it does not have one. The difference between 'A camel is an animal' and 'A camel is a herbivore' may be brought into focus by noting that the first can also be expressed as an entailment, '*being a camel* entails *being an animal*', and the second can not — *being a camel* does *not* entail *being a herbivore*. Nothing is more plain than that being a camel is logically consistent with being a herbivore and also with not being a herbivore, and that experience alone, not penetration into the meanings of the words 'camel' and 'herbivore', will show whether it is a herbivore or not.

To come back to the philosophical claim that a necessary proposition is verbal, it can easily be seen that even though it is expressible in the form 'All necessary propositions are verbal', it is not put forward as a generalisation which issues from an examination of instances. Instead, it is put forward as a statement to which there can, in principle, be no exception, or as one whose universality is 'strict'. Construed in this way it can be restated as an entailment: *being logically necessary* entails *being about the use of terminology*. But looked on as making an entailment claim we are puzzled to understand the continued disagreement which revolves around it. There is no debate over whether *being a camel* entails *being an animal*; and if philosophical conventionalism did actually come down to a straightforward, elementary entailment claim, to the effect that *being logically necessary* entails *being verbal*, there is no question but that the debate over it would have been brought to an end long ago. But if the conventionalist thesis is not to be taken as an entailment statement, correct or incorrect, then truly a familiar view is turned into an enigma. We do not know *what* the conventionalist is asserting, nor do we know what we are disputing. There can, of course, be no doubt that in some way we do understand the view and the arguments for and against it; and the conclusion would thus seem to be that our understanding of the view, like our understanding of our dreams, is hidden from us. No one who lets himself become a curious observer of the philosophical scene can fail to entertain the idea that philosophy is an activity which takes place in one of the obscurer parts of the mind. Conscious understanding of the apparent entailment statement should help us understand the nature of philosophical views in general. For if, as Wittgenstein has declared, philosophical propositions are not empirical, then it is natural to suppose them to be *a priori* and to be making entailment claims. Again, as in the case of the conventionalist position, what needs to be seen is what makes possible the continued disagreement centring on them. For example, if the philosophical statement 'A sense datum is private' is an entailment statement, it is one which is turned into a mystery by the continuing disputation over it. The only hope of dispelling the mystery and arriving at an undistorted perception of the philosophical theory lies in clarifying how a logically necessary proposition is related to the sentence which expresses it; or, to put it generally, how logical necessity is related to language.

In the *Tractatus* Wittgenstein makes a number of remarks about tautologies which throw light not only on tautologies but also on all statements having logical necessity, whether analytic or synthetic *a priori*. Proposition 6.1 states that 'The propositions of logic are tautologies', and 6.11 that 'Therefore the propositions of logic say nothing'. The view which comes out of these two propositions is that tautologies say nothing. This view has been linked with the idea that they say nothing about things, that is, with the notion that they have no 'factual content'. Thus in 4.462 Wittgenstein states that tautologies are not 'pictures of reality', the implication being that they give no ontological information. The statement, 'It is either raining or not raining' says nothing about the weather; 'A plant is either an oak or not an oak' says nothing about what a plant is; 'An object is either a plant or not a plant' says nothing about what an object is. This can perhaps be made more perspicuous by considering the negations of these statements. The expressions, 'not both an oak tree and not an oak tree', 'not both a plant and not a plant', do not function as predicates which tell us what a plant or an object is not, unlike 'not both a camel and not herbivorous', which does function to deny what a creature is. To say with regard to anything that it is not both a camel and not a herbivore is to say what the thing is not, and this is because the predicate 'both a camel and not a herbivore' presents a possible 'picture' of the thing. But to say with regard to a plant that it is not both an oak tree and not an oak tree is not to say what the plant is not, in as much as 'both an oak and not an oak' does not have a use to describe any plant, actual or hypothetical. Tautologies say nothing about what there is and what things are like, and contradictions say nothing about what there is not and what things are not like. Predicates of the form 'φ or not φ' equally with 'φ and not φ' have no descriptive content.

These considerations apply to all analytic propositions, and to synthetic *a priori* propositions as well. Kant, and many philosophers after him, have held that synthetic *a priori* propositions, the predicates of which are connected by 'inner necessity' to their subjects, but are not components of them, have factual content; that is, they delineate features of the world. But it will be clear that a true proposition, and hence a logically necessary proposition of whatever kind, will tell us something about what there is only if its negation states something to be the case which in fact is not he case. Kant's claim that the proposition that every change has a cause is *a priori*, although not analytic, has, as is known, been challenged and debated over and over again with a vigour which promises the debate immortality. Without going into its detail, we must say that if *being a change* entails (whether synthetically or otherwise) *having a cause*, then *being a change and not having a cause* will not be a predicate of any conceivable occurrence, and thus will not have a function to describe what does not take place. The conclusion would seem to be that the proposition that a change must have a cause, like a tautology, says nothing about what does or does not take place. Consider for a moment the proposition, 'A red thing is not green'. It clearly is an *a priori* truth, and it could be argued, in the following way, that it is also synthetic. *Being red* entails *not being green*, but the concept *not green* is not discovered by a 'dissection' of the concept *red*: the consequent concept is not a conjunctive part of the antecedent concept. In other words, it could be argued that the consequent is synthetically entailed by the antecedent, and thus that the proposition, 'A red thing is not green', is synthetic *a priori*. But as in the case of a tautology, it says nothing about what things are, if its negation does not present a picture of a hypothetical reality. And since *being red and simultaneously green* is not a predicate of a conceivable object, *not being both red and green* will fail to function as a predicate which says what a thing is not.

It becomes clear now that Wittgenstein's claim that tautologies say nothing can be extended to all propositions which have *a priori* necessity. With regard to tautologies he said they are 'not, however, nonsensical. They are part of the symbolism, just as "0" is part of the symbolism of arithmetic' (4.4611). The implication of this would seem to be that a sentence which expresses a proposition that says nothing is not a nonsensical combination of words like 'Duplicity reclines on the first odd prime'. It would generally be maintained that an indicative sentence which is not nonsensical — that is, one which is literally intelligible — must say something. To put it equivalently, a sentence which says nothing whatever would be said to be nosensical or to have no literal meaning. The idea behind this claim is that an intelligible declarative sentence must be about something, actual or imaginable, that it must have a subject about which it makes a declaration. A sentence which expresses an empirical proposition puts forward a claim about the world; it says something about what in fact is the case or is not the case, and has some sort of subject of discourse. A tautology, which says nothing, but nevertheless is not nonsensical, must therefore have some subject-matter about which it makes a declaration.

Some philosophers have identified the subject of *a priori* statements as the structure of the world. In his *Notebooks 1914–16* Wittgenstein wrote: 'The great problem about which everything I write turns is: Is there an order in the world *a priori*, and if so what does it consist in?' (p. 53e). And in the *Tractatus* there is the suggestion that the subject of tautologies is identified as the structure of the world. In his own words, 'The propositions of logic describe the scaffolding of the world, or rather they exhibit it. They have no "subject matter" . . . It is clear that something about the world must be indicated by the fact that certain combinations of symbols — whose essence involves the possession of a determinate character — are tautologies' (6.124). The implication of these words is not that tautologies have no subject-matter, but rather that their subject-matter is not of a certain sort. They are 'about the world' in a particular respect, namely, about its basic structure, and this, not the specific contents of the world, is their subject-matter.

This notion would seem to be in accord with Leibniz' view that necessary propositions are true for all possible worlds. Leibniz' distinction between necessary, or identical, truths, and truths of fact is that the latter hold only for particular possible worlds, true for some and false for others, while identical truths hold for every world, for the existing world as well as for non-existing possible worlds. The underlying idea is that an *a priori* truth has some sort of ontological import. It is about the world, just as an empirical proposition is, but it is not only about this world. We may gather that Leibniz had the idea, whether or not he was fully aware of it, that an *a priori* necessity refers to that which is invariant in all possible worlds, to what might be called a cosmic content; and this is the structure to which all possible worlds conform.

Wittgenstein's way of putting this is summed up in (6.12): 'The fact that the propositions of logic are tautologies shows the formal — logical — properties of language and the world.' Some philosophers have characterised the three Aristotelian laws of thought as laws not only to which thinking must conform but also as laws to which things must conform. The proposition that nothing can be both an oak tree and also not an oak tree is a different kind of law from a law of physics, e.g. the law that every particle of matter is attracted to every other particle with a force that varies directly as the product of their masses and inversely as the square of their distance apart. A law of logic may be said to apply to special laws of nature as well as to the specific charcteristics of things. The idea behind the views of Wittgenstein and Leibniz is that any system of things, together with the laws governing their behaviour, however, different from any other system of things and their laws, will fall under the same laws of logic, and more generally, the principles embedded in all *a priori* propositions. The cosmic picture linked with this idea is that *a priori* statements give the structure to which all things and laws, actual and possible, must conform. Contingent truths refer to the contents of the present cosmos; the totality of *a priori* truths details its logical structure. Thus, equally with empirical propositions, tautologies have a subject: the invariant structure of all possible worlds. Wittgenstein's two statements, 'Tautologies say nothing' and 'They are not nonsensical', would seem to imply, on his own accounting, that tautologies say nothing about what there is in the world but nevertheless do have a subject: the structure of reality which they explicate, or in some way reveal.

A philosopher who perceives that a tautology says nothing, for example, that 'It is either raining or not raining' says nothing about the weather, but who does not deny that it is intelligible will, if his thinking is governed by the formula 'An intelligible statement cannot be about nothing', *find* something which it is about. For a time Wittgenstein identified the subject of *a priori* truths as the structure of the world, but this seems to have been only a transitional view. The insight that necessary propositions have no factual content may develop into the perception that they convey no sort of information whatever about the world; and this seems to have occurred in Wittgenstein's thinking. One consideration which shows that tautologies have no factual content also shows that they are not about the structure of the world either. The negation of a logically necessary truth presents us, in Locke's words, with an 'impossibility of thought'. The negations of 'A red thing is not also green' and of 'A physical particle which is in one place is not at the same time in another place' result in combinations of terms which stand for impossibilities of thought, namely, the expressions 'a red thing which is green' and 'a physical thing which is in two different places simultaneously'. They present us with conceptual blanks, so to speak. It will be clear that if these phrases denoted concepts, instances of which we could imagine, then instead of denoting impossibilities of thought they would present us with conceivabilities, that is, with 'thinkable states of affairs'.[8]

To suppose, however, that they apply to hypothetical instances is to imply that it is possible to conceive of what would upset a necessary proposition. It would thus imply that a necessary proposition is in principle falsifiable. It would imply that we know what it would be like for there to be a red thing which is also green, for a plant to be both clearly an oak tree and also definitely not an oak tree, and for one and the same oak tree to be in a given place and also elsewhere, and hence that we can envision circumstances which would make true a self-contradictory proposition and make false a logically unfalsifiable proposition. Wittgenstein remarked (3.031): 'It used to be said that God could create anything except what would be contrary to the laws of logic. — The reason being that we could not *say* what an "illogical" world would look like.' To this we might add that to deny that God could create something contrary to the laws of logic, or a self-contradictory state of affairs, is not to imply that there is something which God cannot do. For a putative descriptive expression which involves a contradiction has no descriptive content, i.e. has no use to describe anything, actual or not. Hence, to say that God can create nothing which goes against the laws of logic, or that God cannot create a state of affairs which answers to a self-contradictory expression , is not to use language to state what cannot be done. Wittgenstein appears to have intended this in 3.032: 'it is . . . impossible to represent in language anything that "contradicts logic".'

The implied difference between a phrase which denotes a logical impossibility and an expression which denotes a physically impossible state of affairs, one which, if it existed, would cancel an immutability in nature, is that the second presents us with a thinkable state of affairs — to use Wittgenstein's word, a state of affairs we can *picture* to ourselves (3.001) — and the first does not. Thus the negation of a necessary proposition neither shows nor represents nor exhibits nor depicts what the structure of the world cannot be. Hence a necessary proposition does not represent or exhibit or depict a structure that the world must have. If the one does not show *what* the structure of reality cannot be, or perhaps better, does not exhibit a structure to which reality could not conform, then the other does not depict a structure to which reality must conform. The statement, 'A thing can be in one place only at a given time', would tell us something about what must be with regard to things in space only if 'A given thing is in two separate places simultaneously' *described* what cannot occur in space. In this regard 'A thing must be in one place only at a given time' is completely different from 'A thing is gravitationally influenced by other things in space'. The second describes what happens in space, the first does not.

Giving up the idea that the subject-matter of tautologies is the structure of the world does not mean giving up the idea that they must have some sort of subject-matter. Parenthetically, it is not difficult to see that the expression 'the logical structure of the world' is a made-up expression to which no clear meaning has been assigned. Its apparent function is to serve as the 'name' of the subject-matter of tautologies, devised in the course of looking for the subject-matter under what might be called the 'regulative' formula that a literally meaningful statement must be about something. A philosopher who thinks that tautologies are in no way whatever about reality and who rejects the metaphysical claim that the meanings of general words are abstract entities might then fix on the use of terminology in a language as the subject-matter of tautologies, and in general of *a priori* statements. A philosopher like Wittgenstein, who later saw more deeply into the workings of philosophy than anyone else and eventually arrived at the idea that a philosopher rejects a notation under the delusive impression that he is upsetting a proposition about things, will in the course of his intellectual odyssey try out various 'theories' regarding the subject-matter of *a priori* statements. Wittgenstein certainly tried out conventionalism, which represents the use of terminology as what necessary statements are about.

Elsewhere I have tried to show that the philosophical theory is a gerrymandered piece of terminology which, because it is presented in the ontological form of speech, tends to create an illusion that conceals what is being done with language. Without elaborating this here, it needs to be pointed out that an ontologically presented re-editing of terminology can have either of two purposes which do not necessarily conflict with each other. It can have the purpose of highlighting in a graphic way a point of usage; it can also have the purpose, undoubtedly unconscious, of creating an illusion that a theory about things is being advanced. In Wittgenstein these two purposes do not stand out in clear separation from each other. It is safe to say that the conventionalist position which he sometimes took is the usual variety, which itself is a philosophical theory, that is, a 'theory' with a built-in possibility of endless disputation. The insight which goes beyond conventionalism, and does not issue in a philosophical theory, is to be found in his later writings; but he never presented it in clear articulation, unobscured by metaphor.

Traditional conventionalism is one of the theories which appears to be adopted in the *Tractatus*. Thus, he wrote (6.126):

> One can calculate whether a proposition belongs to logic by calculating the logical properties of the *symbol*. And this is what we do when we 'prove' a logical proposition. For, without bothering about sense or meaning, we construct the logical proposition out of others using only *rules that deal with signs*.[9]

This position also makes its appearance in some of his later work. Moore, in discussing some things Wittgenstein said about tautologies in his 1930–33 lectures suggests that Wittgenstein identified a statement of the form 'it is logically impossible that *p*' with the statement 'the sentence "*p*" has no sense'.[10] Moore went on to remark, 'why he thought (if he did) that "It is logically impossible that *p*" means the same as "The sentence '*p*' has no sense", I cannot explain'.[11] He also reports him as having stated that:

> the proposition 'red is a primary colour' was a proposition about

the word 'red'; and, if he had seriously held this, he might have held similarly that the proposition or rule '3 + 3 = 6' was merely a proposition or rule about the particular expressions '3 + 3' and '6'.[12]

Moore observed that:

> he cannot have held seriously either of these two views, because the *same* proposition which is expressed by the words 'red is a primary colour' can be expressed in French or German by words which say nothing about the English word 'red'; and similarly the *same* proposition or rule which is expressed by '3 + 3 = 6' was undoubtedly expressed in Attic Greek and in Latin by words which say nothing about the Arabic numerals '3' and '6'. And this was a fact which he seemed to be admitting in the passage at the end of (I) [notes of lectures in the Lent and May terms of 1930].[13]

It is certainly not rare for a philosopher to hold a view while aware of 'fatal' objections to it. This blitheness of attitude toward refuting evidence is not encountered in the sciences, and its occurrence in philosophy stands in need of explanation. In this connection, Moore's paradox forces itself on our attention: 'The strange thing is that philosophers have been able to hold sincerely, as part of their philosophical creed, propositions inconsistent with what they themselves *knew* to be true.'[13] It may be unkind, but it appears to be true to say that philosophers have not sincerely faced up to this paradox. Instead of being made curious about the nature of their activity, about what it is they are doing with words, they push the paradox out of their mind and go on doing philosophy with what seems to be a determined lack of curiosity. Be this as it may, there is no question but that Wittgenstein at times adopted a conventionalist view about *a priori* necessity, though he did not remain irremovably attached to it. Conventionalism does represent insight into the nature of logically necessary propositions, but presented in the form of a *theory* about *a priori* necessitation it is an obstacle to the understanding of the nature of philosophical statements. Wittgenstein overcame this obstacle and arrived at an understanding of how philosophy works. The following report of the way he began to think about language and necessity shows clearly his growing perception into the special way a sentence which expresses a necessary proposition and the necessary proposition are bound up with each other:

'4' has two different uses: in '2 + 2 = 4' and in 'there are 4 men here'. ... We must understand the relation between a mathematical proposition about 4 and an ordinary one. The relation is that if the word '4' is a word in our language, then the mathematical proposition is a rule about the usage of the word '4'. The relation is between a rule of grammar and a sentence in which the word can be used . . . Now is '2 + 2 = 4' about 4 or not? If the sentence 'I have 4 apples' is about 4, then '2 + 2 = 4' is not about 4 in this sense. If you say it's about the *mark* '4', be careful . . . When do I emphasise the word 'rule'? When I wish to distinguish between '2 + 2 = 4' and 'There are 4 apples on the table'. . . . If I use the word 'rule' it is because I wish to oppose it to something else. . . . If 'There are 2 men here' is about 2, then to say '2 + 2 = 4' is about 2 is misleading, for it's 'about' in a different sense . . . 25 × 24 = 600 isn't used as a rule for handling signs, though it would stand in the relation of a rule to a *proposition* using this equation.[14]

The objections to conventionalism, construed as making a claim regarding what necessary propositions are about, that is, regarding what their 'subject-matter' is, are conclusive. It is unrealistic to think that the theory, taken at face value, could be held by anyone who was aware of them: it would require our having to think that the conventionalist was suffering from an odd mental condition which enabled him in some way to seal off the objections to the view from the view. Looked at through the spectacles of Moore's paradox, we should have to imagine that a philosopher believes a view to be true while aware of objections which he knows show it to be false. The conclusion forced upon us, however strong our resistance to it may be, is that despite its appearance of making a claim regarding what necessary propositions are about, it makes no such claim. To understand what the conventionalist is trying to bring to our attention, consider three of the six sentences given earlier:

(1) A camel is a herbivore.
(3) A camel is an animal.
(5) The word 'animal' applies, as a matter of usage, to whatever 'camel' applies to.

The difference between (1) and (5) is obvious: (5) is about the word 'camel' and (1) is about what the word 'camel' denotes. That is, one is about a word and the other about a thing. (3) is neither about the word 'camel' nor about what in (1) is denoted by the word 'camel': it is neither about a word nor a thing. What we know in knowing that what (1) says is true is something about camels. What we know in knowing that what (5) says is true is a fact of usage, and what is known in these two cases is something in addition to our understanding the sentences. In this regard (3) is different from both (1) and (5). Understanding it is equivalent to knowing a fact about verbal usage, although this fact is not expressed by the sentence. (3) shares its form of speech with (1), the ontological idiom in which words are not mentioned and are usually used to refer to things. Its content, however, what might be called its invisible subject-matter, is shared with (5).

Perhaps this point is best brought out in the following way: the fact that the sentence 'A camel is an animal' expresses a necessary proposition is equivalent to the fact that the sentence 'The word "animal" applies, as a matter of usage, to whatever "camel" applies to' expresses a true verbal proposition. To put it metaphorically, the verbal content of (5) is explicit and visible, while the verbal content of (3) is hidden; it is made invisible by the mode of speech in which the sentence is formulated. (1) has factual content, (5) has verbal content, and (3) has hidden verbal content. (3) is a grammatical hybrid which is sired by (1) and (5) and differs markedly from both. (As an aside, it may be observed that philosophical theories about the nature of necessity are nothing more than academic assimilations of the offspring to one or other of the parents, with the consequence that its relation to one parent is, to use Wittgenstein's expression, hushed up.)

The objections to conventionalism can now be seen to call attention to respects in which (3) is different from (5), and there is a temptation to take them to be objections against identifying (3) with (5). But if we can resist retreating into philosophical fantasy, we can understand how the conventionalist is able to hold his position only by supposing that he has made no such identification, however much his words suggest that he has. Supposing that the conventionalist does not in fact make this identification requires our thinking that conventionalism is not a description of the subject-matter of necessary statements. Instead, it is to be construed as a way of highlighting the likeness between (3) and (5), in disregard both of their difference and of the likeness between (3) and (1). With his pronouncement that necessary propositions are really verbal the philosopher heightens a similarity which seems important to him, while minimising a dissimilarity which seems unimportant to him. This he does by artificially stretching the use of the word 'verbal' so as to cover, if only nominally, necessary propositions. We might say, for the purpose of bringing out the point, that the word 'verbal' has two uses which are made to appear as the same use: the original use to describe the nature of some propositions, and a new descriptively empty use with what might be called a grammatical point. By means of this stretched use he brings nearer to us a similarity, while keeping at a distance a dissimilarity. Being a philosopher he dramatises what he does by presenting it in the guise of a theory to which, it must be said in his defence, he himself falls dupe. Instead of saying *a camel is an animal* is like *the word 'animal' applies to whatever 'camel' applies to* but is unlike it in not mentioning words, and that it is unlike *a camel is a herbivore* in not being about camels, he says 'The proposition *a camel is an animal* is *really* verbal'. When a philosopher uses the word 'really', he appears to be reporting a discovery, whereas, as Wittgenstein remarked, 'what he wants is a new notation'.[15] A new use of 'verbal' is presented in a way which creates the impression that the true nature of necessary propositions is being revealed.

To return for a moment to Moore's objection against saying that the proposition that $3 + 3 = 6$ is about the expressions '$3 + 3$' and '6', the objection, namely, that the same proposition which is expressed by '$3 + 3 = 6$' is expressible in other languages by words which say nothing about the Arabic numerals '3' and '6'. It is a fact that the sentences '$3 + 3 = 6$' and 'drei und drei macht sechs' mean the same, or express the same proposition; and they would not if the first said something about the use of '3' and '6' and the second said something about the use of 'drei' and 'sechs'. For the first says nothing about the German words and the second says nothing about the Arabic numerals. Since the two sentences express the same proposition, neither sentence can say anything about the symbols which occur in it. As is known, some metaphysically inclined logicians have adopted a view according to which these sentences and others like them are about abstract entities.[16] To revert to sentences (1)–(6), one difference between 'A camel is a herbivore' and 'A camel is an animal' is, on the Platonic theory, that the first is about camels and the second about abstract camelhood. Here no more can be said about the metaphysical difference of 'subject-matter' (in the one case things, and in the other case supersensible entities) than that the Platonic theory, like the cosmic structure theory, is the product of thinking which is governed by the formula that an intelligible indicative sentence must be about something.

To continue the explication of Moore's point, by reference to the sentences (1)–(6), it is correct English to say that (1) and (2) — that is, 'A camel is a herbivore' and 'Ein Kamel ist ein Pflanzenfresser' — have the same meaning. It is correct English to say that (3) — 'A camel is an animal' — and (4) — 'Ein Kamel ist ein Tier' — mean the same; but it is not a correct use of English to apply the phrase 'mean the same' to the pair of sentences, (5) — 'The word "animal" applies, as a matter of usage, to whatever "camel" applies to' — and (6) — 'The word "Tier" applies, as a matter of usage, to whatever "Kamel" applies to". Sentences (1) and (2) have a subject-matter, as do sentences (5) and (6); but (3) and (4) have only a contrived subject-matter, which is to say they are made to appear to have a subject-matter. Neither (3) nor (4) says anything about words or about things, and this fact has led some philosophers to hold that they say nothing. Sentences (1) and (2) say the same thing about the same subject. This feature of the pair of sentences gives us one condition for the correct application of the phrase 'mean the same'. Sentences (5) and (6) do not satisfy this condition: they say similar things about their subjects, but their subjects are different, which makes it incorrect to apply the phrase 'mean the same' to them. By contrast, (3) and (4) have no subjects; but it is correct English, nevertheless, to say that they mean the same. They have the same meaning, although they make no declaration about anything. We might, in order to bring out a point, say that 'mean the same' does not have the same meaning in its application to (1) and (2) that it has in its application to (3) and (4). Although (1) and (2) translate into each other, and (3) and (4) likewise, (1) and (2) are about the same subject, while (3) and (4) have no subject.

Nevertheless, it is not true that (3) and (4) say nothing, or that they are literally meaningless. To put the matter briefly, understanding them comes down to knowing facts about the use of terminology, although terminology is not the subject of these assertions. The sentence 'A camel is an animal' is a grammatical crossbreed with one foot, so to speak, in the correlated verbal sentence in the same language and the other in related non-verbal fact-claiming sentences. (3) and (4) translate into each other, which is a feature that makes it correct to apply the term 'mean the same', or 'have the same meaning', to the sentences, despite their not being about anything.[17] But a person who understands both sentences will know facts of usage in different languages, while a person who understands only one of the sentences would not know the fact of usage exhibited by the other. The phrase 'mean the same' is used to refer to one feature when applied to sentences in the hybrid idiom and is used to refer to a further feature when applied to fact-claiming sentences. But by artificially equating 'mean the same' witn 'say the same thing about the same subject' under the rule that a literally meaningful indicative sentence *must* be about something, a philosopher creates the illusion that (3) and (4) have a special rarified subject-matter, that they are about supersensible objects which can only be grasped by the pure intellect.

A comment of Wittgenstein's is worth noting in this connection:

> 'The symbol "a" stands for an ideal object' is evidently supposed to assert something about the meaning, and so about the use, of 'a'. And it means of course that this use is in a certain respect similar to that for a sign that has an object, and that it does not stand for any object.[18]

When a philosopher like Moore points out that (3) and (4) mean the same and therefore that neither could mean the same as (5) or (6), he is calling attention to a grammatical similarity between sentences which express necessary propositions and those which make factual claims about the world, while pushing into the background the likeness between sentences which express necessary propositions and those which express propositions about usage.

Wittgenstein sometimes characterized necessary propositions as rules of grammar, with the idea in mind that he was stating a theory about the nature of logical necessity. He was able to see past this idea, however, and at other times he called them 'rules of grammar' in order to direct our attention to an important feature of sentences which express necessary propositions. Probably part of his reason for wishing to stress the verbal aspect of necessary propositions was to remove the idea that they are about mysterious things, and thus to dispel the occult air which tends to settle over them. But more important than this, he undoubtedly felt that having a clear understanding of the nature of necessary statements is required in order to see how philosophy works. Seeing what breed of theory conventionalism is, which comes to seeing what a conventionalist does with the word 'verbal' or equivalent expressions, is the final step towards understanding the theories of philosophy. The conventionalist theory is one of a large family of theories, and to gain an inside look into it is to gain an inside look into the other members of the family.

Wittgenstein has said that what the philosopher needs in order to solve, or to 'dissolve', his problems is to 'command a clear view of our use of words'.[19] We might add that what he needs is a better understanding of sentences which express or are put forward as expressing necessary propositions, and to see how they both conceal their verbal content and also create the impression of being about phenomena. It will be recalled that Wittgenstein stated that philosophical theories are not empirical, and that he also said that a philosopher rejects an expression under the delusive impression that he is upsetting a proposition about things. This idea about the nature of philosophical theories and philosophical refutations is deeply rooted and, according to him, 'pervades all philosophy'.[20] The conventionalist theory will be recognised now as falling under Wittgenstein's characterisation. It is not empirical, it is restatable as making the entailment claim that being a necessary proposition entails stating verbal facts. Reformulating it as an entailment statement dissolves the notion that it is an inductive generalisation, and it also changes our idea of what a philosopher is doing who, to all appearances, is demolishing by unanswerable arguments a widely-held theory about what a necessary proposition is. It brings into clearer view what the theory is not and it also puts us on the way to a correct understanding of what it is.

It is easy now to see why the conventionalist can hold his position against all conclusive objections. He is presenting a stretched use of 'verbal', a use which artificially covers necessary propositions, and is not using the word 'verbal' in the normal way to make a false statement about them. Like the philosopher who satisfies himself that he has refuted the conventionalist theory, the conventionalist can survive refutation after refutation and remain satisfied that, none the less, his theory is not incorrect. Both the philosopher who holds the conventionalist theory and the philosopher who rejects it suffer from the fallacy which pervades all philosophy: namely, the false notion that the dispute centres on the truth-value of a theory rather than on the academic redistricting of a term.

II

This understanding of what the conventionalist theory comes to has direct application to the philosophical problem of the privacy of experience. Consider the following words:

When philosophers assert that experience is private, they are referring to a necessary proposition. It would be a contradiction to speak of the feelings of two different people as being numerically identical: it is logically impossible that one person should literally feel another's pain. But these points of logic are based on linguistic usages which have, as it were, the empirical facts in view. If the facts were different, the usage might be changed.[21]

When we consider these words with care, we discern in them three claims. One, explicitly stated, is that the sentence 'experiences are private' expresses a necessary proposition, a second is the conventionalist view that the necessary proposition is really verbal, i.e. 'the points of logic' are 'based on linguistic usages'; and a further claim is that in some way a matter of fact about experience is involved. What comes through quite distinctly in the words that the 'points of logic are based on linguistic usages which have, as it were, the empirical facts in view', and that 'if the facts were different, the usage might be changed' is the idea that experience is private, as a matter of empirical fact.

It is by no means uncommon for a philosopher to hold explicitly that his utterance expresses an *a priori* truth, and also to imply that it refers to an empirical fact; and in the present case the implication stands out in bold relief. To put the matter shortly, what is being held is that the proposition expressed by 'Experience is private' both is logically necessary and also has 'factual content', i.e. makes a factual claim about feelings, pains, and the like. Wittgenstein's observation that philosophical problems are not empirical carries with it the implication that philosophical answers to philosophical questions are not empirical. But it should no longer be necessary to remark that the philosophical statement that experience is private has its absorbing and continued interest for philosophers because, for one thing, of the empirical picture associated with it, the picture of our having experiences which no one is privileged to share with us.

The contradiction implied by the conjunction of philosophical claims is blatant, and it parallels the contradiction frequently pointed out in the view that necessary propositions are really verbal, or that they are 'based on linguistic usages'. Philosophers are not too troubled by contradictions like these; indeed, such contradictions become permanent additions to the content of philosophy. Anyone who is realistic about philosophy will find it hard not to think of it as a growing collection of contradictory theories which are not given up, and of paradoxes which remain in permanent suspension. A further contradiction can now be added. This is the contradiction that is implied by the conventionalist view of logical necessity in combination with the tacit claim that at least some necessary propositions are about things — in the present instance, the contradiction which comes from holding that the proposition that experience is private is 'based' on the use of terminology and that it also states a matter of fact. To put the matter in terms of the *sentence* 'Experience is private', holding that it expresses a necessary proposition amounts to stating, on the conventionalist thesis, that it is *about the use* of the terms 'experience' and 'private', and thus that the sentence *does not use the terms* to make a statement about what they are ordinarily used to refer to. The contradiction which emerges is that a sentence which is about words rather than things is nevertheless about things. Perhaps a more perspicuous way of making this contradiction explicit is the following. On the conventionalist view, to hold that the sentence 'Experience is private' expresses a necessary proposition amounts to holding, in part at least, that the phrase 'non-private experience' has been given no application to anything, i.e. that it has no descriptive function in the language. And to hold in immediate conjunction with this, that the sentence refers to an empirical fact about experience, is to embrace the contradiction that a phrase which has no descriptive use nevertheless has one. It is important to try to understand what makes it possible for a philosopher to accept this and related contradictions, and treat them as if they somehow do not go against their views. The insight reached into the nature of the conventionalist view helps us toward an understanding of why a contradiction in mathematics eliminates a proposition, but does not do this in philosophy.

The passage cited at the beginning of this section tacitly implies that the phrase 'feels another's pain' refers to what is logically impossible, and thus that it does not have a use to describe a conceivable occurrence. It states, also, that if the empirical facts were different usage might be changed, which is to say that the phrase might then be given a descriptive use. It is not clear what the empirical facts are which the linguistic usages keep in view. The only facts which, so to speak, *fit* the case are those which would be described by 'feels another's pain', and which, if they obtained, might make us *give* a descriptive use to this combination of words. The passage is labyrinthine in its ambiguity, but what makes itself evident is the idea, which probably all philosophers have, that an expression for a logical impossibility describes what never in fact happens.

One philosophical logician said: 'That which necessarily is the case is also as a matter of fact the case',[22] and it is fair to infer that he also has the idea that what is logically impossible never occurs as a matter of fact. It cannot be pointed out too often that a phrase which expresses what is logically impossible, e.g. the phrase 'soundless crash of thunder', does not have a use to *describe* what is not or what cannot be: it simply has no descriptive function in the language in which it occurs. It may be useful to point out that the proposition that an expression which denotes a logical impossibility has no descriptive content is not itself an experiental proposition, but rather declares an entailment to the effect that being an expression for a logical impossibility entails being devoid of descriptive content. The assertion that an expression refers to what is logically impossible is incompatible with the assertion that it describes what in fact never occurs. If it describes what does not occur, it does not refer to a logical impossibility, and if it refers to a logical impossibility, it does not describe what does not happen.

If the sentence 'Experiences are private' does refer to a necessary truth, in virtue of the ordinary conventions governing the use of 'private' as well as of experience-denoting terminology,[23] then it makes no declaration about experiences. It exhibits, without expressing, what is stated by the sentence 'The word "private" correctly applies to whatever "experience" applies to, such that the phrase "an experience which is not private" has no descriptive use'. And if the phrase 'feels another's pain' does, in virtue of the rules governing the words occurring in it, refer to what is logically impossible, then it does not describe what one cannot feel, or feelings that one cannot have. Now, a philosopher who holds both that 'feels another's pain' has no descriptive use and also that it describes what never happens, and declares that if what does not happen were to happen we might then *give* a descriptive sense to 'feels another's pain', would seem to have lost his way. It is tempting to think that anyone who states that a term which lacks a descriptive use might be given one if situations answering to it came into existence is making a mere mistake, which for some odd reason he fails to see. The terms 'eternity bone' and 'phlogiston' fell into disuse when it was finally

decided that nothing existed which answered to them and, undoubtedly, if the facts had been different the terms would not have fallen
into disuse. But these cases are not comparable to the philosophical
case, which is like that of being told that the expression 'prime
number between 13 and 17' might be given an application if such a
number were discovered.

There is a strong temptation to think that our opponents in
philosophy make mistakes which are plainly visible to us but which
they do not have the wit to see. Hardly any philosopher fails to
succumb to it, not only because it makes him feel superior but also
because it sustains the truth-value façade which hides from him the
real nature of philosophy. The importance for the correct understanding of philosophy of putting aside the truth-value spectacles
through which philosophers look at their work will be realised by
anyone who is not on the defensive about the unexplained difference
between the chronic condition of philosophy and the condition of
the experimental and mathematical sciences. To put the matter in
terms of a probability evaluation, it has now become more probable
that philosophical assertions have no truth-value than that they
do have truth-values which philosophers have been unable to
agree on.

If we keep separate the statement that it is logically impossible for
one person to feel another's pain, from the statement that no one as
a matter of fact ever feels another's pain, and suspend the idea that a
mistake is involved, we can see how the two statements work with
respect to each other to produce the philosophical theory that
experience is private. Consider first the claim that it is logically
impossible to feel another's pain, which is linked with, and in fact
derives its importance from, the empirical picture of contents which
are not accessible to more than one person, comparable in some
ways to the contents of a bank box to which only one person has the
key. If the claim about the impossibility of feeling another's pain is
an *a priori* truth, understanding a sentence which expresses it is
equivalent to knowing that the descriptive part of the sentence (the
phrase 'feels another's pain', in the English sentence) has been
assigned no use to describe anything.

It will be clear thus that if the phrase 'feels another's pain'
expresses what is logically impossible, the words 'another's pain' do
not have a use in the language to distinguish between pains that a
person is able to feel and pains he is prevented from feeling, for one
reason or another. It will also be clear that a philosopher who asserts

the impossibility of feeling another's pain draws from his assertion the consequence that a person can feel only his own pains. The background picture linked with the consequence is that of someone who is *confined* to feeling certain pains. But the picture turns out to be inappropriate to the words 'A person can feel only his own pains'. For 'feels his own pain' is semantically connected with 'feels another's pain' in such a way that if the second expression has no use to describe anything, neither does the first. The terms 'another's pain' and 'his own pain' serve to make a contrast, such that if in a certain context 'another's pain' describes nothing, in the same context 'his own pain' will describe nothing. Thus, if in the sentence 'By contrast to another's pain, which I cannot feel, I can feel my own pain', the phrase 'another's pain' does not describe what I cannot feel, then the phrase 'my own pain' does not describe what I can feel. Put somewhat differently, 'his own pains' will have a use to set apart pains a person can feel from pains he does not or cannot feel only if 'another's pains' also has a use to set off pains a person does not or is unable to feel from those he does or is able to feel. To imitate Bishop Butler, the sentence 'A person can feel his own pain and not another's pain' says nothing about what a person can feel, if the required contrast is cancelled by the failure of one of the terms to have a descriptive function. Either both terms have a use or neither term has a use. Hence if the philosopher of the privacy of experience followed through on the consequences of his claim with regard to 'feels another's pain', he would have to allow that 'feels his own pain' has no use to describe what a person is limited to feeling. But this, quite obviously, he does not wish to do. If he did maintain, whether explicitly or indirectly, that both expressions lacked descriptive sense, his 'theory' would vanish, cancel itself out of existence.

Wittgenstein has characterised as a typically metaphysical mistake [24] the use of one of a pair of antithetical terms in what might be called linguistic dissociation from its antithesis, i.e. retaining one of the terms while deleting the other by the artful technique of 'showing' by an argument that the other stands for a logical impossibility. He described at least some of his later work as consisting of 'bringing words back from their metaphysical to their everyday usage'.[25] The semantic fact about antithetical terms is that if one of a given pair is stripped of its use in the language, without being replaced by a term to do its work, the other also loses its use. By bringing back words from their metaphysical to their everyday use, which is to say, by restoring to them their former use, the words which normally function as their antitheses *recover* their use. Wittgenstein's language sometimes suggests the idea that the metaphysical use of a term, as against its everyday use, is an actual use which assigns to a word the role of describing occult realities or real as against merely apparent states of things. It is clear, however, that a metaphysical use is not given to a term *independently* of the semantic suppression of its antithesis. Instead, its metaphysical use is *the result of*, and thus is created by, the ontologically reported suppression of the word. Instead of speaking of the metaphysical use of a term, it would be less misleading to speak of the metaphysical role a term acquires when its antithesis is (academically) cast out of the language. When one of a pair of antithetical terms is suppressed the other loses its function to describe and takes on a metaphysical, illusion-creating role.

A term which is shorn of its descriptive use by making its antithesis stand for a logical impossibility does not spontaneously acquire a new descriptive use. Any new use it has it must be given, and if it is not in fact given a use, the use it appears to acquire is one in appearance only. The problem is to explain how the illusion is brought about of its having a use to describe reality, how, in the present context, the appearance is created that a dramatic claim is being made by the words 'A person can feel only his own pains'. If we go back to our interpretation of the conventionalist position, we can get a behind the scenes look at the semantic props which are used to bring to life the scene at the front of the philosophical stage. The props which produce the delusive picture of everyone being enclosed by a wall over which no one else can look are not either the wrong use of 'feels another's pain' and 'feels only his own pain', nor the mistaken descriptions of their actual use in the language. The props are academic, linguistically idle alterations, which when held up against everyday, unrevised language give rise to the delusive impression that a fact about the nature of feelings and sensations is being disclosed.

The assertion that it is logically impossible to feel another's pain, which is linked with the declaration that a person is limited by logical necessity to feeling his own pain, embodies a piece of gerrymandered terminology. The result is to *deprive* an expression of its use, as part of a game that is being played with language. The fact that the game is conducted in the non-verbal mode of speech conceals its verbal nature. What is being done with words is hidden all the more effectively by the fact that the use they have in everyday language *remains intact* in everyday language, which thus serves as a backdrop and gives to the game the appearance of a discovery. Wittgenstein has said that a philosophical problem arises when language goes on holiday; and it seems that the philosophical view that experience is private is, as we might say, an image thrown on the language screen by an ontologically presented, non-workaday revision of grammar.

It is unrealistic to think that the verbal game by itself is so entirely captivating as to make it worth while. Its ability to keep thinkers in permanent intellectual thralldom requires us to suppose that something else is involved, something which it is difficult to recognise consciously. A brief speculation is permissible at this point, and it may be enlightening. The suggestion that part of the mind is a dark area whose contents are inaccessible to us tends to be received not only with the expected rejection but also with a kind of grudging fascination. Philosophers perhaps more than other intellectuals resist the idea that the mind contains a submerged Atlantis; but there can be no doubt that they, too, and perhaps even more than others, sense that something in their own mind is inaccessible to them, something from which they feel estranged and to which, try as they may, they cannot find their way back. It is not to indulge in wholly remote speculation to think that the philosopher is disturbed by this state of affairs within himself. And it need not come as a complete surprise to discover that his ambivalence about the submerged part of his own mind, both his inner perception of its existence and his denial, finds expression in his philosophical work. In view of the fact that a sentence which expresses a philosophical theory does not, despite appearances, describe or assert the existence of a state of affairs, supposing that an unconscious thought finds expression in it helps us understand what holds the philosopher spellbound to his view and also keeps it at a comfortable distance from his curiosity.[26]

The philosophical view that a person's experiences are private carries with it the idea of inaccessible mental contents, and this idea suggests a connection of the view with the inaccessible unconscious. The view itself says nothing about our pains and feelings, but appears to be a veiled way of expressing the perception of the existence of the unconscious and also of mitigating its disturbing quality. By his theory the philosopher reports his perception of the noumenon[27] within himself in an inverted way, in the form of a projection. He deflects the perception away from himself and onto others, who thus become externalised surrogates for his own unconscious. In the fantasy which accompanies this projection he also represents to himself his unconscious (his own mind in relation to other people), and in this way denies the fact that it is alien territory which lies beyond his reach. The words 'The experiences a person has are private to himself' gives rise to the false notion that they have descriptive content; and the spell they are able to cast can be explained only by supposing they *do* have unconscious content. One concealed thought which the words might very well express is that the unconscious is outside of us and also that the contents of the unconscious are really no different from the contents of the conscious part of the mind. The philosophical 'view' that experiences are private, or that no one's experiences are accessible to anyone else, seems to be a mask for stating that the unconscious exists but that its contents are conscious.[28]

Several remarks Freud made throw light on the way some people cope with the uneasy perception that part of their mind is a lost land that lies beyond the horizon of consciousness. They are especially revealing in the present connection. What he said needs to be quoted at some length and merits being read with care.

the study of pathogenic repressions and of other phenomena which have still to be mentioned compelled psychoanalysis to take the concept of the 'unconscious' seriously. Psychoanalysis regarded everything mental as being in the first instance unconscious; the further quality of 'consciousness' might also be present, or again it might be absent. This of course provoked a denial from the philosophers, for whom 'conscious' and 'mental' were identical, and who protested that they could not conceive of such a monstrosity as the 'unconscious mental'. There was no help for it, however, and this idiosyncrasy of the philosophers could only be disregarded with a shrug. Experience (gained from pathological material, of which the philosophers were ignorant) of the frequency and power of impulses of which one knew nothing directly and whose existence had to be inferred like some fact in the external world, left no alternative open. It could be pointed out, incidentally, that this was only treating one's own mental life as one had always treated other people's. One did not hesitate to ascribe mental processes to other people, although one had no immediate consciousness of them and could only infer them from their words and actions. But what held good for other people must be applicable to oneself. Anyone who tried to push the argument further and to conclude from it that one's own hidden processes belonged actually to a second *consciousness* would be faced with the concept of a consciousness of which one knew nothing, of an 'unconscious consciousness' — and this would scarcely be preferable to the assumption of an 'unconscious mental'.[29]

III

It is of special interest to apply the later Wittgenstein, or rather that part of Wittgenstein's later work which some philosophers find hard to fit into the continuity of his thought, to several philosophical statements in the *Tractatus*. Although it has become almost a commonplace, it is worth repeating that our mind works at several different levels simultaneously, and that what we are aware of at one level we can obliterate from our mind at another. John Wisdom has described the case of a person who, under hypnosis, saw a blank space wherever the definite article occurred on a page of print. The explanation of this curious state of affairs is that part of his mind blotted out what he saw with another part. This suppressing, or blotting out, mechanism seems to be used by philosophers who read Wittgenstein's later writings with intellectual blindness to the revealing things he said about philosophy. It has to be granted that the iconoclastic perceptions to which he gave expression do not belong to the continuity of his *philosophical* thought, but rather, are breaks in it. They are remarkable departures from conventional philosophy. This is, perhaps, one reason why philosophers have been able to read Wittgenstein with a Parmenidean eye that eliminates the unconventional things he said about conventional philosophy.

As is known, Wittgenstein rejected the *Tractatus*, even though some of his later thought is continuous with it; and this rejection can be best understood if we look at it through the metaphilosophical spectacles he has given us. Consider the following selection of statements.

What can be described can happen too, and what is excluded by the law of causality cannot even be described. (6.362)

Belief in the causal nexus is *superstition*. (5.136)

A necessity for one thing to happen because another has happened does not exist. There is only *logical* necessity. (6.37)[30]

Just as the only necessity that exists is *logical* necessity, so too the only impossibility that exists is *logical* impossibility. (6.375)

The impression these pronouncements make on us is that they advance factual claims about what exists or does not exist, and about the irrationality of a common belief about how changes are brought about in things. Read in conjunction with each other, the sentences 'A necessity for one thing to happen because another has happened does not exist' and 'Belief in the causal nexus is superstition' give rise to the idea that propositions like 'The light must go out when the current is turned off' and 'A hummingbird cannot carry off a hippopotamus' are all being declared false. They also suggest the notion that a person who believes any of them to be true is holding a pre-scientific belief, one which, like the belief that heavy bodies fall faster than light ones, has been shown false by science. It is factual claims like these that Wittgenstein seems to be giving expression to by his philosophical sentences. But if we pause to reflect on them and relate them to other of his statements, we shall realise that what he seems to be saying here is, to use a favourite expression of Bradley's, mere appearance.

If we dispel the mists generated by the empirical talk with which philosophical theories about causation are surrounded, we can see that they are not empirical. A philosopher who declares that causation is a logically necessary connection between classes of occurrences is, obviously, not holding an empirical view about causation. Logical connections are not discovered by observing the behaviour of things, in Wittgenstein's words in the *Notebooks, 1914–16*, 'none of our experience is *a priori*'.[31] But neither does a philosopher give expression to an empirical claim who says that there is no causal nexus, or says that causation is nothing more than constant conjunction. For he has ruled himself out from being able to say what else might supplement mere constant conjunction. Wittgenstein said in his *Notebooks* that whatever can be described at all could also be otherwise.[32] The implication of this is clear. The sentence 'A causal nexus [or productive causation] does not exist' expresses an empirical proposition only if the term 'causal nexus' has a use to describe something which, if it did exist, would make false what the sentence asserts. The sentence would express an empirical proposition only if matters could be other than it declares them to be. Since it does not describe what could be otherwise, it does not express a proposition about what is or is not the case.

We come to the same conclusion if we bring in statement 6.362 above: 'What can be described can happen too, and what is excluded by the law of causality cannot be described.' The implication of these words is that the law of causality has no describable exception; which is to say that nothing can be described such that if it existed it would upset the law. It is clear that a philosopher who holds that the law of causality has no conceivable or describable exception implies that, as *he* construes the words which give expression to it, they do not state an empirical proposition. It may be useful to point out that to say that 'what is excluded by the law of causality cannot be described' is to imply that *nothing* is excluded by it; otherwise it would be possible to say what is excluded, i.e. it would be possible to say what exceptions to the law would be like. On this claim about the law of causality, taken at face value, it has the character of a tautology, which also excludes nothing. This in general is the character of an *a priori* true proposition: it excludes no describable state of affairs. Whether or not the words 'A necessity for one thing to happen because another has happened does not exist' are being used to express an *a priori* proposition, it is clear that they do not express one that is empirical, i.e. one that *excludes* a describable state of affairs. The sentence which follows from these words makes this evident, namely, the sentence 'There is only *logical* necessity'.

A philosopher who states that 'the only necessity that exists is logical necessity', or that 'the only impossibility that exists is logical impossibility', has not arrived at his claim by an inductive proce- dure, or by anything comparable to an inductive procedure. The difference between his sentences and a sentence like 'The only horses that exist are wingless horses' stands out. One is empirical and excludes what *can* be described, the other is used by the philosopher in such a way as to preclude his describing possible exceptions. The phrase 'the only' does not function in his utterance in the way it functions in the non-philosophical sentence. Its function in the philosophical sentence is more like the one it has in 'The only even prime number is two'.

Seeing this makes it natural to think that a philosopher who says, 'The only necessity that exists is logical necessity', has the idea that he is using terminology in the accepted way to express an *a priori* truth. It also makes it natural to think that he has the idea that the sentence, 'A necessity for one thing to happen because another has happened does not exist', expresses an *a priori* truth. Without going into an explanation of the nature of logical necessity again, it can be seen that if he had this idea he could be charged with being in error about actual usage — that is, with having the mistaken idea that the use of 'necessary' is no wider than the use of 'logically necessary'. Again without repeating reasons elaborated in similar connections elsewhere, the conclusion that he has this idea has to be rejected, and with it the notion that the philosopher labours under the idea that he is making *a priori* pronouncements.

The alternative conclusion, which invariably provokes emotional resistance but nevertheless has great explanatory power in its favour, is that instead of being stubbornly fixated to a mistaken idea about usage, he is in some way retailoring usage, artificially contracting or even suppressing terminology. Instead of supposing him to think that the use of 'necessary' coincides with that of the term 'logically necessary' and that the use of 'impossible' coincides with that of 'logically impossible', this alternative requires us to suppose him to be contracting 'necessary' and 'impossible' into part only of their actual use, which he announces in the ontological mode of speech. Philosophers like to show contradictions or vicious infinite regresses in each other's views, and they do succeed sometimes in momentarily embarrassing each other, which is the sum total of what is achieved. In philosophy showing a contradiction of one sort or another in a view does not remove it from the collection of optional theories. The philosophical view that the only necessity which exists is logical necessity, or that only logical necessity is real necessity, construed as making a factual claim that equates the terms 'necessary' and 'logically necessary' is subject to the obvious objection that it implies an infinite regression, comparable to the regression G. E. Moore pointed out in the ethical view that an act's being right is identical with its being thought right.[33] The metaphilosophical[34] construction of the view that represents it as belonging to the family of 'theories' of which conventionalism is a member, offers an explanation both of how an astute thinker can overlook an obvious difficulty, why he is not embarrassed by having it brought to his attention, and also why the difficulty does not remove the theory from the collection of optional philosophical theories.

Wittgenstein has said that a philosopher rejects a form of expression under the illusion that he is refuting a proposition about things. This remark applies to his philosophical theories about causation and necessity in the *Tractatus*. The artificial contraction of the use of 'necessity' and 'impossibility' and the suppression of causal verbs (there is no 'causal nexus') is conducted in the style of discourse which we use to talk about things and which we also use to express necessary propositions. Presented in this way the words create the false but vivid impression that indubitable theories about the existence or nature of phenomena are being stated. There can be no doubt that this illusion answers to an unrelinquished yearning in the depths of the minds of philosophers, who continue to think that they can obtain knowledge of things without taking the trouble to go to them. The recent words of an important metaphysical philosopher strengthens this idea:

> What philosophers have supposed they were doing was pursuing truth; they were thinking about the ultimate nature of things — more critically than the common man, more profoundly than the scientist, more disinterestedly and precisely than the theologian.[35]

Notes

1. See, for example, 6.53, *Tractatus Logico Philosophicus* (1922), New York: Harcourt Brace & Co., London: Kegan Paul, Trench, Traubner & Co., trans C.K. Ogden.

2. *Philosophical Investigations* (1953), Oxford: Basil Blackwell, p. 19.

3. Ibid., p. 51.

4. This phrasing of the idea follows the phrasing in 'The Yellow Book', which consists of notes take by A. Ambrose and M. Masterman in the intervals between dictation of *The Blue Book* in 1933–34.

5. Wittgenstein has brought out the same point with the help of his own use of the term 'grammar': 'The way you verify a proposition is part of its grammar. If I say all cardinal numbers have a certain property and all men in this room have hats, the grammar is seen to be different because the ways of verification are so different'; (Lecture notes, 1934–35). Wittgenstein undoubtedly uses here his word 'grammar' to refer to the difference in the logic of the two statements, the difference in their 'logical grammar'.

6. *An Analysis of Knowledge and Valuation* (1946), Lasalle, Ill.: Open Court, p. 91.

7. p. 53e.

8. This phrase is taken from 3.001.

9. Wittgenstein's emphasis brings out the point.

10. *Philosophical Papers* (1959), London: Allen & Unwin, p. 275.

11. Ibid., p. 276.

12. Ibid., p. 291.

13. Ibid., p. 41.

14. Lecture notes, 1934–35, taken by Alice Ambrose. Compare the last sentences with *Tractatus*, 6. 126.

15. *The Blue Book* (1958), Oxford: Basil Blackwell, p. 57.

16. For discussions of the views that propositions and the meanings of general words are abstract entities, see especially 'Understanding Philosophy', in *Studies in Metaphilosophy* (1964), London: Routledge & Kegan Paul; and 'The Existence of Universals', in *The Structure of Metaphysics* (1955), London: Routledge & Kegan Paul, by M. Lazerowitz.

17. It should be noted that 'mean the same' does not apply to all sentences which translate into each other, for example, to equivalent nonsensical sentences in different languages. A person who insists that sentences which translate into each other *must* mean the same is stretching the expression 'sentences which mean the same' so as to give it the same range of application that 'sentences which translate into each other' has.

18. *Remarks on the Foundations of Mathematics* (1956), ed. G. H. von Wright, R. Rhees and G. E. M. Anscombe, trans. G. E. M. Anscombe, New York: Macmillan, p. 136.

19. *Philosophical Investigations*, p. 49.

20. The Yellow Book.

21. A. J. Ayer (1956), *The Problem of Knowledge*, Harmondsworth: Penguin Books, p. 202.

22. G. H. von Wright (1968), 'Deontic Logic and the Theory of Conditions', *Critica*, vol. 2, no. 6, p. 3.

23. It is hardly necessary to call attention to the fact that the philosophical use of the word 'experience' does not correspond to its everyday use. We should not, for example, say of a person in pain that he is having an experience.

24. *The Blue Book*, p. 46.

25. *Philosophical Investigations*, p. 48. This is easily recognised as 'linguistic therapy' for avoiding metaphysics.

26. It also helps us understand why philosophers experience so much hostility to the notion of an unconscious part of the mind. The suspicion, which they may very well harbour, that the sole ideational, non-verbal content of a philosophical theory is a cluster of unconscious thoughts would naturally provoke a strong reaction against the idea of an unconscious.

27. Kant's notion of a noumenal mind behind the conscious self is easily recognised as referring to the unconscious.

28. At a more superficial level the philosophical view would seem to express a self-revelation: a felt inability to empathise with others.

29. *An Autobiographical Study* (1946), trans. James Strachey, London: The International Psychoanalytical Library, Hogarth Press/The Institute of Psychoanalysis, no. 26, pp. 55–6, 2nd edn.

30. Trans. C. K. Ogden.

31. p. 80e.

32. Ibid.

33. *Ethics* (1912), London: Home University Library, Williams & Norgate; New York: Henry Holt, pp. 123–4.

34. For an explanation of the term 'metaphilosophy', see my note in *Metaphilosophy* (1970), vol. 1, no. 1, p. 91.

35. Brand Blanshard (1970), review of *Philosophy and Illusion, Metaphilosophy*, vol. 1, no. 2, p. 178.

2 FACTUAL, MATHEMATICAL AND METAPHYSICAL INVENTORIES

Proposition 1 of Wittgenstein's *Tractatus* reads: 'The world is everything that is the case.' But what does 'everything' cover? Apart from its generality, its reference to the world, the question would seem to be clear and unambiguous enough, and to have a straightforward answer. Under 'everything' we should list trees, buildings, human beings, animals, etc. However, when a philosopher asks the question 'What is there in the world?', something more than this kind of simple-minded, commonplace answer is expected. In G. E. Moore's opinion the attempt to answer it is of first importance. He wrote, 'it seems to me that the most important and interesting thing which philosophers have tried to do is . . . to give a general description of the *whole* of the Universe, mentioning all the most important kinds of things which we *know* to be in it.'[1] In part, what makes the question important and interesting is that it presents some sort of difficulty, as is evidenced by the fact that philosophers have for centuries been divided on what kinds of things there are — whether there are material objects, minds, relations, properties, numbers, propositions, facts or only some selection of these, or even none at all. The divergence of opinion is very different from that occurring in a disagreement over whether there are people or gold deposits within a certain region, or over whether there are prime numbers between 2000 and 2031. The difference between the disagreements parallels the difference in the kinds of tasks undertaken by the census taker, the miner or the mathematician, on the one hand, and the metaphysician on the other. The metaphysician keeps a ledger of reality and unreality, of what exists and what does not exist, which would seem to rule out many run-of-the-mill inventories. Thus, if according to his ledger there are no material objects, a warehouse inventory is ruled out; if there are no relations, then one can spare oneself concern over the relatives who are to benefit under one's will, etc. Yet we all recognise that in fact warehouse inventories, censuses of cities, existential proofs in mathematics are made without regard to what the metaphysician's ledger records as real. The metaphysician is not consulted. Questions as to how many people there are in a city or how many cars come off an assembly-line or how many primes there are within a given sequence of numbers may have conflicting answers; but it is known in a general way how to decide between answers. The situation is very different with regard to existence questions and answers in metaphysics; it is in fact so different that doubt arises whether metaphysical statements refer to the world at all. Indeed, the suspicion arises whether the metaphysician has set himself a task of inventory which is only a semblance of a task. In this essay I shall maintain the impossibility of such an inventory, not because the task is beyond our powers but because there is no task.

It would seem that to say there are things, properties, numbers, facts, etc. is to state what there is in the universe, and that like other existence claims it should be possible to ascertain whether they are true. To maintain that it is impossible to ascertain their truth suggests the presence of a logical or psychological obstacle. In both the *Notebooks* and *Tractatus* Wittgenstein characterised *thing, fact, function, number*, etc. as 'pseudo' or 'formal' concepts, to contrast them with what he called 'proper' concepts, declaring that the sentences '1 is a number', 'M is a thing', 'There are *n* objects' are senseless.[2] He said: 'To ask whether a formal concept exists is nonsensical. For no proposition can be the answer to such a question' (4.1274).[3] It is clear that according to his early writings there could be no deciding the correct answer to such a question, not because its answer poses insuperable difficulties but because there is no question.

In this essay I do not wish to maintain that such questions are nonsensical. But I do want to argue that the answers do not state what there is in the universe. I shall try to show that in a roundabout way they are verbal rather than factual in import. In support of this claim I call attention first of all to differences and similarities between three types of existence statements: (a) those asserting a fact which might be otherwise, (b) existence propositions of mathematics, and (c) metaphysical propositions stating the existence of the most general categories of things. Their similarity is of course obvious. In particular, the last two kinds have as their verbal model statements of the kind (a) — such statements as record, for example, the contents of a drawer, a warehouse, a gallery, an archaeological excavation. There seems merely to be a difference in the boundaries within which things of each kind are located — in the case of (a), spatio-temporal, in the case of (b), neither spatial nor temporal, in the case of (c), universe-wide, or without boundaries. That persons and artifacts are discovered by a different area of the mind than are irrational roots or propositions seems as inconsequential a difference as the difference in boundaries within which discovery is made. All are discoveries in the cosmic warehouse. The functions 'x is a young person', 'x is an irrational root of $x^2 = -2$', 'x is an attribute' seem to be on the same ontological footing and merely to take different sorts of values, and the statement that there exist values of these functions seems to use 'exist' in the same way. To claim that metaphysical sentences differ so radically from existential sentences of everyday life and mathematics that they do not tell us what there is, challenges both of these apparent facts.

On the face of it, their relation to contingent statements and to the necessary existential statements of mathematics appears to be that of the more general to the more specific. The impression that this is so is strengthened by seemingly unobjectional entailments between specific existential statements of classes (a) and (b) and the general existential statements of (c). In fact a metaphysician might argue for the truth of existence statements of the most general class (c) by adducing some such entailments as the following. (Take '→' to mean 'entails'.)

1. There are rickshaws in Shanghai → There are rickshaws → There are things.
2. There are rickshaws in Shanghai → There are rickshaws → There is the property of being a rickshaw → There is a property.
3. There are prime numbers between 10 and 15 → There are prime numbers → There are numbers.
4. That there are planets is a fact → There is a true proposition → There is a proposition.

And the existence of properties might be argued as follows. If there were no property of being a tree, for example, there could be no instances of it, i.e. no trees. But since there are trees there is at least one property. These entailments make the proof of metaphysical statements about what there is seem very simple indeed.

We know, however, at least in the case of the long-standing controversy over the existence of universals, that entailments which are asserted above to have the existence of universals as their consequents are subject to challenge. According to W.V. Quine, these consequents 'follow from the point of view of a conceptual scheme', whereas 'judged within another conceptual scheme an ontological statement . . . may be adjudged false'.[4] In other words, one can perfectly well admit there are rickshaws while holding it to be false that there is the attribute of being a rickshaw. So far as I can see, 'the conceptual scheme by which one interprets all experiences',[5] to which 'one's ontology is basic',[6] is either just the ontology under debate or else presupposes it logically. To say the existence of universals follows from 'casual statements of commonplace fact'[7] according to one conceptual scheme and not according to another is a simple denial that it follows from these casual statements alone, and provides no reason against its being held to follow. The puzzle is why it cannot be settled once and for all whether it follows or not. I think the question whether an entailment holds remains unsettled because it is unclear what the sentence 'There are universals' asserts — if indeed it asserts anything. So the similarity of 'There are things', 'There are attributes', 'There are numbers', etc. to 'There are rickshaws in Shanghai' and 'There are primes between 10 and 15' must be matched by differences which create an obstacle to coming to a decision on these matters. Quine writes: 'Our acceptance of an ontology is, I think, similar in principle to our acceptance of a scientific theory.'[8] If a survey of the differences among these sentences leaves them with only an outward, verbal similarity, Quine's claim may seriously come in question, and what, in truth, there is may appear not to be a question at all.

One important fact of difference which bears on the continuing indecision concerning the entailments 1–4, and stands in the same need of explanation, should be noted at the start. This is the fact that existential statements of metaphysics, unlike commonplace factual statements and unlike statements of mathematics, have their truth-values chronically in dispute with no prospect of a settlement. Admittedly, we may be a long time discovering the truth-value of 'There are other inhabited planets' and of 'There are three consecutive 7s in the development of π'. But in the first case we could describe getting to know which truth-value it had, and in the second, even though we might not be able to describe getting to know this without being able to describe the proof, we should at least be in agreement, once a proof was produced, regarding what its truth-value is. The difficulties standing in the way of discovering the truth, or falsity, of factual and mathematical statements are quite different from each other, but in the case of neither sort is one presented with the puzzling features peculiar to the difficulties of discovering that it is true, or false, that there are in the universe things, or relations, or propositions, or numbers. One cannot specify what the obstacles are which prevent reaching a decision. For example, one finds that a philosopher who denies that there are things is unable to say under what conditions he would be constrained to allow that there are. And similarly a philosopher who denies the possibility of knowing they exist is unable to say what would have to be done in order to acquire this knowledge. Again, could one say what would show the proposition that there are numbers to be false? and how would one show it to be true in the face of a philosopher's challenge? Quine writes: 'When we say, for example $(\exists x)$ (x is a prime. $x > 1,000,000$), we are saying that *there is* something which is a prime and exceeds a million; and any such entity is a number, hence a universal.'[9] Suppose a philosopher denies that there are universals?

Metaphysical propositions differ from factual and mathematical propositions not only in the respects that they are in permanent dispute and in want of any specification of what would be required to determine their truth-values. They differ also in respect of their so-called proofs and disproofs, though here metaphysical propositions are more akin to mathematical propositions than to factual propositions. Traditionally, metaphysicians have presented arguments for and against existence claims which resemble arguments in mathematics. Bradley, for example, argued that it is self-contradictory that things, properties and relations exist. But unlike proofs of self-contradictions in mathematics, his arguments gain no general acceptance and at the same time are not shown, by those who reject them, to be guilty of any generally acknowledged logical mis-step. A commonsense philosopher like Moore, who retorts that since he knows he had breakfast before he had lunch he knows that a temporal relation, and hence a relation, exists, does not point out an error in the argument. And presumably Bradley already knows that such expressions as 'breakfast before lunch', '3 < 4', etc. are not self-contradictory expressions in current English. Despite his argument, he continues to use specific relation words exactly as Moore does, and it is doubtful whether he could be made to feel, by Moore's translations into the concrete, that consistently with his view the word 'before' is in the same position as the phrase 'related to'. One gains the impression that in his eyes this phrase has been shown to be self-contradictory and hence without use in descriptive phrases but that his argument leaves untouched the use of specific relation terms, like 'less than' and 'before'. Thus he could agree with Moore that he had had breakfast before lunch and deny the reality of relations. Similarly, philosophical mathematicians might agree that 'There is a prime number between 4 and 6' expresses something true while dividing on the existence of numbers.

It would appear that what one might call category concepts occurring as the entire predicate of existence propositions have a quite different function, if they have a function at all, from specific concepts, or 'proper' concepts, as Wittgenstein called them. Evidently differences between these concepts are responsible for the differences just cited between metaphysical propositions and others. It will be useful, then, to compare the terms 'related to' and 'before', 'quality' and 'colour', 'number' and 'prime number', 'thing' and 'rickshaw', with an eye to their differences. Wittgenstein denied that the first term in each of these pairs is a generic name.[10] 'Red', to use W. E. Johnson's terminology, is a determinant under the determinable 'colour', and 'scarlet' is a determinant under the determinable 'red'; but the behaviour of the category concepts puts in question whether 'colour' is a determinant under the determinable 'quality', and 'rickshaw' a determinant under the determinable 'thing'. It is natural to suppose they are. To say that the concepts denoted by these words are related as the more generic to the more specific is another way of saying that 'There are rickshaws' entails 'There are things' and that 'There are shades of red' entails 'There are qualities'. Whether these are entailments is just the question at issue. At any rate, supposing they are entailments, the further question is whether they figure in demonstrations of the contents of the universe.

That these concepts are not related as the more generic to the more specific is suggested by various considerations. Take first the concept *thing*, which appears to be the most general of the concepts in the series, *rickshaw, conveyance, thing*. The word 'thing' seems to be a general name, only more general than 'conveyance', just as 'conveyance' is a general name, only more general than 'rickshaw'. Several considerations indicate that this way of looking at the terms is mistaken. First, teaching the use of the word 'thing' is not at all analogous to teaching the use of either 'conveyance' or 'rickshaw'. One could explain these latter by pointing to things to which each applied, and also to some to which they did not; for example, 'rickshaw' does not apply to carts or sleds. And one could test a person's understanding by asking him to point out rickshaws and conveyances. Obviously the learner could fail the test by pointing out some other kind of thing. We should know he had failed to understand 'rickshaw' if, for example, he pointed to a sedan chair or a gig, i.e. if he pointed to other species of things falling under the genus *conveyance*. This is the kind of mistake a person could make who failed to differentiate properly among *kinds* of things to which the word 'rickshaw' sensibly, even though falsely, applies. These considerations about teaching the use of the word show what the function of a generic name is; namely, to distinguish among kinds of things.

Consider now a person learning the word 'thing', and the type of mistake he could make, as contrasted with a person learning the word 'rickshaw'. A person who pointed to a gig and said, 'That's a rickshaw' would make the mistake of assigning a false value to the variable in the function 'x is a rickshaw'. He could also make a mistake if he had an hallucination, or pointed to a shadow or a mirage, where hallucination, shadow and mirage were all similar to a rickshaw. But a mistake of this kind is entirely different. It would consist of failing to distinguish appearance from reality, whereas the mistake of a person who pointed to a gig would consist in not distinguishing properly among kinds of conveyances. The expression 'x is a rickshaw' might be said to have two ranges of significance, which one could characterise as its 'reality' range and its 'appearance-reality' range. The one would comprise rickshaws and other kinds of real objects, the other, rickshaws and delusive rickshaw appearances. There are thus two kinds of situation in which 'rickshaw' would have the function of a generic name to set off objects within its range of significance from others. But this is not so for 'x is a thing'. 'Thing' functions like a generic name to set off things from appearances, but not to distinguish among *kinds* of things. Nothing within its 'reality' range of significance could fail to be a thing. That is, all sensible substitutions on 'x' in the expression 'x is a thing', save for demonstratives designating shadows and the like, would yield something true. Unlike 'x is a rickshaw', there would be no possibility of assigning, from its reality range, a false value to the variable. The kinds of mistake a person being taught the word 'thing' could make are thus limited to mistaking appearances for reality. And this difference sets off 'thing' from proper concept words like 'rickshaw'. Of course, these two are alike in that one could so far fail to understand both as to take them to apply to processes, events, qualities, relations or numbers. If one cited any of these and said, 'That's a rickshaw' or 'That's a thing' one would in each case utter nonsense, as English is at present used. But the difference between the two is that barring such mistakes or a confusion of reality and appearance, there is no other mistake a person being taught the word 'thing' could make.

This difference between the category concept *thing* and concepts like *rickshaw* shows up in a difference in the verifications of the existential generalisations of '*x* is a thing' and '*x* is a rickshaw'. Since both antecedent and consequent of the entailment '*x* is a rickshaw → *x* is a conveyance' have within their reality range of significance both true and false values, both success and failure in establishing their existential generalisations are possible. This is a feature of any empirical verification. But compare the entailment '*x* is a conveyance → *x* is a thing'. Within the reality range of the antecedent there are both true and false values, but within that of the consequent there are only true ones. There is nothing within this range which could fail to be an instance of the concept *thing*, which is to say that by choosing from this range one could never fail to establish that there are things. It is doubtful whether we should call a procedure which could not fail empirical, or that we should say we had established anything by it.

The lack of analogy between 'There is a conveyance' and 'There is a thing' with respect to establishment has its counterpart in a lack of analogy with respect to disproof. It is clear that we could not, by way of disproof of 'There are things', show someone that he was mistaken about each of the objects within the reality range of '*x* is a thing' (as we could with '*x* is a conveyance') — we could not urge that they were in fact not things. A philosopher like Bradley, who wishes to prove that things are unreal, makes no pretence of using empirical methods to do so. Instead he attempts to show that it is logically impossible that there should be things. I think the difference between the two kinds of concepts, the category concept *thing* and the generic concepts like *conveyance* and *rickshaw*, is the source of differences (a) between establishing the existence of conveyances and the existence of things, which is not paralleled by a difference in establishing the existence of rickshaws and the existence of conveyances; and (b) between disestablishing the existence of conveyances and things, which is not paralleled by a difference in disestablishing the existence of rickshaws and of conveyances.

Let us see whether any similar considerations hold in the case of existentials involving the category concepts *number*, *quality*, *relation*, *proposition*. Take first the sequence *even prime number*, *prime number*, *number*, of which *number* appears to be the most general concept. Consider the method for determining whether something is an instance of each sort. Numbers are obviously what we should test, i.e. only numbers fall within the range of significant application of these concepts. It is clear in the case of the first two concepts what calculations we should make in order to determine whether a number was an even prime, or a prime. But it is also clear that no similar calculation is involved in determining whether 31, say, is a number. '31 is an even prime', '31 is a prime', and '31 is a number' are on a quite different footing, in the following respects: whereas the denial of the first two results in a necessary truth and a necessary falsity, respectively, the denial of the third is an absurdity of language. Its denial is on a par with pointing out a chair to someone and saying 'This chair is not a thing'. This consideration connects with two considerations which are analogous to those pointed out in the case of the concept *thing*: first, a person could be taught the use of the terms 'even prime' and 'prime' by citing numbers to which these words applied and numbers to which they failed to apply, but in teaching the word 'number' one could not cite anything, within its range of significant application, which was not a number. This is to say that the word 'number' does not serve to distinguish amongst kinds, as do 'even prime' and 'prime'. It does not single out a species from a genus. One can say it singles out a logical type from others; but this is to say that '*x* is a number', unlike '*x* is a prime', does not have true and false values, but only true and nonsensical ones. Second, the method of establishing either that there is an even prime or that there is a prime among the integers is irrelevant to establishing what we are here supposing to be entailed by them, that there is a number. For as long as one is confined to the range of significance of 'number' one cannot cite anything to which the word 'number' fails to apply. Its truth range and its range of significance are the same.

I think the situation with respect to the concepts *quality*, *relation*, *proposition* is in important respects analogous. To throw into doubt whether these category concepts are generic concepts, to which others are related as more specific to more general, one has but to consider such sequences of concepts as *scarlet*, *red*, *quality*; *nearness*, *relation*; *true proposition*, *proposition*. Suppose in these sequences the appropriate entailments hold: *a* is scarlet → *a* is red → *a* has a quality; *a* is near *b* → *a* is related to *b*; *p* is a true proposition

→ *p* is a proposition. One could explain the application of 'has the quality scarlet', 'has the quality red' by pointing to scarlet things and to red things. 'Scarlet' and 'red' both distinguish things which are scarlet or red from those which are not. But in explaining what it is to have a quality there would be nothing one could point to of which 'having a quality' was a distinguishing feature. For there could be nothing that fails to have a quality. Similarly with relations. 'Being near to' could distinguish the objects *a* and *b* from the objects *a* and *z*. But 'being related to' could not distinguish any pair of things from any other pair. This is to say that *quality* and *relation* do not have the usual function of generic concepts. A further disanalogy with proper concepts shows up when one considers the differences in testing whether something is red or has a quality, whether two objects are near each other or are related. Similar disanalogies to those canvassed for the concepts *quality* and *relation* obtain in the case of the category concept *proposition* in contrast to *true proposition*. Only propositions fall within the range of application of these concepts, and it is clear that whereas there is a test for a proposition's being a true one, there is no test for 'There are other inhabited planets' being a proposition.

Differences between category concepts and others show up when one tries to represent them in another notation than English, the notation of logic. In the *Tractatus* Wittgenstein wrote: 'Formal concepts cannot, in fact, be represented by means of a function, as concepts proper can' (4.126).

> Wherever the word 'object' ('thing', etc.) is correctly used, it is expressed in conceptual notation[11] by a variable name. For example, in the proposition, 'There are 2 objects which . . .', it is expressed by '$(\exists x, y)$ . . .'. Wherever it is used in a different way, that is as a proper concept-word, nonsensical pseudo-propositions are the result. So one cannot say, for example, 'There are objects', as one might say, 'There are books'. And it is just as impossible to say, 'There are 100 objects', or 'There are $\aleph_0$ objects'. And it is nonsensical to speak of the *total number of objects*. The same applies to the words 'complex', 'fact', 'function', 'number', etc. They all signify formal concepts, and are represented in conceptual notation by variables, not by functions or classes (as Frege and Russell believed). (4.1272)

In the *Notebooks* he refers to 'There are *n* things' as a pseudo-proposition, which 'shews in language by the presence of *n* proper names with different references' 'what it tries to express'.[12]

In connection with these statements there are two points which need to be made. One point is that it is not intended that translatability into the notation of logic is to be taken as a test of the sense or nonsense of a corresponding English expression, but rather that peculiarities which show up in the logical notation highlight the peculiarities of English. The other point is that the notation of logic, in particular the quantifiers, may, and in fact does, leave open the matter in dispute between philosophers, namely, the status of existential sentences involving category words. To consider the second point first, quotations above from Wittgenstein make it clear that he takes such sentences to be nonsense. On the other hand, Quine takes quantification in certain contexts to commit one to an ontology, that is, to the truth of certain existence statements. It would appear, according to him, that one is committed to holding that things, propositions, classes, attributes exist if individual variables, propositional variables, class variables and functional variables are quantified over. He says:

> To be assumed as an entity is, purely and simply, to be reckoned as a value of a variable . . . this amounts roughly to saying that to be is to be in the range of reference of a pronoun. . . . The variables of quantification, 'something', 'nothing', 'everything', range over our whole ontology, whatever it may be; and we are convicted of a particular ontological presupposition if, and only if, the alleged presuppositum has to be reckoned among the entities over which our variables range in order to render one of our affirmations true.[13]

The 'criterion of ontological commitment [is]: an entity is presupposed by a theory if and only if it is needed among the values of the bound variables in order to make the statements affirmed in the theory true.'[14] To say that a theory T 'presupposes an entity' is to say that T entails the existence of that entity. Clearly Quine takes it to be either true or false that such an entity exists. That is, he takes the indicated entailment in such a statement as '$(\alpha)(\exists\beta)(x)(x\epsilon\alpha \ . \ \equiv \ . \ x\epsilon\beta)$: $\rightarrow$. There are entities over which α, β, and x range' to hold. And even though a schema such as $(x)Fx \equiv Fx$ involves no quantifier ($\exists F$) . . ., to say that this schema is valid involves 'an appeal to classes'.[15] For this is to say that the schema is true 'for all values of its free (but bindable) variables under all assignments of classes as extensions of the schematic predicate letters'.[16] He adds: 'By treating predicate letters [or class letters] as variables of quantification . . . we precipitate a torrent of universals . . .'[17] Though some schemata involving quantifiers over classes and attributes can be re-expressed as schemata free from commitments to classes or attributes, and although validity in first-order quantification theory can be redefined by reference to rules of proof which Gödel has shown to be complete, there remain, according to Quine, schemata in class theory and in elementary number theory (like $(\alpha)(\exists\beta)(x) \ldots$) which will not reduce to schemata devoid of quantified class variables.[18] It is an extremely curious fact that on the matter of what is entailed by a statement containing bound variables there should be such a divergence of opinion. Quine takes it as inescapable that certain occurrences of bound (class) variables 'convict [us] of an ontological presupposition'. But he admits that Carnap's 'attitude is . . . that quantification over abstract objects is a linguistic convention devoid of ontological commitment'.[19] And Wittgenstein no doubt would have denied in the *Tractatus* that there is such a presupposition, on the ground that the phrase 'existence of numbers, classes, etc.' makes no sense.

It is curious also that Quine makes no objection to supposing the quantifiers $(\exists x) \ldots$ and $(x) \ldots$, which he reads as 'There is some entity x such that . . .' and 'Each entity x is such that . . .',[20] presuppose the existence of 'individuals'. What is puzzling is not merely the divergence of opinion, between him and Wittgenstein, over whether the phrase 'existence of individuals' makes sense, but that he makes no attempt to represent an ontological presupposition in logical notation. What happens when one tries to translate 'There are individuals', 'There are attributes', etc. into logical notation is an indication of the difference between these category concepts and generic concepts. 'There is at least one individual', which is proved in *Principia Mathematica* as proposition 24.52, i.e. $(\exists x).x\epsilon V$, involves the function $x = x$, a property which according to Russell is 'possessed by everything'.[21] ('V' is defined as the class $\hat{x}(x = x)$.) It is interesting also that such a proposition could occur amongst the propositions of logic — that it should count as valid.[22] Of '$(\exists x).x = x$', which one might take to express 'There is at least one thing', Wittgenstein said in the *Notebooks* that 'it might be understood to be tautological since it could not get written down at all if it were false'.[23] And yet he was constantly unsure whether it, or its negation

$\sim (\exists x).x = x$, was a proposition at all.[24] Thus, 'Can we speak of the class $\hat{x}(x \neq x)$ at all? — Can we speak of the class $\hat{x}(x = x)$ either? For is $x \neq x$ or $x = x$ a function of x?'[25] Furthermore, 'Supposing that the expression "$\sim (\exists x).x = x)$" were a proposition, namely (say), this one: "There are no things", then it would be a matter of great wonder that, in order to express this proposition in symbols, we had to make use of the relation (=) with which it was really not concerned at all.'[26] Is there a way of saying in the logical notation, 'There are things'?

If one does not attempt to express it solely in the notation of logic, the natural treatment of 'There are things' is as the existential quantification of the function 'x is an individual'. Analogously for the statements 'There are attributes', 'There are numbers', 'There are propositions', etc. That is, it is natural to treat the terms 'individual' (or 'thing'), 'attribute', etc. as predicates, like 'book', 'prime', etc. But this is misleading, because it slurs over the important difference between the concept *thing* or *individual* and generic concepts. As has already been pointed out, 'x is an individual' does not have both individuals and non-individuals within its reality range of significance, unlike 'x is a book', whose range of significance comprises both books and non-books. Any values other than individuals yield nonsense when substituted for 'x' in 'x is an individual'. A similar point is imbedded in the following from the *Tractatus*:

> There are certain cases in which one is tempted to use expressions of the form '$a = a$' or '$p \supset p$' and the like. In fact, this happens when one wants to talk about prototypes, e.g. about proposition, thing, etc. Thus in Russell's *Principles of Mathematics* 'p is a proposition' — which is nonsense — was given the symbolic rendering '$p \supset p$' and placed as an hypothesis in front of certain propositions in order to exclude from their argument-places everything but propositions. (It is nonsense to place the hypothesis '$p \supset p$' in front of a proposition, in order to ensure that its arguments shall have the right form, if only because with a non-proposition as argument the hypothesis becomes not false but nonsensical, and because arguments of the wrong kind make the proposition itself nonsensical.) (5.5351)

What are we to say of the expressions 'p is a proposition', 'x is an individual', 'N is a number', 'ϕ is an attribute', 'R is a relation', and the existential quantifications of these? Certainly they do not appear to be nonsensical. But if not nonsensical, must one then admit that the values of the functions will constitute the items in a cosmic inventory? Is this the alternative? What must one conclude from the differences between '*p* is a proposition' and '*p* is true', '*x* is an individual' and '*x* is red', 'ɸ is an attribute' and 'Jones has ɸ', '*N* is a number' and '*N* is prime'? I have argued that the fact that the range of significance of the category functions and their truth range are identical shows 'individual', 'attribute', etc. not to be generic concepts. The bearing of this on the possibility of listing what there is in the universe has now to be examined. I shall assume that the existential sentences 'There are individuals', 'There are numbers', etc. make sense. But I shall argue that their import is so different from factual existential statements like 'There are cougars in Arizona' and from mathematical statements like 'There are primes between 10 and 15' as to preclude our supposing they declare the existence of things in the cosmos. We need to look again at these three types of statements.

With regard to factual statements like 'There are cougars in Arizona', it is clear that they make no reference to any verbal fact. It may be remarked that if the sentence 'There are cougars in Arizona' expresses something true, the expression 'cougar in Arizona' applies to an instance of the concept *cougar*, and if it expresses something false, 'cougar in Arizona' fails to apply to anything. But in neither case does the sentence make a declaration about this expression, either overtly or covertly. I think it will become evident that the other two types of statements do not have this complete removal from verbal fact. Philosophers have sometimes distinguished existential statements of mathematics from factual statements by saying either of two things: (a) that the word 'existence' in mathematical statements means something different — that mathematical entities have a different kind of existence from cougars and the like — or (b) that 'existence' means the same in the two contexts but that the entities said to exist are different.[27] Distinguishing between factual and mathematical existence statements has sometimes been treated as a matter of deciding which characterisation is the proper one. Philosophers who dispute over the two characterisations evidently share the assumption that, as in the case of factual propositions, the existence or nature of a kind of object, abstract rather than concrete, is in question. The assumption implies that mathematical propositions, like factual propositions, are not

verbal in import. But it seems to me that the necessity of propositions of number theory, say, which so radically differentiates them
from factual propositions like 'There are cougars in Arizona',
depends just on some fact about the use of words.

Consider the statement 'There is no greatest prime'. It is like the
non-necessary statement about cougars in that it does not mean the
same as a statement about a verbal fact, that is, it is not synonymous
with any statement referring to words or phrases. 'There is no
greatest prime', unlike '"Brother" means male sibling' which
mentions the word 'brother', does not mention the phrase 'greatest
prime'. Yet what one knows when one sees that 'There is no greatest
prime' expresses a necessary truth is exhausted by one's knowing
that 'greatest prime' does not have a descriptive use. The fact that
this sentence expresses a necessity derives simply from the use
assigned to terminology — mathematical usage precludes the
English phrase 'greatest prime' from describing any number. By
contrast, no fact about the use of the descriptive term of such a
sentence as 'There are no dinosaurs', which expresses a contingent
truth, precludes the term from applying to anything. To know this
matter of fact about the word 'dinosaur' is to know something in
addition to knowing the usage of 'dinosaur'. That 'dinosaur' does
not apply to anything is assured by a non-linguistic fact, to be determined by observation of the world. The word has a descriptive use
and so *could* apply to an animal; but it does not, and this does not
affect the use assigned to it. One cannot similarly say, as English is
used, that 'greatest prime' could have an application but that an
inspection of numbers bears out the fact that it does not. We can
form the self-contradictory expression 'greatest prime', but once we
have a proof that there is no greatest prime we know that the phrase
has no conceivable application. What I am saying here is not that the
sentence 'There is no greatest prime' *means* that 'greatest prime' has
no use, but that in knowing it expresses a necessary truth this is the
fact that we know; and there is no further fact to know. That is, to
know that the sentence 'There is no greatest prime' expresses a
necessity is just to know the empirical linguistic fact that 'greatest
prime' has no use to describe a number.[28] The point is perhaps
clearer in the case of necessary propositions for which no proof is
required, like 'There are no round squares'. To show someone that
it is true one does not ask him to survey geometrical figures. Instead,
one appeals to criteria for the use of the words 'round' and 'square'.

Since we wish to compare both existential and non-existential propositions of metaphysics with outwardly similar contingent and mathematical propositions, it will be useful to complete our account of mathematical propositions by exhibiting the linguistic character of existential propositions, in contrast with the non-existential ones just cited. For to do this is less simple than to indicate the verbal import of 'There is no greatest prime' or 'There are no round squares'. Consider the sentence expressing the necessary truth that there is a prime between 10 and 15. When we know that this sentence expresses a necessity, with what verbal fact are we acquainted? First of all, that the expression 'prime between 10 and 15' has a use to describe at least one number. But something more than this needs to be said in order to distinguish the fact that this sentence expresses a necessary truth from the fact that the sentence 'There are cougars in Arizona' expresses a contingent truth. For it might be said that in knowing these two facts one knows there are objects which the expressions 'prime between 10 and 15' and 'cougar in Arizona', respectively, describe. Further, it might be said that in each case a non-linguistic fact, established by observation, informs us that these expressions have application. The difference, of course, is that criteria for the use of 'prime between 10 and 15' informs us that the expression applies to a number and observation informs us that there is an animal to which 'cougar' applies. Explication of this difference will I think show up the verbal import of the proposition that a prime exists between 10 and 15.

Consider the translation into quantifier notation of the sentence 'There is a prime between 10 and 15': '$(\exists x)$. x is a prime . x is between 10 and 15'. The fact that this sentence expresses a necessity is equivalent to the fact that some sentence resulting from substitution on 'x' in 'x is prime . x is between 10 and 15' expresses a necessity. This is to say that within the language of numerals at least one numeral, 'a', is so used that 'a is prime and between 10 and 15' expresses a necessity. Take 'a' to be '11', and consider the fact that '11 is prime and between 10 and 15' expresses a necessity. What do we know in knowing this fact? That the criteria for the use of the component expressions prevent the expression '11 and not both prime and between 10 and 15' from having a use. What is logically impossible cannot, even in theory, have instances, and since '11 and not both prime between 10 and 15' expresses a logical impossibility, knowing this fact comes to knowing that it has no theoretical application. And this is precisely what we know in seeing that '11 is a prime between 10 and 15' expresses a necessary truth. To say the necessary proposition expressed by the sentence 'There is a prime number between 10 and 15' has verbal import only is to say that in knowing that some specification of the sentence '*a* is prime and between 10 and 15' expresses a necessity we know a fact about the use of a numeral.

Something should be said here in answer to the contention that a non-linguistic fact, namely that 11 is a prime between 10 and 15, established by an examination of numbers, informs us that the phrase 'prime between 10 and 15' applies to something. I have argued that the proposition '11 is a prime and between 10 and 15' is verbal in import. But suppose my claim is countered by the claim that inspection of numbers between 10 and 15 assures us that the phrase 'being prime' stands for an internal property of two of them, just as inspection of animals shows that 'being a cougar' stands for an accidental property of at least one animal. This counter-claim suggests the idea that numbers are objects, that 'being a number' is a generic name for them, and that 'prime between 10 and 15' is a description setting off one class of objects from another. It is clear that at this point we have arrived at a metaphysical position, namely, that numbers are objects and that they exist. We turn now to an investigation of these and other propositions of metaphysics, both existential and non-existential, to determine whether they are such as to assert what there is, or is not, in the universe. I wish to argue that they are, like mathematical propositions, verbal in import. They are like mathematical propositions in this respect but yet are different.

Two differences are apparent at once. One is that they are all somehow idle. 'There are numbers' has no role in any number theory proof. And 'There are attributes', 'There are relations', 'There are propositions', 'There are things' are not the kinds of sentence one would utter in anything but a 'philosophic moment'.[29] Likewise for their negations. The second difference is that two philosophers can dispute, without hope of coming to a decision, over whether there are such entities as numbers, attributes, relations, etc. while both are in the presence of the same facts and neither is blind, either psychologically or physically. This latter fact indicates not only that their statements are unlike assertions within mathematics, for which arguments adduced have a finality about them. It also indicates that the dispute is not empirical, that is, that the metaphysical propositions are like those in mathematics. Philosophers who deny the existential metaphysical claims under discussion here either refuse to accept the entailments of which they are consequents (e.g. that there are rickshaws entails the existence of things and of the attribute of being a rickshaw; or that there are primes between 10 and 15 entails the existence of such entities as numbers), or else they refuse to accept the truth of the entailments' antecedents. (For example, some philosophers object to Moore's 'proof' of an external world on the ground that it begs the question: they may grant that 'Here is a hand' entails the existence of an external object, but not accept that here is a hand.) It is interesting that those who deny existence claims in metaphysics (a) refuse to accept *any* evidence in support of those claims, and (b) argue demonstratively for their own claims. That is, they proceed as though their views were *a priori*. In assessing the status of these views let us consider first those which deny the existence of certain categories of things, as their treatment presents fewer difficulties. Because they each occur within the context of general philosophical positions which dictate rather different arguments in support of them, we cannot go into the detail of each view. But certain similarities will appear which bear on my claim that they are verbal in import.

Consider first Bradley's claims that there are no things, no qualities, no relations. These are made within the context of a philosophical position according to which things, qualities and relations have the status of appearances. We leave aside for the moment the matter of their status in order to highlight the important fact about what appear at first to be empirical claims, the fact namely, that the arguments for them are *a priori*, directed to showing that the concepts *thing*, *quality*, *relation* are self-contradictory. The procedure is similar to the proof that there is no greatest prime, and we may justifiably assume that Bradley intends his statements to express necessary truths. We can therefore treat the propositions he asserts in the same way as comparable propositions in mathematics, i.e. as having only verbal import — to use Findlay's expression, as 'reflecting' usage.[30] But do these metaphysical propositions in fact reflect usage? As a matter of English, the sentence 'There is no greatest prime' expresses a necessity; linguistic conventions being what they are, 'greatest prime' has no use. But it is obviously false to say that the words 'thing', 'quality', 'relation' have no use. Although they are not generic names for a thing or quality or relation, as are 'house', 'red', or 'north of', it is undeniable that in English they can be conjoined with 'proper' concept words without literal nonsense resulting. To know that 'There are no things, no qualities, no relations' expresses a necessity we should have to be knowing that 'thing', 'quality', 'relation' are deprived by current conventions of any function. But there are no such conventions, and of course, a philosopher who utters these sentences knows this.

If, then, his sentences express neither a necessary proposition nor an empirical one, and at the same time are not nonsense, what are his arguments intended to do? The explanation is I think that set out by Lazerowitz:[31] this is that his arguments are persuasive devices, devices unrecognised by the philosopher who uses them, for altering present language in a non-workaday way. A metaphysical argument purports to demonstrate a necessary truth, but since present linguistic conventions prevent the sentence concluding the sequence of proof sentences from doing what it purports to do, the argument can plausibly be taken to have another purpose: to induce one to accept other conventions. Wittgenstein wrote in *The Blue Book*:

> [The philosopher] is not aware that he is objecting to a convention. He sees a way of dividing the country different from the one usual on the ordinary map. He feels tempted, say, to use the name 'Devonshire' not for the county with its conventional boundary, but for a region differently bounded. He could express this by saying: 'Isn't it absurd to make *this* a county, to draw the boundaries *here*?' But what he says is: 'The *real* Devonshire is this.' We could answer: 'What you want is only a new notation, and by a new notation no facts of geography are changed.[32]

As Quine remarks, 'What there is [does not] depend on words'.[33] But the illusion that the existence of something is being asserted or denied or debated can depend on words. And a demonstration charged with no logical flaw can indeed create the illusion that some question is being settled about what should be listed in a cosmic inventory.

The use of words in a natural language is not so precisely circumscribed as to rule out their employment in argumentation eventuating in the most startling conclusions, for example, that the concept *relation* is self-contradictory. How in particular this is effected has to be ascertained afresh for the argumentation for each 'view'. The point I wish to make is that the sentence expressing a view, though it fails to assert a necessity, in purporting to do so has verbal import none the less. In the case of those metaphysical sentences which are advanced as if they express the necessary falsity of some existential proposition, the desired linguistic effect is evidently to preclude from use some word or phrase which now has a function. To argue that things, qualities, and relations *cannot* exist has the effect of producing reasons for linguistic revisions. The concluding sentence of the sequence of sentences used in setting out a demonstration fails because of actual usage to express a necessity; but in a revised language it would express one, and the point of the proof can be to justify *taking it* to express a necessity rather than showing that it does express a necessity. Such a revision would have no practical appeal. For the language in which words are so used that the sentence 'There are no things, qualities, or relations' expresses a necessity would be one precluding the use of 'thing', 'quality', 'relation' in existence sentences. The revision can be made less drastic by doing what Bradley did. On a linguistic level, he assures the continued use of these words in appearance sentences[34] in assigning to things, qualities and relations the status of appearances. In effect, what he does is to stretch the use of 'appearance' to apply to whatever thing-, quality- and relation-phrases normally apply to. So the use of the latter is contracted rather than rejected altogether. The belief the metaphysician has that he has shown things, qualities and relations to have the status of insubstantial appearance is an illusion produced by his unconsciously redrawing linguistic boundaries.

When Moore objects to Bradley's views and in defence of common sense opposes it with the claim that things and relations exist, it is most natural to take him to be asserting a plain matter of fact, even though it would be unnatural to assert such a thing in any ordinary circumstances. But construed as a reply to Bradley's position that they *cannot* exist, i.e. as a counter to a purportedly necessary proposition, the matter appears otherwise. Moore's claim has on the verbal level the effect of preserving the linguistic *status quo*. To see this it is useful to make the supposition that 'There are things', 'There are qualities', 'There are relations' assert empirical propositions and to examine the character of the sentences resulting from substitution on the functions 'x is a thing', 'ϕ is a quality', 'R is a relation'. If the propositions asserted by the original sentences are empirical and non-verbal, the propositions asserted by 'This (say, a house) is a thing', 'This (say, red) is a quality', 'This (say, north of) is a relation' would serve to substantiate them. I think it must be admitted that the only circumstance under which the first proposition would be non-verbal in import is that in which it serves to inform someone that he is not seeing a shadow or a mirage, or having an hallucination. In such cases the word 'thing' would function like a generic name to set off objects within its range of significance from others. But if a philosopher were to justify his claim that there are things, qualities and relations by asserting 'A house is a thing', 'Red is a quality', 'North of is a relation', clearly each of the statements he makes is necessary. And this tells us something about the logical character of the propositions they are supposed to support: they, also, will be *a priori*. The necessity of his supporting statements is guaranteed by the linguistic fact that in the sentences expressing them the words 'house', 'red', 'north of' have as part of their meanings *thing*, *quality*, *relation*, respectively. And this is what knowing that 'A house is a thing', etc. express necessities amounts to. The status of philosophical existential propositions which are used to counter the Parmenidean denials now becomes easier to assess. If the propositions supposedly supporting them are verbal in import, then 'There are things, qualities and relations' must likewise be verbal in import. For propositions whose sole informative force is verbal could not support propositions informing us about what there is in the world. Within the context of a dispute in which one of the disputants asserts the self-contradictoriness of the concepts *thing*, *quality*, *relation*, to insist that there are things, qualities and relations has the effect of urging that the words 'thing', 'quality', 'relation' retain the use they already have in English.

Existence claims about numbers, attributes, relations and propositions, when made by a Platonist, require a somewhat different treatment from existence claims a commonsense philosopher makes in denying the view that the world of appearances is unreal. A philosophical assertion that something exists has to be investigated in relation to what is being denied. In the case of the Platonic position, the objection is that the Platonist is understood to assert certain objectionable entailments, of which some 'casual statement of commonplace fact' may be the antecedent and an objectionable metaphysical statement the consequent. Consider the assertion that the proposition 'There is a prime greater than 10 and less than 15' is necessarily true. The Platonist would maintain that this entails the existence of a proposition, of an attribute, of at least one number, and of a relation, and that the existence of each of these entails the existence of an entity, one which is abstract rather than concrete.

That is, 'Propositions, attributes, numbers, relations are entities' is held to be necessarily true. Nothing will induce the Platonist to admit to the non-existence of a world of universals which, according to him, he clearly perceives by the eye of the mind. The fact that other philosophers fail to report such a finding does not shake him.

But of course if the sentence 'Propositions, attributes, numbers, etc. are entities' did express a necessary proposition then in point of English usage 'entity' could be used wherever 'proposition', 'attribute', etc. are used, just as 'sibling' can be used wherever 'brother' is used. It is obvious that the phrases 'true proposition', 'personal attribute', 'prime number' are proper English, whereas 'true entity', 'personal entity', 'prime entity' are not. Hence the philosopher who holds that 'Numbers are entities' states the essence of numbers, that it expresses what is undeniably because necessarily true, commits himself to a false proposition about English usage, unless the point of his claim is taken to be something else: to say, not that 'entity' does in fact classify numbers, but that it should. A revised language, in which 'Numbers are entities' expresses a necessity would do what is desired, classify numbers as entities. When the Platonic view that numbers have being is challenged by the rejoinder that numbers are scratches on paper, we may take the exchange as a family quarrel over what kind of entities they are, whereas as language is now used it is not a fixed convention that 'entity' describes numbers at all. The Platonic philosopher redraws the boundaries of the word 'entity' — extends it, and by this linguistic manoeuvre creates the illusion that he is asserting the existence of things not hitherto noted. Russell observed: 'Seeing that nearly all the words to be found in the dictionary stand for universals, it is strange that hardly anybody except students of philosophy ever realises that there are such entities as universals.'[35] His comment is made in the language of factual record, and the style of speaking is an important factor in creating an atmosphere which makes it difficult not to think the existence of something is being asserted. Although, as Quine remarked, what there is does not depend on words, the use of words to induce a new classification can produce the illusion that a *correct* classification of what exists is being made. Occam's injuction against the multiplication of entities can be interpreted as an injunction against creating the illusion, by language, that the existence of entities is being asserted. Language cannot create entities; but a philosopher can so use it that its point appears to be the factual assertion that something exists, whereas its point is verbal, not factual.

If what I have said about the import of existential and non-existential propositions of metaphysics is correct, then the disputes about them, and their 'proofs', have been misconceived. It is clear in general that if a statement is verbal in import it gives us information about a language but tells us nothing about the world to which the language is used to refer; it tells us nothing about what there is in the world.

Notes

1. *Some Main Problems of Philosophy* (1953), London: Allen & Unwin, London, p. 1.

2. *Tractatus Logico-Philosophicus*, 4.1272; and *Notebooks, 1914–1916* (1961), Oxford: Basil Blackwell, p. 108e.

3. From the translation of D. F. Pears and B. F. McGuinness (1961), London: Routledge & Kegan Paul. Unless noted otherwise, this translation is to be used throughout.

4. 'On What There Is' (1961), in *From a Logical Point of View*, Cambridge, Mass.: Harvard University Press, revised edn, p. 10.

5. Ibid.

6. Ibid.

7. Ibid.

8. Ibid., p. 16.

9. 'The Reification of Universals', in *From a Logical Point of View, op. cit.*, p. 103.

10. From the lecture notes of Alice Ambrose, 1934–35.

11. The German words translate literally as 'conceptual notation', rather than as 'logical symbolism' (C. K. Ogden's translation, Harcourt Brace, 1922), but in the context it is reasonably clear that Wittgenstein is referring to Russell's logical notation.

12. p. 20e.

13. *From a Logical Point of View*, p. 13.

14. Ibid., p. 108.

15. Ibid., p. 115.

16. Ibid.

17. Ibid., p. 123.

18. See discussion, *Methods of Logic* (1959), New York: Henry Holt, pp. 227–8, revised edn.

19. *Methods of Logic*, p. 208.

20. *From a Logical Point of View*, p. 102.

21. *Principia Mathematica* (1925), Cambridge: Cambridge University Press, 2nd edn, p. 216. $(x) . x = x$ is proved as proposition 50.53.

22. See Russell's discussion of the way in which the logical primitives guarantee that 'there is something'. *Principia Mathematica*, pp. 226, 335.

23. p. 11e.

24. See *Tractatus*, 5. 5352.

25. *Notebooks, 1914–1916*, p. 16e.

26. Ibid., p. 47e.

27. Quine says in *Methods of Logic*, p. 198: 'When the Parthenon and the number 7 are said to be, no distinction in the sense of "be" need be intended. The Parthenon is indeed a placed and dated object in space–time while the number 7 (if such there be) is another sort of thing; but this is a difference between the objects concerned and not between senses of "be".'

28. For an elaboration of this treatment of necessary propositions, see M. Lazerowitz's 'Necessity and Language'.

29. G. E. Moore's phrase.

30. 'Can God's Existence be Disproved?' (1948), *Mind*, vol. LVII, no. 226, p. 182.

31. See especially 'The Existence of Universals' (1955), in *The Structure of Metaphysics*, London: Routledge & Kegan Paul; and 'Moore and Philosophical Analysis' (1964), in *Studies in Metaphilosophy*, London: Routledge & Kegan Paul.

32. p. 57.

33. *From a Logical Point of View*, p. 16.

34. For this thesis and its elaboration, see M. Lazerowitz's 'Appearance and Reality', in *The Structure of Metaphysics*.

35. *The Problems of Philosophy* (1943), London: The Home University Library, Oxford University Press, p. 146.

3 A PRIORI TRUTHS AND EMPIRICAL CONFIRMATION

C. I. Lewis has distinguished between 'explicitly analytic' statements, such as 'All cats are necessarily animals', and 'implicitly analytic' statements, such as 'The class of (existent) cats is included in the class of animals', which affirms that something '(which *is* necessarily true) is actually true'.[1] He uses this distinction to justify holding that implicitly analytic statements, which are nevertheless 'genuinely analytic',[2] might be established by a procedure comparable to that used to infer empirical generalisations, namely, examination of cases. In his own words:

> that the class of (existent) cats is included in the class of animals can be assured by reference to the meanings of 'cat' and 'animal' without recourse to further and empirical evidence. But also it might be established — as well established as most laws of science, for example — by generalisation from observed instances of cats.[3]

In natural science examination of cases is a means either to render a generalisation probable or to disestablish it by exhibiting a counter-instance. Lewis writes that 'we may be able to discover that an implicitly analytic statement, like "All cats are animals", is *true* by empirical investigation, and without discovering that it is analytic'.[4] So what is seemingly implied — if not explicitly stated — in these remarks is the philosophical claim that a logically necessary general statement is open to being rendered probable by an examination of cases. It thus implies that a proposition can be both analytic and true as a matter of fact.

The point of confining the class of cats to the class of *existent* cats is obscure until we realise that Lewis's claim requires the class of cats to be non-empty. One cannot discover by an empirical investigation that all cats are animals unless cats exist: that is, there is no generalising from observed instances of cats unless there are cats. Lewis's account is only applicable (if indeed it is applicable) to necessarily true general propositions whose subject-class is non-empty. It is inapplicable to such a proposition as *All dinosaurs are animals*. It becomes clear that a proposition such as *All (existent) cats are animals* is to be viewed as a conjunction, of which one component is an empirical proposition — in the present example, *There are cats*. It now becomes unclear how Lewis arrives at the philosophical view that an *analytic* statement can be established in this manner, for this 'implicitly analytic' statement seems not to be 'genuinely analytic', that is, 'certifiable from examination of meanings',[5] as he claims it is. The existence of cats cannot be certified by analytical means.

As against Lewis, Wittgenstein has stated (*Tractatus*, 6.1222): 'logical propositions cannot be confirmed by experience any more than they can be refuted by it. Not only must a proposition of logic be irrefutable by any possible experience, but it must also be unconfirmable by any possible experience.' This characterisation can easily be seen to cover any necessarily true proposition p, regardless of whether p is of the form $\sim \diamond \sim p$. Although *All cats are animals* does not assert that all cats *necessarily* are animals, it is nevertheless analytic, and according to Lewis can be known to be such: by knowing 'the corresponding *explicitly* analytic statement . . . that all cats are animals is a logically necessary fact, whose contradiction involves an inconsistency'.[6] If one knows this with regard to any proposition p, one knows that there is no possibility of there being a counter-instance. To falsify by experience an analytic proposition would be to establish by experience a logically impossible one. That part of Wittgenstein's claim, *viz*. that a proposition of logic is irrefutable by any possible experience, is thus obvious.

At first glance the other part of Wittgenstein's characterisation of logical propositions — namely, that they cannot be confirmed by any theoretical experience — might seem to be in a more questionable position than the claim that they are irrefutable. Within mathematics analogous general propositions — analogous in the sense that they are *a priori* — can properly be described as having instances on which the generalisations are based. It is proper to speak of supporting cases; at least it must be considered proper if 'supporting case' has a characterising use in the language of mathematicians. Regarding certain mathematical laws Polya wrote that they are 'suggested by special cases, the results being found by induction and proved later'.[7] Hardy described Ramanujan as 'proceeding by induction from numerical examples',[8] which confirm a general conjecture. The process of finding confirming cases of the proposition that any even number is the sum of two primes (e.g. finding that $100 = 97 + 3$) has been given as an example of collecting 'empirical evidence'.[9]

What needs to be emphasised here is the vast difference between the uses made of special cases of general propositions in mathematics and in natural science. Special cases in mathematics can serve as a basis for conjecture and thus as a prelude to a demonstration. No mathematician would go about *establishing* a general proposition by marshalling instances of it. A generalisation is not established until a demonstrative proof is at hand. And the latter is an entirely different activity from finding confirming cases. When Lewis speaks of generalising from observed instances of cats as a relevant procedure for establishing that all cats are animals, it is plain that what he has in mind is intended to parallel the natural scientist's procedure of generalising from observations which render the generalisation probable. But in natural science, repeatedly finding confirming instances of a generalisation is not a prelude to a *demonstrative* proof. There is no such thing as a demonstrative proof of a law of nature, i.e. an *a priori* proof of an empirical proposition. In this respect what is required to make a scientific generalisation secure is different in kind from what is required to make a mathematical law secure. A scientific law is never secure in the sense that a counter-instance is unimaginable. To be secure in this sense a scientific law would have to be necessary, i.e. 'genuinely analytic'.

Looking on *All cats are animals* as a generalisation, and at the same time as analytic, it is clear that no instance of it could fail to be a confirming instance. It is instructive to examine what its confirming instances must be like on Lewis's view that the same inductive procedure used in natural science can establish it. Confirmation would be effected by verifying in the case of each examined cat that it is an animal; that is, observation would establish the truth of each of a set of singular propositions, *This cat is an animal*, *That cat is an animal*, etc. There being no discovered counter-instances, one goes on by induction to *All cats are animals*.

It is obvious that these supporting instances differ in important respects from instances, say, of cats that are mousers. The sentences, 'This cat is an animal' and 'This cat is a mouser', use the demonstrative 'this', whose customary usage is to select particular things from an assemblage. The proposition, *This cat is a mouser*, implies the possibility of there being cats that are not mousers. But no similar possibility is left open by *This cat is an animal*. The word 'this' occurring in the expression of the latter is a spurious demonstrative, as it has no selective function. Nor could any such singular proposition be evidence for the supposedly factual generalisation. If it could be, then *This cat is not an animal* would *per impossible* count as evidence against it. These dissimilarities raise the question whether it is possible for 'empirical investigation' to have any relevance to establishing *All cats are animals*.

Although the general propositions of number theory are not empirical, something like empirical investigation does occur when the truth-value of a given proposition is unknown. The search for examples and counter-examples parallels in an obvious way the search for examples and counter-examples of natural laws, and the talk surrounding the search is similar. Gamov writes, concerning Fermat's theorem that for all $n > 2$, $x^n + y^n \neq z^n$, 'the possibility, of course, always remains that the theorem is wrong, and that an example can be found in which the sum of two equal powers of two integers is equal to the same power of the third integer'.[10] Entertaining this possibility involves a seeming paradox, for if the theorem is true, no logical possibility of its being 'wrong' exists — i.e. there would be no logical possibility of a counter-example. Yet although Gamov's language is such as to make Fermat's theorem analogous to an empirical generalisation, one having both truth-values open to it, his language can be so interpreted as to escape objections to which Lewis's treatment of *All cats are animals* as an empirical generalisation is subject.

The difference rests on the character of necessary propositions. We can describe their character indirectly by reference to the sentences expressing them: That a sentence$_1$ expresses a necessary proposition is equivalent to the fact that a sentence$_2$, to the effect that some related expression in the language in which sentence$_1$ occurs has no descriptive use, expresses a verbal truth: e.g. that the sentence$_1$ 'All cats are animals' expresses a necessary proposition is equivalent to the fact that the sentence$_2$ 'The expression "cat but not an animal" has no application'[11] expresses a true verbal proposition.[12] It is, of course, clear that it is a fact of language — an empirical fact — that 'cat but not animal' has no descriptive use. This fact is ascertainable by reference to our language. But inspecting usage in the case of the sentence, 'For all $n > 2$, $x^n + y^n \neq z^n$', is of no help: it does not give the information required to cast out of the language of mathematics the expression 'sum of two equal powers of two integers equal to the same power of a third integer'. Proof of Fermat's theorem would have this linguistic result. The paradox of asserting that special cases of $x^n + y^n \neq z^n$ ($n > 2$) make it probable that the inequality holds can be avoided by describing their function in a similar way: as making it probable that for $n > 2$ the *expression* '$x^n + y^n \neq z^n$' denotes a self-inconsistency, i.e. as making it probable that it has no descriptive place in mathematical language. Probability talk, when directed towards an empirical matter — whether an expression has a use — is paradox-free.

By contrast, in the sentence 'All cats are animals' the use of the terms is already known, and amassing instances as a means of establishing the generalisation is not construed by Lewis as making probable that 'cat but not an animal' does, or does not, have a use to refer to something. He envisages the empirical investigation of cats as a way of establishing a non-verbal proposition, analogous to inferring a scientific generalisation from cases. As is known, in his system of strict implication, Lewis demonstrated the two theorems $\sim \Diamond p < \sim p$ and $\sim \Diamond \sim p < p$ (18.41 and 18.42).[13] '[F]or any statement asserting something to be logically necessary', he writes, 'there is a correspondingly implicitly analytic statement, which asserts only that something is factual'.[14] To keep to his illustration, the second theorem would be exemplified by: If all cats necessarily are animals, then it is a matter of fact that all cats are animals. From the consequent of this statement it follows that finding a cat that is not an animal would be a matter of fact impossibility, like finding a cat with three tails. Now a factual impossibility does not eliminate a logical possibility, and in consequence the factual statement, *All cats are animals*, would leave open the possibility of there being a cat that is not an animal. The term 'cat but not an animal' would denote the null class, but could, in principle, denote a membered class. Not only does this go against Wittgenstein's claim that an *a priori* proposition has no possible refutation; holding that *All cats are animals* is analytic and at the same time factual implies a contradiction, namely, that it is both impossible and possible for there to be a cat that is not an animal. If analytic, the term 'cat but not an animal' is not linked with any theoretically possible experience, and if factual, it is linked with the non-existence of a possible experience.

Lewis's position in respect of the consequence it appears to have is like the positivist view that necessary propositions are really verbal. The proposition with which positivists equate an *a priori* general truth is about usage, and thus empirical, so that the positivist view has been charged with the contradictory consequence that a necessary proposition is not necessary. One cannot reasonably assume that Lewis was unaware of what it is natural to take to be a simple consequence of his view, that an *a priori* true proposition can be falsified. It is as though he preferred not to see something he knew perfectly well. This calls for an explanation. How could he be aware of the difficulties in his view and fail to admit it is untenable? The explanation must be like that for the positivist, who certainly knew that a necessary proposition is not empirical. His seeming to embrace a contradiction must be thought to have no more substance than an appearance. There is no actual contradiction. We have to think that his claim that an *a priori* general proposition can be established by observation of instances is not what on the surface it suggests. Lewis represents himself as having made a discovery about a relation between an *a priori* proposition and an inductive procedure. One possible explanation of how he can appear to do this is that he makes a hidden semantic manoeuvre in which language is in some way being revised rather than being used to state a fact.

Again and again in philosophy views are put forward as though they announced some new fact about things or relations. When classical materialists asserted that everything is material they gave the impression of presenting a scientific discovery. Yet if one is sensitive to their behaviour, for example, their refusal to accept any describable phenomenon as being a counter-instance, coupled with their being unable themselves to describe one, it is easily seen that their account of the nature of phenomena is in no way comparable to the discovery, say, of Brownian motion. What has happened is that one of a pair of antithetical terms — in this case the pair 'material' and 'mental' — is artificially deprived of its application, while the other term to all appearances is not. However, the latter remains in the language by academic courtesy, so to speak, for it has in fact lost its former characterising function. When the term 'mental' is cast out by philosophical fiat, the retained antithetical term loses its use; it no longer functions to distinguish among phenomena.

To return to Lewis's claim that a general statement which has been analytically certified can also be established by an inductive procedure in the way in which a law of physics is established. If knowingly holding a contradictory view is not to be imputed to Lewis, his claim has to be interpreted otherwise. One possible explanation which helps clear up the paradox is that Lewis has reclassified an *a priori* general proposition, in what might be called the spirit of a semantic game, as an inductive generalisation. In the normal use of 'induction', adding confirming instances of a general statement may increase its probability.[15] In such a case as *All cats are animals*, it is impossible for there to be instances which make probable, or increase the probability of, its truth. Examination of instances not only fails to render probable the general proposition, it is a procedure which has no relevance to establishing it. To put it in the verbal mode of speech, the expression 'examination of instances' does not refer to a procedure. We cannot, however, suppose that Lewis has misapplied the expression, the use of which he knows perfectly well. One possible explanation of what has happened is that an innovation in familiar terminology has been introduced; one which *stretches* the expressions 'generalisation from observed instances' and 'inductive generalisation' to cover *a priori* propositions. The stretched use is such that 'inductive generalisation' is made, by fiat, to apply to *all* general propositions. Like the use given the term 'material' by the Hobbesian metaphysician, which artificially deprives the term 'mental' of its use in the language, the antithesis of 'inductive generalisation' is deprived of its use. The unnoticed consequence of this innovation is that 'inductive generalisation', although it ostensibly remains in the language, has lost its use to distinguish among general propositions. If its antithesis, 'non-inductive general proposition', is brought back into the language, then Wittgenstein's characterisation of an *a priori* proposition as having no confirmation (as well as no refutation) is preserved.

Notes

1. *An Analysis of Knowledge and Valuation* (Open Court, 1946), p. 91.
2. Ibid.
3. Ibid.
4. Ibid., p. 93.
5. Ibid.
6. Ibid.
7. *How to Solve It*, pp. 103–6.
8. *Proceedings of the London Mathematical Society* (1921) (2), XIX, p. lviii.
9. R. Courant and H. Robbins, *What is Mathematics?* (Princeton), p. 30.
10. *One Two Three . . . Infinity* (NAL, 1947), p. 41.
11. Although the individual words do have application.
12. Alternatively, to the fact that the sentence$_2$ 'The word "animal" applies to everything the word "cat" applies to' expresses a true verbal proposition. For a detailed account of necessary propositions, see Morris Lazerowitz, *The Language of Philosophy*, pp. 11–13. It should be clear that it does not state any equivalence between a necessary proposition and the sentence expressing it.
13. C. I. Lewis and C. H. Langford, *Symbolic Logic*, p. 163.
14. *An Analysis of Knowledge and Valuation*, p. 92.
15. In some cases in which a law of nature is established, it would be ridiculous to suppose that its probability might be increased by doing more tests: e.g. the combination of hydrogen and oxygen to produce water when repeated in a laboratory demonstration does not strengthen the probability of the same result in future cases.

Goldbach asked Euler whether he could prove that every even number is the sum of two primes or could disprove it by producing a counter-example. As is known, mathematicians have conjectured that Goldbach's proposition is true, and their conjecture is supported by its having been verified by at least 200,000,000 numbers; but the problem put to Euler still remains. Fermat's proposition, and the proposition that there is no last pair of primes of the form p and $p + 2$, are similar examples of unsolved problems. And each of these can be shown to involve a philosophical paradox. The paradox is bound up with the fact that number theory propositions, unlike empirical propositions, have only one theoretically possible truth-value. The truth-value they have, they have by inner necessity, to use Kant's characterisation. It would seem, however, that conjecturing or believing them to be true allows the possibility of their not being true, and thus to imply the possibility of their having a truth-value other than the only one open to them. When there are two opposing beliefs with regard to a given proposition p, since each belief is a *possible* belief, each attributes a possible truth-value to p. Hence, in the case in which p is necessarily true but believed false, p would be both necessarily true and also possibly false; and in the case in which p is necessarily false, but believed true, p would be necessarily false and possibly true.

Where mathematical propositions have been shown to be impossible, prior to disproof it seems proper to describe believing them to be true as believing what is logically impossible. For what is shown to be logically impossible was impossible before the demonstration. The belief, and the discovery of the demonstration, have a date, but what is demonstrated does not. Mathematics provides many examples of the discovery of impossibilities previously supposed not to be such. There was a time when it was supposed possible to find two integers s and t such that $s/t = \sqrt{2}$. And the myriad attempts to trisect an angle with straight edge and compasses attest to the existence of the belief that this is possible. Fermat once supposed that all numbers of the form 2^{2^n} are prime, but was soon beset by doubts which Euler 100 years later showed were justified. 2^{2^5} is factorable. In each case a supposition was made of the possible truth of some proposition. What the proof showed was that it was not possible. To be sure, no one knowingly supposes to be possible something that is impossible. But after a demonstration has been found one can ask *what* it is that was supposed, and one can be made to feel that it was impossible that one should have made a supposition. It is puzzling to know what people who said they were trying to trisect an angle with straight edge and compasses thought they were actually doing. For what was apparently supposed possible could not even have been conceived. Yet the original question whether a given proposition p is true is what initiated the investigation. And the question seems to imply that p's truth is one possibility, regardless of the fact that this possibility is not theoretically open to it.

Entertaining the possible truth, or possible falsity, of an empirical proposition poses no similar problem. Establishing its actual truth-value does not eliminate the theoretical possibility of its having an opposite truth-value: an empirical proposition *has* two possible truth-values no matter what its actual truth-value is. We can assert the conjunction $\Diamond p . \Diamond \sim p$ without contradiction, and we can assert without contradiction either conjunct with p *is true* or with p is false. That is, p may possibly be the case without actually being the case, and similarly for $\sim p$. To illustrate, we can conjecture that a suspect committed a certain crime, and finding that he did not raises no question about the possibility of his having committed the crime or about the possibility of our having made the conjecture. The detective can use the hypothesis that he is guilty in a piece of reasoning. For example, he can reason that if the suspect Smith, who is a cripple, were guilty, he would have had to have an accomplice. By establishing that no more than one person was involved, Smith would be found not guilty. His innocence is no longer open to conjecture; the possibility of his being guilty has been eliminated. But the theoretical possibility of his being guilty remains, even though what we might call the factual possibility has been removed. The established truth-value of an empirical proposition does not crowd out the theoretical possibility of the alternative truth-value. It does of course crowd out the factual possibility.

A *reductio ad absurdum* piece of reasoning in mathematics, though of the same general form, p implies q, not-q, therefore not-p, is entirely different from one whose constituents are all empirical propositions. For example, from the supposition that there is a rational number $s/t = \sqrt{2}$ it follows that s (or t) is both even and odd, and hence that the supposition is logically impossible. Solving a crime is different in kind from solving a mathematical problem. To prove the suspect Smith is innocent of the crime one does not show both that not more than one person was involved in it and that more than one was involved. That is, one does not establish the logical impossibility of his guilt. But when it is shown that 2^{25} is factorable, or that there is no theoretically conceivable way to trisect an angle with straight edge and compasses, what was once believed is ruled out as logically impossible.

In mathematics there would appear to be no gap between what is possibly the case and what is actually the case, and between what is possibly not the case and what is actually not the case. If p is possibly true, then p is necessarily true. For if p has the possibility of being true it is because truth is internal to it, which is to say it is true necessarily. If the possibility that 2^{25} is prime did lie within it, it would *be* prime. By contrast, where p is an empirical proposition, although the evidence for its possible truth may be relevant to its actual truth, the evidence for its possible truth may fall short of being sufficient for its actual truth. In mathematics there is no such 'distance' between possibility and actuality. As Wittgenstein put it, 'The feeling is that there can't be possibility and actuality in mathematics. It is all on *one* level. And is, in a certain sense, actual.'[1]

Once we recognise the peculiar character of mathematical propositions the question arises whether supposing to be possible what is logically impossible is a paradox infecting every *reductio ad absurdum* proof and every belief associated with an unsolved problem, or whether the paradox is a philosophical invention which has only a 'dissolution', to use Wittgenstein's word. We know that there is the question about Goldbach's proposition, for example, and also that proof by *reductio ad absurdum* is a standard procedure in mathematics. Still, there seems no escaping the question whether we are really making a *supposition* when we say 'Suppose Goldbach's proposition is true', and whether we are really assuming anything when we start the proof of the irrationality of $\sqrt{2}$ by saying 'Suppose there is a rational number $= \sqrt{2}$'. In the latter case the end result of the demonstration implies that we could not have conceived what we stated we were supposing. Are we merely going through the verbal motions of making an assumption or asking a question, without actually doing so? One can utter the words 'I am in two different places simultaneously', but are we using the words to express something we are entertaining? Analogously, we can utter the words 'Suppose p', where the outcome of the demonstration is that *p* is logically impossible. And the question is whether the words 'Suppose *p*' ask us to entertain a concept like *being red all over and also green*, and if so, whether we are simply going through the motions of making a supposition. Certainly we are taken to be making a supposition.

Some light on why this difficulty should arise in connection with modal propositions which are assumed, believed or conjectured is shed by a closer look at modal propositions. It will be useful to examine certain features of *a priori* propositions which conventionalists have called attention to. For the use they make of what they have perceived is in some respects analogous to what mathematicians do when they begin a proof with the words 'Suppose that . . .'. Seeing the analogy may help us see through the paradox which seems to be implied by supposing or believing the contrary of an *a priori* true proposition. The conventionalist notes, and stresses, a dissimilarity between *a priori* and empirical statements. In contrast to an empirical statement, an *a priori* true statement makes no sort of claim about things in the world,[2] for if it did, it could be falsified by changes which might occur in the world. Since a necessarily true proposition is unconditionally true, no possible condition could affect its truth-value. With respect to what there is, it remains true no matter what comes into existence or passes away. This being the case, it says nothing about what the world is like, either about what there is or about the nature of what there is. However, a sentence such as 'Cerise is a colour' or 'A horse is an animal', like an empirical sentence,[3] has literal meaning. This fact seems to suggest that it therefore must say something, and hence must have a subject-matter to which it refers.[4] The subject-matter according to Platonic philosophers are abstract entities, according to conventionalists, language.

Wittgenstein has said that we have the idea that the meaning of a word is an accompaniment of it; that is, a kind of object which coexists with the word, so that we can say 'Here the word, there the meaning'.[5] Against this idea he maintains that the meaning of a word is nothing in addition to its use. As he puts it, 'For a large class of cases — though not for all — in which we employ the word "meaning" it can be defined thus: the meaning of a word is its use in the language.'[6] The implication of this remark is that the Platonic conception of the meaning of a word as being a kind of object accompanying it rests on a mistaken notion about the use of the word 'meaning'. One reason for this notion according to Wittgenstein is that we tend to look for a substance when we encounter a substantive.[7] It is to avoid the temptation of the Platonic fantasy that he urges replacing talk about the meaning of a word with talk about its use. His well-known comparison is that language is like a box of tools.

To return to conventionalism. It is denied by conventionalists that the subject-matter of a sentence denoting an *a priori* proposition are abstract objects. The alternative to the rejected Platonic claim is that what it refers to is language. The phrase 'has literal meaning' is equated with 'is about something'; and what an *a priori* sentence is about — the only information it yields — is the actual use of terminology. Accordingly, on the conventionalist theory, the sentence 'Cerise is a colour' means the same as the sentence 'The word "colour" applies to whatever "cerise" applies to'; the two are substitutable for each other. The conventionalist theory about necessity, as is well known, is to the effect that propositions expressed by sentences like 'Cerise is a colour', 'Even numbers are of the form $2n$', 'A horse is an animal', are really verbal.

The conventionalist claim, taken at face value as asserting an identity between a necessary proposition and a verbal proposition, can easily be seen to lead to unacceptable consequences. To mention one familiar objection, the verbal proposition with which *Cerise is a colour* is equated is empirical, which implies that an *a priori* proposition is not *a priori*. To put it somewhat differently, the implication is that a proposition having only one theoretically possible truth-value has more than one. Further, if necessary propositions were verbal, then *all* propositions would be empirical. The consequence is that the term 'empirical' (and its equivalents) would not have the use it now has in the language to distinguish between kinds of propositions. The meaning of the expression 'empirical proposition' would be absorbed into the meaning of the word 'proposition'. It is plain that '*a priori*' also would no longer have its use to characterise propositions. Wittgenstein has remarked that antithetical terms from which one of the antitheses has been removed are like a tiller without a rudder. We might add that when one term is deprived of its function, so is the other: remove the rudder, and the tiller loses its function as a tiller. To cite another objection to the conventionalist theory, the sentence expressing the proposition that cerise is a colour does not mention words, i.e. is not about words, whereas its counterpart, '"Colour" applies to whatever "cerise" applies to', is about words. Thus the verbal fact expressed by the latter sentence cannot be what is expressed by the non-verbal sentence 'Cerise is a colour'.

Nevertheless, there are certain facts about *sentences* expressing necessary propositions which the conventionalist has perceived and from which he appears to infer that the *propositions* expressed are verbal. Whether he makes a mistaken inference, or does something else, requires further investigation. The facts on which he appears to base his claim are as follows: (1) that there is a logical equivalence between:

(a) the fact that the sentence 'Cerise is a colour' expresses an *a priori* truth; and
(b) the fact that the sentence 'The word "colour" applies, in point of usage, to whatever "cerise" applies to' says what is true; and alternatively, between (a) and
(c) the fact that the sentence 'The phrase "cerise but not a colour" is prevented by the use of "cerise" and "colour" from having a descriptive function in the language' says what is true.

(2) *Knowing* (a) is the same as knowing (b) or (c). That is, in knowing that 'Cerise is a colour' expresses an *a priori* truth, what we know is a fact of usage — either that 'colour' correctly applies to what 'cerise' applies to, or that 'cerise but not a colour' has been provided with no application in the language. And in as much as 'Cerise is a colour' is uninformative about things in the world, this is all that we know.

However, the equivalence of (a) to (b) and to (c) does not warrant concluding that the sentence 'Cerise is a colour' *means the same as* 'The word "colour" correctly applies to whatever "cerise" applies to', or that it *means the same as* 'The phrase "cerise but not a colour" has been given no descriptive function in the language'. What we nevertheless can say is that if these facts about the words 'cerise' and 'colour' did not obtain, the sentence 'Cerise is a colour' would not express a necessary proposition. Because this sentence is in the non-verbal form of speech we cannot say that it expresses a linguistic fact. However, what we might say is that it 'alludes to', without expressing, what its counterpart, '"Colour" applies to whatever "cerise" applies to', explicitly asserts. We might bring out the point by saying that the content of the verbal counterpart is the *unexpressed content* of 'Cerise is a colour'. As should be clear by now, a sentence whose meaning is an *a priori* proposition is unlike its verbal counterpart, whose meaning is an empirical proposition. But the unlikeness is, in John Wisdom's words, 'an unlikeness not of subject-matter but of manner of functioning'.[8]

If the conventionalist view were what it is natural to take it to be, a theory about the nature of necessary propositions resting on facts (1) and (2), then the objections against it would be conclusive, and the philosopher who held it would have to give it up. But there is the possibility that the view is not what it is taken to be by conventionalist and non-conventionalist alike. If this is so, it would help explain why the conventionalist does not feel refuted by the objections. It may be that he is not stating a mistaken theory, and is therefore not committed to its consequences, but not because what he states is true. There is an alternative interpretation of what he is doing when he appears to advance a theory about necessity, one which fits in with his holding the view in the face of apparently overwhelming objections to which he has not replied in any satisfactory way. It will be instructive to examine this alternative because of its analogy to an alternative account of what the mathematician is doing when he says 'Suppose there is a rational number $= \sqrt{2}$'.

In the case of the conventionalist, 'has literal meaning' and 'being about something' are equated. As applied to sentences expressing necessary propositions, what they are claimed to be about is actual usage. The alternative explanation is that the conventionalist is not making a mistaken claim about the relationship of 'having literal meaning' to 'being about something', but instead is *stretching* 'has literal meaning' so as to cover everything to which 'is about something' applies. His assertion of their identity is a statement of a preferred, contrived use of 'literal meaning' rather than a mistaken application of the term. The statement of a semantic preference, unlike a factual claim, does not have the consequences the factual claim would have. When Humpty Dumpty declared 'There's glory for you!', his widening the use of 'glory' is taken to be the intent of his exclamation, even though it is not about the word 'glory'. The irrelevance of citing non-verbal facts to contradict him is obvious. Humpty Dumpty was explicit about his intentions, as the conventionalist is not, when he retorted, 'When *I* use a word it means just what I choose it to mean'. The conventionalist conceals his intent, from himself as well as others, by expressing his preference in the language appropriate to the expression of a theory: 'Cerise is a colour' is about words. By semantic decree the sentence 'Cerise is a colour' is, by the device of stretching the term, *made* to mean the same as the sentence '"Colour" correctly applies to whatever "cerise" applies to'. What it is that we know in knowing that 'Cerise is a colour' expresses an *a priori* truth is 'converted' into the meaning of the sentence. A game is being played, to use Wittgenstein's words, with the term 'literal meaning', which is stretched to cover what is only obliquely referred to by an *a priori* sentence.

The point of doing this is not to urge the practical adoption of a change in the use of the term 'literal meaning' but to highlight a likeness between indicative sentences which express *a priori* truths and indicative sentences which express propositions about the use of terminology. The conventionalist does this by the technique of semantic exaggeration. He exaggerates the similarity between sentences which are about usage and their non-verbal *a priori* counterparts; and at the same time he minimises the difference in their form of expression. Under the guise of announcing a theory about the nature of necessity he stresses the fact that *a priori* sentences are like sentences about usage in respect of the information they convey. He minimises, to the vanishing point, the fact that what they convey is not what they express. In a concealed way a verbal innovation in the use of 'literal meaning' is presented in the form of a theory.

In the so-called 'Yellow Book' Wittgenstein is reported as saying:

> The fallacy we want to avoid is this. When we reject some form of symbolism we are inclined to look at it as though we had rejected a proposition as false. . . . This confusion pervades all of philosophy. It is the same confusion that considers a philosophical problem as though such a problem concerned a fact of the world instead of a matter of expression.[9]

To bring this into connection with the conventionalist–Platonic controversy, his words might be reformulated as follows: The confusion involved in the controversy considers the philosophical problem as though it concerned a fact about the nature of necessary propositions instead of an altered use of an expression.

We are now in a better position to reach a proper understanding of how we can suppose or conjecture the truth-value of a logically single-valued proposition, *as if* it could have a truth-value other than the one it has. A *reductio ad absurdum* proof in mathematics appears to ask us to assume or suppose the truth of a proposition which the demonstration shows to be logically impossible. The language used is like that of advancing a scientific hypothesis and by recourse to fact eliminating it. The unlikeness between the mathematical use of 'assume' and its scientific use might lead one to suppose that the mathematical use is mistaken — that it is thought to express an assumption which it has no actual use to express. But the mathematical use is as well established as the everyday use of the term and its use in science, and it is not part of the intention in this paper to raise objections to it. The aim is to understand it.

Since a *reductio ad absurdum* demonstration proceeds *a priori*, the conjunction of sentences expressing it stands for a series of entailments and thus for an *a priori* proposition. In the proof of the irrationality of $\sqrt{2}$, the first of the sentences correlated with each step of the demonstration correctly includes the use of 'suppose' in conjunction with the expression 'rational number $s/t = \sqrt{2}$'. This implies that, unlike the use of 'suppose p' in the empirical case, where the words stand for a theoretically possible concept, their occurrence in *reductio ad absurdum* proofs has no comparable use. A different account of their use has to be given, one not requiring that 'p' denote a proposition capable of either of two truth-values.

The paradox which a *reductio* proof presents, of requiring us to suppose the unsupposable, can be dispelled by an account of the use of 'supposition', 'hypothesis', 'assumption', etc. analogous to the account given of the conventionalist's stretched use of 'having literal meaning'. Since these terms have an accepted use in mathematics and hence cannot be said to be used incorrectly, the mathematical use can only be properly understood as a *stretched* use, one in which the terms are made to cover cases in which conceivability does not enter. To imitate the language of geometry where, for example, the term 'point' is sometimes defined as a circle with zero radius, we might say that the mathematical use of 'supposition' and similar terms is defined to mean 'zero hypothesis'. This use indeed departs from its everyday use, but since it is a correct use, we can conclude that paradox only arises from treating it as if its use were in all contexts the same. We might surmise that the use 'supposition' has in mathematical contexts was re-edited in such a way as to bring the language of *reductio ad absurdum* demonstrations into line with the language of argumentation from empirical counter-factual suppositions. Regardless of whether mathematicians were explicitly aware of their terminological departure from the usual uses, the departure has been effectively concealed by the form of language used to introduce and continue it. It is a hidden alteration in a familiar nomenclature which brings the proofs of the irrationality of $\sqrt{2}$ and the infinity of primes into conformity with e.g. Archimedes' rejection of the artificer's claim that Hiero's crown was fashioned of pure gold. Starting from the hypothesis that the metal of the crown was unalloyed, Archimedes reasoned that it would displace a volume of liquid equal to that displaced by an equally heavy lump of pure gold, and then inferred from the fact that the crown displaced a greater volume that the hypothesis was false.

A *reductio ad absurdum* demonstration verbally parallels an argument employing a counter-factual hypothesis. But a *reductio* argument does not eliminate a possibility, as there is no possibility to be eliminated. This means that the use of 'Suppose *p* . . .' at the beginning of a demonstration does not imply the existence of a possibility which '*p*' stands for. In as much as the unexpressed content of the *a priori* conclusion is verbal, what the proof does eliminate is an expression from mathematical language.[10] Some expression in the sentence which stands in the position of a hypothesis is shown to have no use in the language of mathematics.

Believing or conjecturing the truth of a mathematical proposition whose truth-value is unknown can be analogously explained. In the case where a belief turns out to be impossible, the use of 'believe' is extended in the same way as the use of 'suppose' in a *reductio* proof.[11] We might sum up by saying that the hypothesis expression of a *reductio* proof does not express a hypothesis; nor does the expression of a belief in mathematics express a belief. Nevertheless it is not improper to speak of the one as expressing a false hypothesis and the other a false belief.

Notes

1. *Philosophical Remarks* (1975), ed. R. Rhees, Chicago: University of Chicago Press; trans. of *Philosophische Bermerkungen* (1964) by Raymond Hargreaves and Roger White, Oxford: Basil Blackwell, p. 164.

2. It is a frequently held view that some *a priori* propositions state an essential feature of things, for example, *A horse is an animal. Being an animal* is said to be an essential attribute of a horse. But this is another way of saying that *being a horse* entails *being an animal*. Thus an essential property of a thing turns out to be a property entailed by another property.

3. 'Empirical sentence' is here used as short for 'sentence expressing an empirical proposition': similarly for '*a priori* sentence'.

4. In a conversation some years ago with Professor J. L. Austin, he urged that since mathematical propositions are true, they must be about something.

5. *Philosophical Investigations*, p. 49.

6. Ibid., p. 20.

7. *The Blue Book*, p. 1.

8. *Philosophy and Psychoanalysis* (1953), Oxford: Basil Blackwell, p. 48.

9. *Wittgenstein's Lectures, Cambridge 1932–35*, from the notes of Alice Ambrose and Margaret Macdonald, ed. Alice Ambrose (1979), Oxford: Basil Blackwell, p. 69.

10. 'We have not excluded any case at all, but rather the use of an expression.' *Wittgenstein's Lectures, Cambridge 1932–35*, p. 63.

11. The case in which what is believed turns out to be necessarily true requires separate discussion.

5 INVENTION AND DISCOVERY

'It is the merest truism, evident at once to unsophisticated observation that mathematics is a human invention.'[1] Quite evidently mathematics did not appear as such to G. H. Hardy, who wrote, 'I believe that mathematical reality lies outside us, and that our function is to discover or *observe* it, and that the theorems which we prove and which we describe grandiloquently as our "creations" are simply our notes of our observations.'[2] Proponents of the respective views that mathematics is invention and that mathematics is discovery would, I think, agree that both views cannot be true, and that certainly one must be false: the form of words in the two cases indicates that antithetical positions are being asserted. The difficulty is that no prospect of a decision between them presents itself. And this hopelessness of justifying either position suggests, not that there is some third compromise position which would satisfy both proponents, but that they misconceive the nature of the views they advocate and the point of the arguments they adduce for them. At least it suggests that a new investigation is in order, one which examines the nature of the rival theories and of the arguments for them rather than takes for granted that they are what they appear to be. Most probably Wittgenstein had something like this in mind when he wrote, 'what a mathematician is inclined to say about the objectivity and reality of mathematical facts, is . . . something for philosophical *treatment*'.[3]

In this essay I shall use Wittgenstein's general thesis that philosophical positions arise from misunderstandings concerning the use of words.[4] I shall maintain that we are misled by language when we accept either of the two rival views of the nature of mathematical investigation. And it will be most important to ascertain the precise nature of the views we are misled to accept and what their semantic sources are. It is natural to assume that if we are misled by language we are persuaded to accept something false. But if two positions are each other's contradictories then it cannot in both cases be *falsities* that we are misled to accept. I shall assume that being misled into either of two rival philosophical theses (whether or not they are each other's contradictories) is to hold as true something which taken literally is neither true nor false. If it can be shown precisely how language is used to create the illusion that something true is being established and the illusion that the counter-view is false, then with the exposure of the illusion both 'positions' reduce to pseudo-positions. To expose an illusion in these cases is not to show a *theory* to be illusory (i.e. false), but to show an assertion to be but the illusory appearance of a theory. It is this which I wish to show in connection with the two apparently antithetical claims, 'Mathematics is a human invention', and 'Mathematics is a record of discoveries in its special domain of objects'.

Wittgenstein said that philosophy, as he did it, 'in the end can only describe the actual use of language'.[5] And the actual use of language when compared with its philosophical use sheds some light on the latter. Language used in the actual doing of mathematics and also language correctly descriptive of various aspects of doing mathematics lead very naturally to what appears to be a theory when one *talks about* mathematics. And I want to say that in the hands of the philosophical mathematician advantage is taken of certain verbal analogies to gain acceptance of a manner of speaking about mathematics which has the semblance of a theory. This is what mustering support for a philosophical position comes to. Argumen-tation apparently in support of a position is a means of rationalising the adoption or retention of a certain description of mathematics. It is the source of a 'theory' but not the justification of a theory's truth. To make plausible this extraordinary claim on my part I shall need to show the sources of the 'views' and of the argumentation for them in the language used in the practice of mathematics and in the language correctly describing it. It will be useful first to record the different philosophical pronouncements made on mathematics as discovery and as invention in order to have before us the 'talk about' mathematics of which we wish to trace the semantic genesis.

We begin with certain philosophical questions, to which these pronouncements are answers, and shall translate them into the concrete by directing them to various of the following examples: $2 + 2 = 4$, $2 - 4 = -2$, $x^3 + x^2 + x + 1 = 0$ has one real root and two imaginary roots, there are infinitely many primes. The questions, which, it will be noted, are not of the sort which need be answered in order to *do* mathematics, are as follows: What are these proposi-tions *about*? Were the number -2 and the roots $\pm\sqrt{-1}$ invented, or only the symbolism for them? Can one invent, as opposed to discover, what necessarily exists? *Was* it *true* that $2 - 4 = -2$ and that $\pm \sqrt{-1}$ were roots of $x^3 + x^2 + x + 1 = 0$ before the domain of numbers was extended to negative and complex numbers? Is what we agree on as being a truth imposed upon us or decided by us?

To the first question, about the subject-matter of mathematics, philosophers have given an answer which, judging by its persistence from antiquity, it is entirely natural to give, and for which the resources of our language provide a powerful bulwark. It is expressed in Theaetetus's answer in the *Sophist*[6] to the question of the Eleatic Stranger, 'And number is to be reckoned as a among things which are?': 'Yes, surely number, if anything, has a real existence.' 'Uncreated and indestructible',[7] numbers for the arithmetician, 'the absolute square and the absolute diameter'[8] for the geometrician (who uses the visible forms only as an aid), lie open to the eye of the mind even more assuredly than the world of sense lies ready to inspection by the organs of the body. More than 20 centuries later the Platonic tradition appears again in Russell:

> the statement 'two and two are four' deals exclusively with universals, and therefore may be known by anybody who is acquainted with the universals concerned and can perceive the relation between them which the statement asserts. It must be taken as a fact, discovered by reflecting upon our knowledge, that we have the power of sometimes perceiving such relations between universals, and therefore of sometimes knowing general *a priori* propositions such as those of arithmetic and logic.[9]

It is obvious that on this account the mathematician is an observer, a discoverer — not an inventor. 'Invention' properly characterises new symbolism; for example, expressions for negative numbers, irrationals, complex numbers, transfinite cardinals. But this symbolism is merely a convenient notation for what the mathematician perceives. Investigation in arithmetic and number theory is like an empirical investigation, but of a non-empirical reality. A field lies before our minds for exploration, and these branches of mathematics are but 'the natural history of the domain of numbers'.[10] As for truth, what could not conceivably be otherwise lies beyond our power to create or destroy.

> Mathematics is independent of us personally and of the world outside, and we can feel that our own discoveries and views do not affect the Truth itself but only the extent to which we or others see

it. Some of us discover things in science, but we do not really create anything in science any more than Columbus created America.[11]

The remarkable agreement among mathematicians on the truth of a theorem results from the fact that the truth imposes itself upon any thinking person.

It scarcely need be said that this philosophical position has not gained unanimous assent. Indeed, to some people it has seemed without any merit, while the counter-position has appeared to be compelling: 'we have overcome the notion that mathematical truths have an existence independent and apart from our own minds. It is even strange to us that such a notion could ever have existed.'[12] Within this position, which might be broadly characterised as 'conventionalist', we find a quite different account of the subject-matter of mathematics and of necessary truth. Where Hardy says *2 + 2 = 4* is about numbers, Hilbert says it is about marks. Symbols are of course invented, and mathematicians who speak of the invention of numbers seem to equate this with the invention of symbols. Courant refers to *i* as 'purely a symbol',[13] and asserts that 'extension of the number concept was made possible by the creation of new numbers in the form of abstract symbols like 0, −2, and $\frac{3}{4}$'.[14] 'By introducing new symbols'[15] the domain of numbers is said to have been extended. And the behaviour of those numbers is decreed rather than observed:

> rules for the addition, multiplication, and equality of our symbols are established by our own definition and are not imposed upon us by any prior necessity other than that of usefulness for the application we have in mind.[16] . . . It took a long time for mathematicians to realise that . . . the definitions governing negative integers and fractions cannot be 'proved'. They are *created* by us in order to attain freedom of operation while preserving the fundamental laws of arithmetic.[17]

'We might whimsically decree some other rule for addition, such as

$$\frac{a}{b} + \frac{c}{d} = \frac{a+c}{b+d},$$

which in particular would yield

$$\frac{1}{2} + \frac{1}{2} = \frac{2}{4},$$

an absurd result from the point of view of measuring.'[18] Further, whether or not a generalisation is extended to a new field, as when Kummer extended the theorem that a rational integer is uniquely factorable into primes to a new species of number, ideals, is a matter for mathematicians to *decide*. Precisely what the decision is may for some time remain unsettled. Descartes denied what Gauss later by implication asserted, that $x^3 + x^2 + x + 1 = 0$ has three roots. And this means that mathematicians are the arbiters of what is necessary and what is not. They are governed by quite various considerations, some having to do with the further conduct of their subject (shall existence statements be accepted for which there is no constructive proof?), others with application, as indicated by Courant in the above quotation: for example

$$\frac{a}{b} + \frac{c}{d} = \frac{ad + cb}{bd}$$

is the accepted rule for determining the total amount of land owned by a legatee who has inherited two-thirds of one acre and four-fifths of another. It legislates that 'he owns exactly one acre in consequence of inheriting $\frac{2}{3} + \frac{4}{5}$ acres' shall express a contradiction. 'The mathematical proposition has the dignity of a rule'[19] (a rule concerning the use of language).

Looked on as a rule,

$$\frac{a}{b} + \frac{c}{d} = \frac{ad + cb}{bd}$$

is arbitrary, something about which there is freedom of decision to accept or not. And yet it seems anything but arbitrary, a necessity arising from the nature of rational numbers which leaves us no freedom. It seems that there should be one correct description of this arithmetical identity, as a creation or as a discovery. How does it come about 'that mathematics appears to us now as the natural history of the domain of numbers, now again as a collection of rules'?[20] Can one decide which face it presents is the true one and which the false?

I wish to say that neither of the two philosophical positions which purport to be accounts of *the nature* of mathematics is what it appears to be. Neither shows the true face of mathematics. Nor is this to say that both are false, although if taken to be true or false descriptions, it is difficult to explain why the two considerations to follow are not accepted as showing both to be false:

1. Clearly $2 + 2 = 4$ is not about the symbols occurring in its expression — the symbols are used, not mentioned; and this being the case it is not a rule about symbols. Nor can symbols and numbers be identified, as is obvious from the different uses in our language of 'the number 4' and 'the sign "4"'. For example, one can say of the sign but not of the number that it is black.
2. But neither can the signs be taken to name abstract objects open to inspection by the eye of the mind, if one weighs the following fact: that mathematicians, rather than the mathematical facts, decided whether $x^3 + x^2 + x + 1 = 0$ had three roots. Had a different decision been made, a different proposition would have been necessary.

Now on the 'discovery' view, since there *necessarily* are three roots it would be an illusion to suppose there was any freedom of decision in the matter of their number. Mathematicians had only to invent a notation for what lay ready to be found. Yet the fact that the symbol '$\sqrt{-1}$' was invented long before Descartes denied that the equation $x^3 + x^2 + x + 1 = 0$ had three roots, coupled with the fact that Descartes cannot be said to have made a mistake, makes such an account appear extremely unsuitable. The fact is that decisions have been made and followed. Even Hardy lapses into talk in keeping with this fact, for example, when he says 'There are technical reasons for not counting 1 as a prime'.[21]

If the 'creation' and 'discovery' views are understood as purporting to describe the subject-matter of mathematics, i.e. to be true or false descriptions of it, considerations 1 and 2 above would refute both. In the face of these considerations and others like them, what needs to be explained is why through the centuries there have continued to be arguments in support of the conventionalist and Platonic positions.

I wish now to examine the arguments brought forward for each position with a view to showing clearly the analogies from which they stem and the differences which they ignore. The arguments centre on two related topics: the domain of mathematical investigation and the necessity of mathematical truth.

I shall begin with reasons for the view that in mathematics we investigate a special domain of objective fact, that this domain is constituted of abstract entities existing independently of our minds. It is worthwhile looking at one question which prompts such a claim: what are mathematical propositions *about*? It is indisputable that it is proper English to reply 'About numbers', 'About polygons', etc. though there is no very natural, non-philosophical context in which such a question would be asked. One such natural context would be that in which one was asked to explain the meanings of the expressions 'mathematical proposition' and 'proposition of natural history' by someone who did not understand them. One could comply by indicating the subject-matter to which they apply, distinguishing mathematical propositions as being about numbers, figures, series, etc. from propositions about the world of nature such as 'Elephants are a source of ivory' which is about elephants and ivory. Another such philosophically aseptic context would be that in which one referred to propositions about primes, conic sections, convergent series, etc. by giving the page numbers of articles in an encyclopaedia where such assertions are made. But when the philosopher of mathematics refers to propositions about numbers he uses his words to imply that these propositions are about entities constituting a domain which he explores with a view to finding proofs that various truths hold of them. He can be represented as arguing as follows:

(1) Just as the true statements, 'Ruthie was a clever circus elephant' and 'There are owls with tufted ears', are about a certain elephant and about certain owls, so '6 lies between 5 and 7' and 'There are factorable numbers of the form $2^{2^n} + 1$' are about numbers. Further, the latter being true, and their opposites being self-inconsistent, 6, and factorable numbers of the form $2^{2^n} + 1$ must exist. And if there exist factorable numbers of that form there must exist numbers of that form, and from this it follows that there must exist numbers.

(2) If, as Euclid proved, there is an infinity of primes, then the numerals, which at any given time are finite in number, can be nothing more than names for what is there to be named.

(3) The distinction between an empty and a non-empty domain as clearly holds for mathematical propositions as for empirical ones. If there were no numbers of which it is true that a certain class of them, all the composite integers, are uniquely factorable into primes, would there be any difference between this proposition and the proposition that all square circles are square? Both would be true because the subject class was null, which flies in the face of the fact

that mathematicians tested particular composite integers for factorability into primes before proving the generalisation about all of them.

(4) Finally, that the body of mathematics is constantly extended by the addition of new theorems derives from a possibility lying within itself. It is as though the possibility of proof is a mathematical fact.[22] What can be proved is strictly determined, as the impressive rigour of mathematical demonstration indicates. The conceptual connections established by proof exist of necessity, and what more natural explanation of their existence than that they are compelled by the properties of the mathematical objects? The roads to truth are already laid down in the world of mathematics by the nature of the entities in it, and with sufficient cleverness the mathematician can map out the road leading from one truth to another. To appropriate a phrase of Lazerowitz's, he is a sort of cartographer of the supra-sensible — of what, according to Cayley, is 'a tract of beautiful country seen at first in the distance, but which will bear to be rambled through and studied in every detail of hillside and valley, stream, rock, wood and flower'.[23] The picture is in fact somewhat misleading, since the freedom to ramble is limited by the necessity of taking certain roads if one wishes to proceed from one truth to another. What roads are mapped are not subject to the will of the mathematician; only the choice among the possible roads is open. Courant's account of the identity

$$\frac{a}{b} + \frac{c}{d} = \frac{ad + bc}{bd}$$

as 'not imposed upon us by any prior necessity' misdescribes a truth deriving from the essence of rational numbers. If this equality were *created* by definition, then its truth would be determined by a convention which had a date. But if, as this implies, its truth-value had a date, presumably there would have been a time when it was not a truth about rational numbers, and it is inconceivable that there should have been such a time. Its truth may have been discovered at a given time, but it did not come into existence with its discovery. It has no date of creation.

Puzzling questions concerning discovery of mathematical truth I shall leave aside in this paper except as they bear on the question concerning the domain in which discovery supposedly takes place. The Platonic account of that domain makes mathematics out to be 'a physics of mathematical entities'.[24] What now can be said for the claim that what are called discoveries had much better be called inventions,[25] that 'the mathematician is an inventor, not a discoverer'.[26] Some reasons to be adduced for it hinge upon features of necessary propositions which have led philosophers to say such things as that they are 'purely verbal',[27] 'purely about the use of the expressions they connect',[28] or alternatively, that their function is not to describe word usage but to 'prescribe how words are to be used',[29] that they are not really propositions, but 'rules which can be followed or disobeyed'.[30] Clearly symbolism is our invention and its use to some degree subject to our will. If $2 + 2 = 4$, for example, is a rule for the use of symbols, then the clear perception of this fact precludes the notion that it is a truth having an existence independent of our minds. But as has been pointed out, $2 + 2 = 4$ uses but makes no mention of symbols. And when Wittgenstein says of a proof that it 'proves *first and foremost* that this formation of signs must result when I apply these rules to these formations of signs'[31] — a characterisation worthy of a conventionalist — the obvious reply is that proof makes no mention of signs. However unacceptably they state their position, conventionalists nevertheless show an awareness of a connection between the necessity of a proposition and the usage of words, a connection whose importance Platonists totally ignore. This is, to put the matter paradoxically, that the necessity of a proposition rests on arbitrary facts about the words used to express it. What renders a proposition incorrigible is an accepted linguistic convention. To see that a proposition is necessary no special kind of seeing, appropriate to a special domain of objects, is required. In the simplest cases, e.g. 'A cube has six faces', 'Even numbers are divisible by 2', 'A pentagon has five angles', a sufficient means for convincing oneself of their truth is appeal to the dictionary — not appeal to facts of the mathematical world. Necessity rests on a fact of language, and language is our creation and our creature. The remarkable agreement among mathematicians on the necessity of a proposition is a direct correlate of their undeniable agreement in the use of language. If a precondition for their agreement in the use of language were inspection of objects whose properties logically determined their relations, then it would be more than remarkable that conventionalists, who deny apprehending any objects, should manage to convey a proof to Platonist mathematicians.

With this I conclude some of the main reasons which can be put forward for the two positions on the nature of mathematics. I have expounded them as having the aim their proponents intend: to establish the truth of one claim and the falsity of the counter-claim. Despite appearances to the contrary I think that truth or falsity is not at issue here, and that the arguments are not directed to establishing this. But it is obviously incumbent on me to state reasons for thinking so. I shall begin with the strongest case against my thesis — the dispute, couched in the language of truth and falsity, between mathematical Platonists and their opponents over the existence of abstract objects. This is perhaps the most fundamental issue between them. The Platonist affirms the existence of abstract objects denoted by mathematical expressions whereas their opponents, no matter what positive claims they make, all by implication deny the existence of such objects. The claim of certain formalists that numbers are nothing more than numerals, and that it is numerals which $2 + 2 = 4$, for example, is about, if taken literally as a true or false description, is so blatantly false that one can assume its point is in what it denies rather than in what it affirms: it is intended to preclude taking numbers to be objects for which numerals stand, and this is secured by identifying numbers with numerals. Undoubtedly part of the point of Hilbert's claim that '2' and '4' in the expression '$2 + 2 = 4$' are meaningless marks is to deny that there are objects which they *mean*. It is a way of countering the claim that since they have meaning there must be *something* which they mean.

Against claim and counter-claim, each ostensibly to the effect that a certain description of numbers is *true*, I call attention to two curious features of the dispute which argue against its being a truth-value dispute over whether numbers are abstract objects. One is that it should arise concerning a matter so simple and familiar as $2 + 2 = 4$, and the other, that there should be no method of settling it. If the disputants were on unfamiliar ground and could expect to establish their respective theories by finding some new fact which would clinch the matter, their arguments would appear in quite a different light. But in the presence of '$2 + 2 = 4$' there are no new facts to call on, nothing beyond what understanding the sentence yields. How is the discrepancy between the reports on what is found upon inspection to be removed? The Platonist may claim that by an 'organ of the mind' he apprehends ideal objects and truths about how they are related, but he cannot claim to possess an organ lacking to the conventionalist, who reports the apprehension of no such objects. This controversy will of course be recognised as a species of the long-standing controversy over the existence of universals, which also has for centuries remained unresolved despite the presence of all the facts relevant to settling it and the possession of all the requisite faculties on the part of the disputants. Such controversies have no parallel outside philosophy.

Further, to take the position that this controversy is over the truth of a theory commits one to an extraordinarily paradoxical belief about the disputants *vis-à-vis* each other, to see which provides a compelling reason for discarding the natural assumption that we have here a truth-value controversy. That there is a dispute of some sort cannot be doubted, but what must the disputants' attitude toward each other be if the truth or falsity of a theory is at issue? The conventionalist must suppose the Platonist to operate under the persistent illusion that he is apprehending objects which in fact do not exist at all, and that his 'discoveries', e.g. of complex numbers, represent the onset of fresh illusions. On the other hand, the Platonist must attribute to the conventionalist an inexplicable blindness to the objects of his acquaintance and an even more inexplicable confusion of these objects with symbols. Furthermore, the blindness of the conventionalist mathematician must be supposed to be of a most unusual sort. Whatever he may say about the meaningfulness of number symbols in the sentence '2 + 2 = 4', he cannot deny that they have meaning in 'I have two apples and four pears', which expresses an empirical proposition. And if he grasps their meanings in this sentence then he must be apprehending the abstract objects which are their meanings. The conventionalist who understands the words yet denies apprehending any such objects must be assumed by the Platonist to suffer from a blindness like that of the person who under hypnosis complies with the order to see a blank wherever the word 'the' appears on the page.[32] Can one believe that either of the disputants makes these suppositions about the other?

These considerations should certainly put in doubt — if not preclude completely — the interpretation of the disputed descriptions of numbers as antithetical factual claims about their nature. But pointing out curiosities of the dispute which shake our conception of it leaves it an enigma how arguments can be marshalled for something which only seems to be a theory, and it leaves us in the dark as to what each seeming theory in fact comes to. By way of explanation I want to show (1) that the arguments rest on misleading analogies between the language of mathematics, both in the doing of mathematics and in talk about it, and the language of empirical fact; and (2) that the arguments do not demonstrate an analytic fact about numbers, but instead support a concealed revision of language whose aim is to justify the description of mathematics as discovery, or as creation. To show this, it is required to show what, specifically, the linguistic analogies are and how being misled by them appears to dictate the divergent descriptions of numbers. We here reiterate the point that showing an analogy to be misleading does not show the description to be false since, for one thing, the two formally contradictory sentences, 'Numbers are abstract objects' and 'Numbers are not abstract objects', could not both express what is false.

The analogies which are the semantic sources of the illusion that theories are being propounded lie in several areas. In investigating these analogies I shall confine myself to one area, the talk about necessary existence. I begin with the first of the specific arguments given earlier for the Platonist position: that just as 'There are owls with tufted ears' is about owls, 'There are factorable numbers of the form $2^{2^n} + 1$' is about factorable numbers; and further, that since the opposite of this latter is self-inconsistent, factorable numbers of this form must exist, from which it follows that numbers must exist. Similarly, if 6 is an even number, it follows that 6 is a number, and from this that at least one number exists. The arguments here are analogical. The pattern of demonstration and the verbal forms of the constituent propositions are similar throughout to an argument establishing the existence, say, of owls. 'The clothing of our language', as Wittgenstein says, 'makes everything alike.'[33] It will be claimed that the only respect in which the argument differs from an argument establishing the existence of owls is that its conclusion is about objects which are ideal, and that these exist necessarily — as if these were small differences. This claim makes clear the construction the Platonist places on 'There are numbers' and '6 is a number': that they are about ideal objects. If now we note the differences hidden under the verbal similarity of 'There are owls', 'There are numbers', 'There are ideal objects', we may be able to discern the semantic sources producing the illusion that 'Numbers are ideal objects' expresses a theory about the nature of numbers.

Leaving aside for the moment the fact that 'There are owls' is contingent and (according to the argument from the necessary existence of factorable numbers of the form $2^{2^n} + 1$) the inferred fact that 'There are numbers' is necessary, there is a more important difference between them. This is a difference which sets off 'There are numbers' from unquestionably necessary existential statements as well; and it is one which helps explain the fact that, apart from attempts such as Peano's to give the properties of natural numbers, there is no occasion to use such an expression as '0 is a number', nor even in the context of Peano's axioms to go on to infer as a necessary consequence that there are numbers. 'There are numbers' is unlike both 'There are owls' and 'There are even numbers between 3 and 9', despite the fact that '$(\exists x) . fx$' is the common form of all of them. An empirical process will determine whether there are owls, and something analogous to an empirical process will confirm that there are even numbers between 3 and 9. But there is no analogous process for confirming that there are numbers. The range of values of 'x is a number' does not include values which are numbers and values which are not, and in this respect it differs both from the function 'x is an owl' and 'x is an even number between 3 and 9'. To put the point otherwise, '$(\exists x) . x$ is a number' cannot be construed as asserting the existence of things in a domain of which it is sensible to say '$(\exists x) . x$ is not a number'. By contrast, '$(\exists x) . x$ is even. $3 < x < 9$' has a sensible correlate '$(\exists x) . \sim (x$ is even $. 3 < x < 9)$'. The range of significance of the two functions 'x is even and lies between 3 and 9', 'it is not the case both that x is even and lies between 3 and 9' is the same. Admittedly certain values in their range of significance will yield a self-contradiction, e.g. '5 is even and lies between 3 and 9'. But in the case of 'x is a number', substitution does not yield something self-contradictory when it fails to yield something necessary. It is clear that any other substitute than number expressions for 'x' in 'x is a number' will yield, not a self-contradiction, but complete nonsense. For example, 'Mauve is a number' is not self-contradictory, but nonsensical in the way in which Russell's example, 'Quadruplicity drinks procrastination', is nonsensical. The range of significance of 'x is a number' is limited to its truth range; it has no falsity range. In this respect it differs from 'x is an owl' and 'x is an even number between 3 and 9', whose ranges of significance are constituted of both a truth range and a falsity range; that is, their possible values comprise two classes.

It is indeed curious that there should be functions which must have values — such functions as 'x is an even number between 3 and 9'. It is perhaps more curious that there should be a function, 'x is a number', none of whose values results in a self-contradiction, whose range of significance is confined to its true values. This feature of 'x

is a number', which distinguishes it from 'x is even and lies between 3 and 9', is paralleled by still another curious feature which sets it apart from other functions. This appears on examination of what it comes to to deny that this function has values. Consider the consequence of supposing it to be true that $\sim(\exists x)$. x is a number, i.e. of supposing that the sentence 'There are no numbers' rather than the sentence 'There are numbers' expresses a necessity. In this case the word 'number' would have no use in the language, and the paradoxical consequence is that there would be no way of expressing the fact that there are no numbers. The resources of language would be inadequate, for the same sort of reason that a language in which there were no numerals and no word 'number' could not frame as a meaningful sentence 'There are no numbers'. The fact that we can frame this sentence implies that the word 'number' has a use, but the assumption that the sentence expresses a necessity implies that the word has no use. From the assumption it would follow that it was no more sensible to say 'There are no numbers' than 'There are no runcibles'. Comparison with the sentences 'There are no centaurs' and 'There are no primes between 13 and 17' is instructive. The fact that the first expresses a contingent truth implies two things, that the word 'centaur' has a use in the language and that as a matter of empirical fact it does not apply to anything. The fact that the second expresses a necessity implies that the phrase 'prime and between 13 and 17' has no use. But its difference from the sentence 'There are no numbers' is that the phrase which has no use has constituents which do have a use, and our language can express the fact that the combination has no use. Were it the case that the single word 'number' had no use the words 'There are no numbers' could not express anything.

This peculiarity bears on the argument, in support of Platonism, to the effect that if there were no numbers then all universal propositions about numbers would be vacuously true, in which case the theorem 'All composite integers are uniquely factorable into primes' would be no different from 'All odd numbers of the form $2n$ are odd'. It will be recalled that the theorem was suggested by the result of testing particular numbers for factorability, and that this process precludes its being true vacuously. If what I have said about 'There are numbers' is correct, there would be no intelligible way of expressing the hypothesis of the above argument for Platonism, and the argument would become a piece of literal nonsense. It must be admitted that the peculiarities of the function 'x is a number' and of the apparent generalisation '$\sim(\exists x)$. x is a number' raise the question whether '$(\exists x) . x$ is a number' can be taken to express a necessity. Its status is very unclear. It will be useful to examine what it comes to for a more usual sentence to express a necessity, in the hope of shedding some light on the following questions: what 'Numbers exist' must express *if* it expresses a necessity, why this sentence plays no role in normal mathematical pursuits, whether necessary propositions of number theory can be said to be about numbers, and finally, what the dispute between Platonist and non-Platonist comes to.

Wittgenstein said that arithmetic propositions say nothing about numbers and geometric propositions nothing about cubes.[34] He could have said a similar thing about the subject of any necessary proposition, e.g. 'Bachelors are unmarried male adults'. Why would he wish to say this statement is not about bachelors when in some sense it obviously is? The reason is that to speak as if it were is to assimilate it to an empirical generalisation, e.g. 'Whales are a source of ambergris', and thereby to obscure the radical difference between them. The difference is this: the fact that a sentence expresses a necessity, unlike the fact that the sentence about whales expresses a contingent truth, gives us only verbal information. If this is the case then it cannot at the same time be held to give information about something the subject term stands for. In support of the claimed difference from which this consequence is drawn I cite the following. To know that the sentence 'Even numbers are of the form $2n$' expresses a necessary truth, and to know this in virtue of knowing the meanings of the involved terms, is to know the following empirical verbal fact, which I shall call the verbal correlate of the sentence: that 'being of the form $2n$' applies to what 'even' applies to, or alternatively, that 'even but not of the form $2n$' has no use. This is not to say that the sentence 'Even numbers are of the form $2n$' means the same thing as the sentence about the phrase 'even but not of the form $2n$'. But it illuminates the position of a necessary proposition *vis-à-vis* an empirical non-verbal proposition on the one hand, and an empirical verbal proposition on the other, to see that understanding the sentence expressing a necessity involves nothing more than knowing that its verbal correlate expresses a true empirical proposition about usage.[35] The fact that a sentence s expresses a necessary proposition is equivalent to the fact that its empirical verbal correlate s' expresses a truth about usage. What makes the non-verbal sentence 'Even numbers are of the form $2n$' express a necessity is the fact that the sentence '"Even but not of the form $2n$" has no use' expresses an empirical truth. In other words, it is not a fact about even numbers which makes the sentence 'Even numbers are of the form $2n$' express what is true, but a fact about the usage of words occurring in it. It becomes apparent why Wittgenstein said that an arithmetical proposition asserts nothing about numbers. To understand the sentence expressing it is to know a fact about words, not about anything the words stand for. This is all that knowing necessary facts about numbers comes to; it is not knowing facts about rarified objects.

With this account of what it is to understand the sentences which express necessary propositions, we can now examine the sentences '6 is a number' and 'There are numbers', assuming that they do express necessities. On this assumption their empirical verbal correlates are, respectively, '"6" is a number-word' and '"Number" has a use'. Granting that the Platonist's argument establishes the necessity of the propositions expressed by the two non-verbal sentences, then what guarantees that these sentences express necessities are entirely trivial facts about the use of the word '6' and of the word 'number'. It is not surprising that mathematicians have no occasion to prove or use such propositions. But the fact that they are trivial leaves in question what the dispute between Platonists and non-Platonists is about. The apparent dispute is over whether there are numbers, but it of course cannot be over whether the word 'numbers' and specific number words have a use. It must be over what both take to be a consequence of 'There are numbers', namely, that there are abstract objects. I think we may assume that the Platonist supposes himself to be asserting the existence of a category of objects, and that 'Numbers are objects' expresses a necessary truth about numbers. The fact that Platonists are not moved from their position by any evidence brought forward by non-Platonists, such as that inspection reveals to them no objects, would indicate that this is the interpretation we must place on this sentence. Further, the Platonists would maintain that 'There are objects' follows from 'There are numbers', and since the latter is necessary, the former also must be necessary.

We have now reached the core of the dispute, whether 'Numbers are objects' does or does not express a necessity. And this dispute is usually conceived of, not as being over what this sentence expresses, but as being over whether what it expresses is true, or false. It is accepted that 'Numbers are objects' expresses a view, whose truth is in question; and this is the assumption I wish to challenge. A comparison of 'Numerals are signs' with 'Numbers are objects' will be instructive. That the first expresses a necessity is guaranteed by the convention for the use of the words 'numerals' and 'sign'. But there is no convention for the use of the words 'numbers' and 'objects' which stipulates that 'object' applies to whatever 'number' applies to, or alternatively, that 'number but not an object' expresses an inconsistency. In order for the sentence 'Numbers are objects' to express a necessity, it is required that an empirical fact about usage be expressed by the sentence '"Object" applies to whatever "number" applies to'. But no such fact of usage exists. This is not to say that there is a *contrary* fact of usage, such as the one which falsifies the claim that 'Numbers are scratches on paper' expresses a necessity. Rather there is no convention at all, despite the Platonist, who seems to deny this by implication. But the consequence of the fact that there is no convention which assures its expressing a necessity, and no counter-convention which precludes its doing so is this: that the sentence itself, 'Numbers are objects', does not express either a truth or a falsity.

What I wish to say is that the Platonist who urges that numbers are objects disguises — perhaps to himself as well as to others — the nature of his claim. His dispute with the non-Platonist is carried out in the language of assertion, i.e. of truth and falsity; it is ostensibly over whether 'Numbers are objects' is *true*. No mention is made of the word 'number' or of any other verbal matter. But if he claims necessary truth for his assertion he commits himself (in the language in which he states himself; here the English language) to the verbal claim that the sentence 'Numbers are objects' expresses a necessity, i.e. that it expresses an entailment between *being a number* and *being an object*. And whether it does so can be readily decided by appeal to established usage, as readily as whether 'Red things are coloured' expresses a necessity. No chain of entailments need be gone through to see whether the end result is necessary. What is required here is quite unlike what would be required to determine whether 'There are no odd perfect numbers' is necessary. It is clear that usage being what it is, it is false that 'Numbers are objects' expresses a necessity. We might then suppose that the Platonist, who apparently commits himself to this false verbal claim, must be saying something false in holding numbers to be objects. But since he knows usage and would know his assertion to be false, I prefer to take it that he is doing something else in making his assertion and arguing for it. He states, as if it were a fact of logic, that 'There are numbers' implies 'There are objects', and he argues this on the ground that arithmetical statements must be about something. As an alternative to supposing that he thereby commits himself to holding that a convention exists which guarantees the necessity of 'Numbers are objects', I suggest that he is urging, in a concealed way (since he mentions no matter of usage), that a convention be accepted. If accepted it would *create* an entailment where none now exists. And the factual idiom in which he frames his arguments is primarily a persuasive device for effecting this. When in recent years Parisian artists disputed whether grey is a colour, one cannot suppose that they did not know the established usage of the word 'grey' to name a colour. One can only construe their arguments as reasons either for retaining established usage or for altering it. In the case of the dispute over whether numbers are objects, the fact that no convention or counter-convention already exists makes it easy to view the dispute as arising from the difficulty of deciding what the essential features of numbers are. But in fact what makes it easy is unfixed usage.

Why the Platonist should wish to settle the essential features of numbers as he does, where 'settling the essential features' is a disguised way of fixing usage, I cannot explain. What is interesting is that his disguise, effected by the non-verbal idiom in which he discourses, results in the illusion that 'Numbers are objects' expresses something true or false, depending on what numbers in fact are. I have already indicated some semantic sources of this illusion in the question 'What is mathematics *about*?' and in the failure to attend to the verbal correlates of necessary propositions. There are other semantic sources which I should like to mention. One is the preoccupation with the noun use of number words, e.g. in '6 > 5', 'There is an even prime', 'the series of numbers', etc. As a concomitant of this preoccupation, the adjectival use of number words in such empirical contexts as 'There are three apples on the table' is ignored. Here the numeral '3' is applied to a collection of objects, and can and does apply to many other collections. But unlike the term 'apple', which is a general name applying to each of a number of things, '3' is a special name for *one* number. '3' is not the general name of a number of things each of which is 3; there is but one number 3. And what is more natural than to go on from 'There is but one number 3' to 'There is but one object that "3" names', as one can rightly go on from 'There is but one Ghengis Kahn' to 'There is but one person whom "Ghengis Kahn" names'? The difference is supposedly summed up in the claim that '3' stands for an ideal object. Of this claim Wittgenstein wrote:

[It] is evidently supposed to assert something about the meaning, and so about the use, of ['3']. And it means of course that this use is in a certain respect similar to that of a sign that has an object, and that it does not stand for any object. But it is interesting what the expression 'ideal object' makes of this fact.[36]

I think we may take it that what this expression does is successfully conceal a fact of grammar. For 'ideal object' is taken as a description of what there is, as though 'ideal' and 'real' were adjectives functioning like 'red' and 'green' to distinguish between objects. 'There is an ideal object which "3" stands for' and 'There is no object which "3" stands for', the one in a disguised way and the other openly, express our recognition of the fact that '3' has not the naming function which 'Ghengis Kahn' has. But there is a metaphysical world of difference between the two forms of words, if I may be forgiven a small levity. Ideal objects, unlike imaginary objects, and unlike no objects at all, require a habitat and enjoy a form of being — albeit less robust than the existence possessed by real objects. The import of the word 'ideal', i.e. *not real*, is forgotten. The picture of an enormous extension created by such phrases as 'the infinity of primes', an extension whose members are named by the numerals as one reaches them by counting, is another result of neglecting, whether intentionally or not, the import of words. Euclid's proof that there is an infinity of primes assures us that the technique of calculating primes 'lacks the institution of an end'.[37] To know that the concluding sentence of the proof expresses a necessity is merely to know that 'greatest prime' has no use in the language of mathematics. There is nothing further to know.

Now if necessary arithmetical propositions are neither about numbers nor about symbols, certain of our original questions disappear, *viz*: Were the number -2 and the roots $\pm \sqrt{-1}$ invented when the domain of numbers was extended to negative and complex numbers? Or was the possibility of an extension discovered? How can one invent objects which necessarily exist? Yet if the roots of $x^2 = -1$ exist necessarily, how account for the historical fact that it was a matter of decision whether there are roots? It is obvious that the language of both invention and discovery suggests a common point of agreement, that mathematical propositions are about objects, the disagreement being over whether they are invented or discovered. A similar point of agreement is evident in the dispute between Platonists and conventionalists over whether mathematical propositions are about ideal objects or marks, namely, that they must be about something. Conventionalists are not content with denying that inspection reveals objects corresponding to numerals: on the assumption that necessary propositions must be about something, what is visible to all, the symbols occurring in their expression, is all that remains for them to be about. The semantic sources of the disagreement thus lie in part in their agreement. I have tried to show that neither the agreement nor the disagreement is about the truth-values of putative views. If they were, then there is no explaining why the existence of objects, whether discovered or invented, should be in dispute by people who have every means at their disposal for coming to a decision and nevertheless continue to dispute.

Notes

1. P. W. Bridgman, *The Logic of Modern Physics* (1927), New York: Macmillan, p. 60.
2. *A Mathematician's Apology* (1941), Cambridge: Cambridge University Press, p. 63–4.
3. *Philosophical Investigations*, p. 91.
4. Ibid., p. 43.
5. Ibid., p. 49.
6. Sec. 238, Jowett's translation.
7. *Timaeus*, sec. 52, Jowett's translation.
8. *Republic*, Book VI, sec. 510, Jowett's translation.
9. *The Problems of Philosophy* (1943), London: The Home University Library, Oxford University Press, pp. 164–5.
10. L. Wittgenstein, *Remarks on the Foundations of Mathematics* (1956), eds G.H. von Wright, R. Rhees, G.E.M. Anscombe, trans. by G.E.M. Anscombe, New York: Macmillan & Co., p. 117.
11. P. E. B. Jourdain, *The Nature of Mathematics*, in James R. Newman, *The World of Mathematics* (1956), New York: Simon & Schuster, p. 71.
12. Edward Kasner and James Newman, *Mathematics and the Imagination* (1940), New York: Simon & Schuster, vol. I, p. 359.
13. R. Courant and H. Robbins, *What Is Mathematics?* (1941), New York: Oxford University Press, p. 89.
14. Ibid., p. 56.
15. Ibid.
16. Ibid., p. 53.
17. Ibid., p. 55.
18. Ibid., p. 54.
19. L. Wittgenstein, *Remarks on the Foundations of Mathematics*, p. 47.
20. Ibid., p. 117.
21. *A Mathematician's Apology*, p. 33.
22. L. Wittgenstein, Lecture notes 1939.
23. Quoted by Alfred Hooper, *Makers of Mathematics* (1948), London: Faber & Faber, p. 382.

24. L. Wittgenstein, Lecture notes 1939.

25. Ibid.

26. L. Wittgenstein, *Remarks on the Foundations of Mathematics*, p. 47.

27. John Wisdom, 'Metaphysics and Verification' (1938), *Mind*, vol. XLVII, no. 188, p. 463, fn.

28. Ibid.

29. A. J. Ayer, 'Truth by Convention' (1936), *Analysis*, vol. 4, nos. 2, 3, pp. 19–20.

30. Ibid.

31. L. Wittgenstein, *Remarks on the Foundation of Mathematics*, p. 80.

32. Example taken from John Wisdom.

33. *Philosophical Investigations*, p. 224.

34. Lectures, Cambridge University, 1933–34.

35. For the detail of this description of sentences expressing necessary propositions, see M. Lazerowitz, 'Necessity and Language'.

36. *Remarks on the Foundations of Mathematics*, p. 136.

37. Ibid., p. 60.

6 MATHEMATICAL GENERALITY

Induction is the process of discovering general laws by the observation and combination of particular instances. It is used in all sciences, even in mathematics . . . We may observe, by chance, that

$$1 + 8 + 27 + 64 = 100$$

and, recognising the cubes and the square, we may give to the fact we observe the more interesting form

$$1^3 + 2^3 + 3^3 + 4^3 = 10^2.$$

. . . Does it often happen that such a sum of successive cubes is a square? . . . In asking this we are like the naturalist who, impressed by a curious plant or a curious geological formation, conceives of a general question. Our general question is concerned with the successive cubes

$$1^3 + 2^3 + 3^3 + 4^3 + \ldots + n^3.$$

We are led to it by the 'particular instance' $n = 4$. . . . The special cases $n = 2, 3$ are still simpler, the case $n = 5$ is the next one. . . . Arranging neatly all these cases, as a geologist would arrange his specimens of a certain ore, we obtain the following table:

1	$= 1 = 1^2$
$1 + 8$	$= 9 = 3^2$
$1 + 8 + 27$	$= 36 = 6^2$
$1 + 8 + 27 + 64$	$= 100 = 10^2$
$1 + 8 + 27 + 64 + 125$	$= 225 = 15^2.$

It is hard to believe that all these sums of consecutive cubes are squares by mere chance. . . . In a similar case, the naturalist would have little doubt that the general law suggested by the special cases heretofore observed is correct. Here the following theorem is strongly suggested by the induction:

The sum of the first n cubes is a square.

. . . In mathematics as in the physical sciences we may use observation and induction to discover general laws. . . . Many mathematical results were found by induction first and proved later. Mathematics presented with rigour is a systematic deductive science but mathematics in the making is an experimental inductive science.[1]

This quotation presents an illustration of the analogies mathematicians find between mathematical and empirical investigations. It makes number theory appear 'as the natural history of the domain of numbers',[2] and it seems entirely natural that it should do so. Proceeding 'by induction from numerical examples',[3] a mathematician will frequently describe his examination of special cases as confirming a conjecture, or supporting a generalisation, and go on to predict that subsequent 'empirical evidence'[4] will bear out the conjecture or generalisation. Propositions which have been 'reached and stated as probably true by induction'[5] may or may not be doubted, depending on the extent and nature of the evidence. The discovery of an exception to a generalisation will justify the doubt that the generalisation holds for the totality of elements in the domain.

Wittgenstein has claimed that such accounts of the mathematician's work, which equally well describe the work of the natural scientist in his laboratory, are misleading. And often he counters them with descriptions which seem quite unnatural. For example, despite its being a proper use of language to say that certain books deal with conic sections or with natural numbers, and to say that this is the subject-matter of geometry or number theory, we find Wittgenstein asserting that arithmetical propositions say nothing about numbers and geometrical propositions, nothing about figures.[6] Such an assertion seems either to be false, or else to have some point which is not immediately evident. What construction is to be placed on his claim that many instances of the ordinary use of language are misleading? It is, of course, obvious that such language does not lead mathematicians astray in the pursuit of their subject. It is also obvious that Wittgenstein's comments are directed to pronouncements which the mathematician *as philosopher* makes. These pronouncements — and their opposites as well — he held to be the outcome of tempting ways of describing what the mathematician does when he tries to prove some mathematical proposition he thinks to be true.

One of Wittgenstein's well-known comments about philosophical views was that they are the products of linguistic confusion, 'misunderstandings concerning the use of words, which are caused, among other things, by certain analogies between the forms of expression in different regions of language'.[7] We have a tendency to assimilate expressions which have different functions in language; we try to talk of very different things by means of the same schema.[8] Ordinary language succumbs to this tendency; witness the differences concealed by 'having a pain', 'having an idea', 'having a pound', 'having a friend'. In this paper my concern is with analogies highlighted and differences minimised by descriptions of what is done in mathematics which are modelled after descriptions of work in the experimental sciences. Wittgenstein represents himself as 'try[ing] to counteract the misleading effect of certain analogies'.[9] Sometimes his own pronouncements appear to be as much pieces of philosophy — as much subject to debate — as the views he supposes these analogies to lead to. If his statements are what they appear at face value to be, then, like the traditional philosopher, he is countering one philosophical position with another, and we must assume that he supposes that these analogies mislead the mathematician into *false* positions of which he should be disabused.

This is one possible construction to be placed on the claim that analogies between the forms of expression in different regions of language are misleading. There is, however, another interpretation, an iconoclastic one, which may be what prompted him to raise the question, 'Where does our investigation get its importance from, since it seems only to destroy everything interesting, that is, all that is great and important?'[10] On this interpretation, showing an analogy to be misleading is the same as showing that it leads to a philosophical view, where the 'view' is merely the semblance of a true or false statement and therefore may turn out to have no truth-value. Wittgenstein said there is a confusion pervading all philosophy, that of looking at the rejection of a form of symbolism as though a proposition had been rejected as false.[11] The implication is that the traditional philosopher misconceives the nature of his theories and their supporting arguments. Accordingly a mathematician's pronouncement on 'the objectivity or reality of mathematical facts' is characterised as 'something for philosophical *treatment* . . . like the treatment of an illness'.[12] Wittgenstein's intention, then, is to cure or prevent the illness. The cure consists, not in solving the philosophical problem which is its cause, but in dissolving it, making it '*completely* disappear'.[13]

It seems to me more plausible that one should be misled into a wrong idea about the nature of a position than that one should be misled into holding a false position, given the history of philosophical fashions, where what was once false now parades as true, and sooner or later falls out of fashion again and is rejected as false. In philosophy, it would seem, truth-value is determined by the prevailing fashion. In the present essay I shall try to illustrate the thesis that linguistic analogies mislead philosophers into the idea that the truth of a position is in debate. The problems under consideration will centre on the character of mathematical generalisations and their relations to singular propositions which instantiate them, and to exceptions which refute them. What we are inclined to say about them — what Wittgenstein calls the 'raw material' of philosophy[14] — takes the form of descriptions analogous to accounts in natural science. The descriptions stress the analogies and consequently mute the differences. Often it is only a short step from these descriptions to a philosophical theory. What I shall try to show is that analogies are employed to justify an altered use of language[15] rather than to support a truth. In Wittgenstein's words, 'what the philosopher wants is . . . a new notation'.[16] The hold of the analogies on our minds is to be broken by emphasising the differences.

It will be useful to begin with certain assertions which clearly parallel assertions about natural science: that generalisations are propositions about a totality of elements; that true existential propositions that contradict them state a truth about some individual within the domain of elements; that singular propositions which suggest a generalisation we believe to be true are themselves discovered by observation; and that a proof of the generalisation at the same time demonstrates what holds for each such special case.

The first reaction to these assertions is that they are unobjectionable, that their similarity to statements in the experimental sciences is open for all to see, and that no harm results from pointing it out. The fact that differences are blurred does not gainsay the similarities. What a little reflection shows, however, is that minimising a difference is related to a philosophical view as a preconscious thought is related to its conscious counterpart. The analogous descriptions just cited all conspire to make a certain philosophical theory seem as natural as the descriptions themselves, namely, the Platonist theory that there is a domain of objects which one needs but observe and explore in order to arrive at truths about them. Except for these objects, what could guarantee the truth of existence propositions and singular propositions? In fact, this question presents a consideration which makes the Platonic view appear as a reasonable answer. Mathematical conjectures, attempts to prove generalisations suggested by observed special cases, the discovery of exceptions which upset generalisations, proofs by mathematical induction starting from cases, all may be described as being about objects which merely differ from the objects of natural science in being abstract or ideal rather than concrete.

Then why not accept the description? What objection is there to taking the analogies between mathematical and inductive generalisations at face value and accepting the philosophical theory to which they lead? What reason is there for supposing that the analogies *mis*lead? There is a short and obvious answer to this question. This is that the existence of counter-views which also claim to be true present what seems — and may well be — a permanent stalemate. While Platonists maintain that the truths of mathematics assuredly hold for a sphere of objects existing independently of the mind and of which the mind is directly aware, others find it 'strange that such a notion could ever have existed';[17] and there is no coming to a clear-cut decision between these positions when taken to be what they appear to be — true or false. It would seem that there is no explaining one philosopher's claim that he is aware of abstract objects when he understands mathematical terms, and the counter-claim of another philosopher that when he understands number expressions, say, he is aware of no such objects.

Analogies between mathematical and inductive generalisations tempt one to hold the Platonic view, but there are considerations, so far not mentioned, which tempt one to deny it and to adopt a counter-view. These considerations call attention to the *differences* between the two types of generalisation. A conventional philosopher takes these differences to bear on the truth or falsity of a theory, and at times Wittgenstein seems to do likewise, although a quite different use of them can be made. Whatever the use, it is important to see what these differences are. Wittgenstein is reported to have remarked, 'We are much more inclined to say "All these things, though looking different, are really the same" than we are to say "All these things, though looking the same, are really different".'[18] He also remarked that facts to which he draws attention are such as 'we know quite as well as he, but which we have forgotten or at least are not immediately attending to'.[19] Obvious facts of difference will be our starting point.

First, a true mathematical generalisation has what Kant called 'strict universality', which is to say that it is not logically possible for there to be an exception to it. This means that its subject and predicate are connected by 'inner necessity', or, what comes to the same thing, that the generalisation can be restated as an entailment.

For example, 'For any polygon of $n + 2$ sides, the sum of its angles is $n \times 180°$' can be restated as: '*being a polygon of $n + 2$ sides* entails *having angles which sum up to $n \times 180°$*'. This feature of universally quantified propositions of mathematics is the wellspring of all other differences: if true, they are *a priori* true. It is logically out of the question for them to have a truth-value other than the one they have. Owing to their necessity, constructions which serve as proofs of geometrical propositions are not experiments, despite the fact that any construction is a particular temporal activity. The interesting thing is that straight edge and compasses can be dispensed with. Mere description, for example, of the division of a line by straight edge and compasses is sufficient to prove the generalisation, 'A straight line can be divided into any number of equal parts by straight edge and compasses'. The actual construction need not be carried out. But description of an experiment is by no means sufficient for establishing the expected result: experimentation on whatever is the subject of the generalisation has to be carried out.[20] Were a Euclidean construction an experiment, 'it could not prove the result for other cases'.[21]

Empirical generalisations and mathematical generalisations, despite looking alike because both have the form 'All f's are g's', differ radically in their relation to singular propositions of the form $fx.gx$ and $fx.\sim gx$, i.e. to what we call instances and exceptions. The difference is that the instances do not confirm in the sense of 'bearing out' a hypothesis; for an entailment holds regardless of instances: instances give no support. Nor is it conceivable that anything of the form $fx.\sim gx$ should upset it. Wittgenstein remarked that it is 'a misfortune that our language denotes such fundamentally different things by the words "question", "problem", "investigation", "discovery". And similarly for the words "conclusion", "proposition", "proof".'[22] An empirical generalisation can have any number of supporting instances, however great, without removing the *possibility* of a falsifying instance. And this possibility is not removed by the truth of the generalisation. With an entailment, neither of the two possibilities of confirmation or falsification, is open to it. For if it is inconceivable for a proposition to have an exception, then instances play no role in supporting it. Where instances cannot in principle falsify they also cannot in principle confirm its truth. If every instance *must*, logically, support the generalisation, then 'supporting instance' means nothing more than 'instance', and the claim that every instance is a supporting instance is quite empty. It shrinks into the empty tautology that every instance is an instance. The question then arises whether a generalisation of the form 'All f's are g's' can properly be said to be *about f*'s.

Mathematical beliefs present another difference, however much 'the clothing of our language'[23] makes them look like ordinary beliefs. We do properly say that we believe no odd number is a perfect number, or that Fermat believed that for $n > 4$, numbers of the form $2^{2^n} + 1$ are prime. In this respect 'believe' seems to have the same correlated contrast term 'know' which it has in the usual, empirical contexts. However, in empirical contexts, it is logically possible both to believe and to know the same proposition. But suppose that 'no odd numbers are perfect', like 'for all $n > 4$, $2^{2^n} + 1$ is prime', is false. Falsity is here self-inconsistency. The marvel, then, is how belief is possible about what is unthinkable. We are reminded of Cardinal Newman's explanation of how those who are ignorant of the Bible because they cannot read may nevertheless be saved: they can believe that what the Bible says is true without knowing *what* it says.

What is it that people believed when they tried to trisect the angle by using straight edge and compasses? And what would it be to succeed? 'It used to be said that God could create anything, except what was contrary to the laws of logic',[24] and presumably He could conceive of every task except what is logically impossible. If there is an oddity about the idea of believing what is unthinkable, there is likewise an oddity about the idea of believing what is thinkable where what is thought of is true necessarily, e.g. $25 \times 25 = 625$. 'Can someone *believe* that $25 \times 25 = 625$?', Wittgenstein asks. 'What does it mean to believe that? How does it show up that he believes it?'[25] Again, usually what one believes one can wish to be the case, even though one's belief is discovered to be false. How different is 'the grammar of belief' in the usual circumstances and in mathematics comes to light when one considers 'whether it makes sense to say: "I wish twice two were five!"'[26] or 'I wish there were an even prime greater than 2'. Not only this, there is some sort of impropriety in saying one wishes for what cannot conceivably fail to be the case, e.g. that one wishes that the sum of the first six consecutive cubes should be a square.

A further interesting difference is that various tenses can be used in the expression of what is believed in mathematics without altering the sense. One can express the same belief, for example, about the division of 1 by 3, by saying either that 3 will recur or that 3 does recur. Except where '3 will recur' is used to predict the digit in a person's calculations, 'will recur' is not temporal. In fact it can be replaced by the tenseless logical 'must'. By contrast, to believe 'He will write "3"' is very different from believing 'He is writing "3"', and clearly neither statement is identical with one in which the logical 'must' replaces the tensed verb. Consequently a mathematical prediction differs characteristically from the prediction of an event which could fail to take place. Once an entailment is established, prediction that it holds for other cases than those considered is like predicting that the fifth day will follow the fourth.[27] Of what is predicted in mathematics it is an impropriety of language to say 'Experience indicates that this will be the case' (e.g. that 3 will recur, or that for the next value of n, say $n = 2$, the polygon having $n + 2$ sides will have angles whose sum is 360°).

Having cited differences which seriously raise the question of how one can talk of believing a mathematical proposition, whether a false one or a true one, it has to be admitted that the answer is that one can. We say we conjecture, as many people have, about the distribution of primes, that we notice a regularity such as Polya describes, and go on to prove that what has been observed must be so, that we make predictions and hazard that something is probably true. What is common talk cannot be dismissed out of hand. At the same time it is paradoxical. There seems to be something wrong about predicting what can have only one possible truth-value; it is like predicting that it will either rain or not rain. (And if the truth-value is falsity, *what* has one predicted? Do the words 'Ten years from now a donkey will be born which is not an animal' make a prediction?) There seems to be something wrong about talk of likelihoods when the probability of the proposition in question must be 0 or must be 1 and cannot sensibly be said to have any intermediate values between 0 and 1. Yet such talk is commonplace.

The following description of *reductio ad absurdum* proof from Polya is a good example of language which bears its meaning on its face, yet at the same time is paradoxical. Suppose

> we wish to prove that it is impossible to fulfill a certain condition, that is, that the situation in which all parts of the condition are simultaneously satisfied can never arise. But, if we have proved nothing yet, we have to face the possibility that the situation could arise . . . although such a situation appears extremely unlikely.[28]

If by assuming p one proves $\sim p$, *what* did one assume? And is there a 'possibility that the situation [assumed in p] could arise'? Yet nothing is more common than *reductio ad absurdum* proofs which begin: 'Suppose p . . .'. Again, it seems correct to describe some specific mathematical truth as having been suggested by observation of several instances of it, and later demonstrated. Undoubtedly it was first discovered by measurements of particular right triangles that the length of the hypotenuse was the square root of the sums of the squares of the other two sides. At any rate the measurements must have been taken as a warrant for the generalisation, just as data about observed cases are taken as inductive grounds for an empirical proposition. But the Pythagorean theorem is demonstrable, whereas what is empirical (i.e. what has two possible truth-values) is not demonstrable (i.e. is not at the same time confined, in principle, to one truth-value).[29]

I wish now to develop one paradoxical consequence of Polya's account of a mathematician's procedure in more detail. In consonance with his account of the 'inductive' procedure preceding a demonstration, he develops a calculus of 'plausibilities' analogous in some ways to the calculus of probability, where plausibility is equated with degree of belief. In as much as no numerical value can be attached to plausibility, with the exception of 0 and 1 (corresponding, respectively, to knowledge of a proposition's refutation and of its proof), he contents himself with an algebra which expresses changes in degrees of belief in a proposition during an investigation rather than attempting to assign an 'absolute' degree of belief to it at the outset.[30] It is unnecessary to go into the detail of this algebra. Suffice it for our purpose to look at his conclusion: 'The plausibility of a theorem can only increase when a consequence of the theorem is confirmed', and 'The plausibility of a theorem can only decrease when a hypothesis of which the given theorem is a consequence is refuted'.[31] The plausibility of a proposition may in the course of an investigation change to 0, if a consequence of it is found to be false, and to 1, if it, or a hypothesis from which it follows, is proved. These limiting values to which the plausibilities tend are of special importance in seeing what is paradoxical about this account despite there being something 'right' about it.

Since empirical investigation is the model here, it is instructive to compare the mathematical case with the case of an empirical proposition which lends itself to being made more and more plausible by the examination of instances. Rendering an empirical proposition certain is a continuation of the procedure which renders it plausible to a degree. Enough confirming instances are amassed to make its denial ridiculous, because investigation of further cases seems ridiculous. (How often must one test whether litmus paper turns red in acid in order to be justified in declaring that this is certain?) But no matter how *factually* absurd its denial becomes, the logical possibility of the denial being true remains. *No* number of confirming instances eliminates the theoretical possibility of a disconfirming instance occurring. It is this theoretical possibility which positivists used to support their philosophical claim that all propositions other than tautologies and so-called basic propositions are nothing more than probable hypotheses. No finite number of favourable cases, they held, could count as *conclusively* verifying an empirical generalisation; nothing short of an infinite number will do. The fact that empirical generalisations can, in principle, always be disconfirmed is bound up with our use of the words 'probable' and 'plausible': a proposition can only be said to be more or less plausible or probable when the same thing could be said of its negation. Experience can render an empirical proposition more and more plausible by fresh confirming instances, or less and less plausible by discovery of the falsity of hypotheses from which it follows. But these same facts also render its negation less and less plausible, or more and more plausible, respectively. Even when an empirical proposition is true and its plausibility changes to certainty, one must allow the logical possibility of its negation being true, or at least of being made plausible.

This is not the case with regard to a mathematical proposition. A mathematical proposition which is made more and more plausible 'inductively' and then *proved* is at the moment of proof shown to be *a priori*. When the value 1 attaches to a mathematical proposition, its negation cannot, in principle, have any of the remaining degrees of plausibility, except 0, which like 1 denotes what is logically necessary, not what is psychologically certain. '"Mathematical certainty" is not a psychological concept.'[32] So Polya's account has the consequence that a proposition can be rendered plausible when it is such that by its very nature its denial cannot be rendered plausible. Given the use of 'plausible' which is the model for his account, a paradox can be elicited. This is that the proposition which fresh trials supposedly make more and more plausible is such as to be incapable of being plausible. Demonstrating that it is true or giving a *reductio ad absurdum* proof of its falsity shows that neither it nor its negative can be plausible. What we shall call Polya's paradox is that his account describes a proposition being made plausible which is such that the concept *plausible* does not apply to it. The source of the paradox lies in treating an entailment proposition as though it could be confirmed by instances. An *a priori* true proposition has no confirmation any more than it has a refutation. However great the appearance of its being inductively confirmable, it is not like 'All crows are black'.

To declare that these features are the characteristic mark of *a priori* propositions is to give them 'a peculiar position among all propositions'.[33] As is well known, Mill boldly made claims which appear to deny to *a priori* propositions any such place. Of 'the Science of Number' he said that 'its first principles are generalizations from experience',[34] 'experimental truths',[35] 'known by early and constant experience'.[36] He cites with approbation Herschel's statement that 'A truth, necessary and universal, relative to any object of our knowledge, must verify itself in every instance where that object is before our contemplation.'[37] Polya puts forward no such theory about the nature of necessary propositions, but his account of the procedure by which a mathematician 'augments or diminishes his confidence in a theorem which is still only a conjecture'[38] treats a generalisation as Mill would have done on the basis of his theory.

It is natural to suppose that mathematical propositions are 'about' something. Mill held that:

> Since . . . neither in nature, nor in the human mind, do there exist any objects exactly corresponding to the definitions of geometry, while yet that science cannot be supposed to be conversant with nonentities; nothing remains but to consider geometry as conversant with such lines, angles, and figures as really exist.[39]

This claim leaves open why the imperfections of drawn figures make no difference to the truth of a theorem. But the only other current position, that geometry, and mathematics in general, is about 'mere symbols'[40] Mill dismissed out of hand. It is to be noted that the question, 'What are mathematical propositions about?', and the various answers to it, are all examples of the 'regulative' principle Lazerowitz discusses in his essay, 'Necessity and Language', *viz.* that a literally meaningful statement must be *about something*. This formula Wittgenstein came to see as a 'grammatical obsession' —

grammatical, according to him, because when we say a reality must correspond to a meaningful statement, instead of asserting a fact we are exhibiting a prejudice in favour of certain grammatical forms.[41] The question, 'What is "Cats are independent" about?', and its answer, 'Cats', act as a model for an analogous question, with its answers, about necessary propositions.

Necessary propositions have two faces, one of which is in eclipse when the other is the focus of attention. And each face has a different and opposing mien. The face they present to most people is that of asserting a fact, and this they do in virtue of the form of speech in which they are cast. The two propositions, 'Red is a primary colour' and 'Red is a colour in many flags', wear the same linguistic dress, the fact-claiming or fact-reporting indicative mood. The appeal, and at the same time the paradox, of Polya's description is a result of emphasising this similarity. The important difference is that the first proposition is such that recourse to the dictionary definition of the phrase 'primary colour' occurring in the expression of it is all that is required to establish its truth. Now it is merely a convention, a quite arbitrary matter, that 'primary colour' is used in English to cover the colours red, blue, yellow and green and only these. That it does so is an empirical fact: the phrase might be used otherwise, and if it were, the statement that it is so used would be false. The fact that the sentence, 'Red is a primary colour', expresses an *a priori* truth thus rests on what is arbitrary, *viz.* the use in the English language of words occurring in it. The sentence stating that 'primary colour' applies, as a matter of usage, to the colour red expresses a contingent proposition. What is *not* contingent is the proposition that red is a primary colour. *Being red* entails *being a primary colour*. About the 'colour system' Wittgenstein remarked: 'Then there is something arbitrary about this system? Yes and no. It is akin both to what is arbitrary and to what is non-arbitrary.'[42] What is arbitrary is the verbal fact about the usage of the terms 'red' and 'primary colour' which make it true that the sentence 'Red is a primary colour' expresses a necessary proposition. This roundabout connection of the necessary proposition with a verbal fact does not make it true to say that the necessary proposition is identical with any proposition *about the terms* 'red' and 'primary colour'. Any statement reporting the usage of a term in a given language is factual rather than *a priori*. Since the proposition to the effect that 'primary colour' applies, as a matter of usage, to the colour red, it follows that the necessary proposition cannot be identified with it.

Conventionalism, as a philosophical position, has made this identification: necessary propositions are 'really verbal'. Certain things Wittgenstein has said about mathematical propositions, and in general about necessary propositions, suggest that at times he held this view. Moore reports that in his lectures of 1930–33 Wittgenstein appeared to hold that 'p is impossible' means the same as '"p" has no use', that '2 is a number' means '"2" has a use', and that 'red is a primary colour' says something about the word 'red'.[43] He also characterised necessary propositions as 'rules of grammar', and asserted that geometry gives the grammar of 'cube' as arithmetic gives the grammar of 'number'.

The effect of these comments is to bring to the fore the second face of necessary propositions, their verbal face, and to make it plainly visible. It turns attention away from their fact-reporting aspect. Since what is right about Polya's account of 'inductive testing' of a conjectured theorem rests on the connection of the theorem with a verbal fact, something more should be said about this connection and especially about Wittgenstein's conventionalism. Keeping in mind that a necessary proposition makes no mention of words, it will be useful to digress here and assess some of the things Wittgenstein said which seem to bear the mark of conventionalism, especially to bring out the *point* he had in mind in asserting that necessary propositions are rules of grammar.

The following account of what, according to Wittgenstein, underlies a philosophical position certainly underlies traditional conventionalism:

> Our ordinary language, which of all possible notations is the one which pervades all our life, holds our mind rigidly in one position, as it were, and in this position sometimes it feels cramped, having a desire for other positions as well. Thus we sometimes wish for a notation which stresses a difference more strongly, makes it more obvious, than ordinary language does, or one which in a particular case uses more closely similar forms of expression than our ordinary language.[44]

Conventionalism as a philosophical view stresses a difference between necessarily true and contingently true propositions, e.g. the difference between knowing that the sentence 'Red is a primary colour' expresses something true, and knowing that the sentence 'Red is a colour in many flags' expresses something true. To know the first requires knowing only a linguistic fact given in a standard dictionary. To know the second requires extra-linguistic knowledge acquired by observation of flags. In another way conventionalism stresses a similarity, namely, that the two statements, 'The sentence "Red is a primary colour" expresses a necessary proposition' and 'The sentence "'primary colour' applies to what 'red' applies to" expresses a true empirical proposition', have the same verification. The fact that 'Red is a primary colour' expresses a true *a priori* proposition is equivalent to the fact that '"Primary colour" applies to whatever "red" applies to' expresses a true verbal proposition. But the sentence, 'Red is a primary colour', does not *state* what it is, i.e. the verbal fact, that we must know in order to know that the proposition it expresses is true. What it asserts is the non-verbal proposition that red is a primary colour.[45] One must take care not to mix the verbal and non-verbal idioms — not to confuse 'The proposition that red is a primary colour is necessary ' with 'The sentence "Red is a primary colour" expresses what is necessarily true', and go on to equate, as do conventionalists, the proposition that red is necessarily a primary colour with the proposition that 'primary colour' applies to whatever 'red' applies to.

Has Wittgenstein committed himself to this kind of confusion? What makes his conventionalism different from its traditional form is the *point* he had in mind in characterising *a priori* propositions as rules of grammar. He knew that calling them 'rules of grammar' did not use the phrase 'rule of grammar' in its usual way to describe propositions about words. *His* rules of grammar are not to be found in grammar books. The point of saying what he did has its explanation in the linguistic illness for which it is a corrective. It must be conceded, however, that the point of his claim appears to be the same as that of any philosophical view, *viz.* to oppose a rival claim. Construing what he says about *a priori* propositions as being itself a philosophical view on a par with any other, we can apply to it his description of the creations of philosophers as stemming from a wish 'for a notation differing from ordinary forms of expression'. The effect of characterising necessary propositions as rules of grammar is to introduce a stretched use of the phrase 'rule of grammar'. (Similarly, conventionalists who express their view in the words 'necessary propositions are verbal' stretch the use of the word 'verbal'.) To extend 'rule of grammar' to cover propositions which make no mention of words is to introduce a linguistic innovation.

The point of this innovation is to bring to the fore a verbal face which sentences for necessary propositions conceal. And the point of doing this is therapeutic: not to show counter-claims to be false, but to remove the temptation to advance them. By exaggerating the verbal aspect of sentences denoting necessary propositions Wittgenstein provides an antidote to Platonic metaphysics. Plato held that numbers 'are to be reckoned among the things that are'[46] and that geometry is about 'the absolute square and the absolute diameter'[47] to which the drawn figures are related as the less accurate to the ideal. Wittgenstein considers this picture an impediment to the proper understanding of mathematical language. A metaphysician who holds that general *a priori* propositions assert an entailment relation between abstract entities has arrived at his view via the regulative principle that they must be *about something*. He *invents* a subject-matter — in name if not in fact — to correspond to substantive terms which do not have a use to refer to things one can point to.

> The question . . . 'What is the number one?' produces in us a mental cramp. We feel we can't point to anything in reply . . . and yet ought to point to something. (We are up against one of the great sources of philosophical bewilderment: a substantive makes us look for a thing that corresponds to it.)[48] On [perceiving that a substantive is not used as what in general we should call the name of an object . . . we can't help saying . . . that it is the name of an aethereal object.][49]

The purpose of Wittgenstein's conventionalism was to avoid the idea that *a priori* propositions, if not about concrete objects, must be about abstract objects, whose entailment relations they assert. Calling them rules of grammar is a therapy directed to 'removing the bias which forces us to think that the facts *must* conform to certain pictures embedded in our language'.[50] The term 'grammatical rule' is stretched in order to break the hold of a linguistic obsession with the name-object pattern.

For one thing, a rule of grammar, being arbitrary, cannot be justified by pointing to objects which verify it. Consider the 'rule of grammar' 'There are four primary colours'. On this he comments that one is not tempted to justify it by saying, 'But there really are four primary colours'. For 'saying that the rules of grammar are arbitrary is directed against the possibility of this justification, which is constructed on the model of justifying a proposition by pointing to what verifies it.'[51] For another thing, calling necessary propositions rules of grammar turns attention to their *use*, namely, to govern the use of language. While recognising that $25 \times 24 = 600$ is not a rule for handling signs, he points out that 'it would stand in the relation of a rule to a *proposition* using this equation'.[52] For example, if one said one had in the period of a year made 24 deposits of £25 each and in the end had a total of £650, the equation would serve as a rule to preclude the statement as an inconsistency. Emphasis on this function diverts attention away from the question as to what the equation is about.

Supposing that mathematical propositions have a subject-matter — abstract entities — may lie at the root of Polya's treatment of them after the model of contingent propositions. What is paradoxical about his account is the idea that a necessary *proposition* might be made plausible by citing confirming instances. If an exception is inconceivable, then instances do not make probable the exclusion of a possibility since there is no possibility to exclude. 'Confirming' cases do not support a mathematical generalisation since they do not reduce the likelihood that there are exceptions.

The fact that a mathematical generalisation can be restated as an entailment is the important difference between it and an inductive generalisation. Sliding over this difference is responsible for the paradox in saying one *believes*, upon examining the first 20 values of n, that all numbers of the form $n^2 - n + 41$ are prime. This requires believing that these cases tend to show that an entailment holds and therefore that it is possible for the generalisation to be true. Suppose now that we try out the value $n = 41$. The result is '41^2 is prime', a contradiction. What this result shows is that the proposition 'for all n, $n^2 - n + 41$ is prime' is an *a priori* impossibility. This being the case, *that* proposition could not have been before one's mind, the one which was thought to be true when values were found that satisfied the function. We cannot say that a proposition was thought to be *a priori* true and that *it* turned out to be otherwise. The truth-value of a proposition of number theory is internal to it. It would not be *that* proposition without having that truth-value. Hence it cannot be said that the necessary singular proposition of the form $fn.\sim gn$ ($n = 41$) which upsets the generalisation shows that its actual truth-value is other than the possible truth-value suggested by the necessary singulars of the form $fn.gn$. Its actual truth-value is identical with its only possible truth-value. The fact that the singular proposition, 'for $n = 41$, $n^2 - n + 41$ is not prime' is necessary, is equivalent to the fact that 'All numbers of the form $n^2 - n + 41$ are prime' is logically impossible, i.e. it shows that there is no entailment.

It is a commonplace that mathematicians do 'make conjectures', 'believe to be true' what they are attempting to prove, and sometimes are 'convinced' by special cases. We all understand the following comment by Descartes:

> In order to show by enumeration that the area of a circle is greater than that of any other figure of the same perimeter, we do not need to make a general investigation of all the possible figures, but it suffices to prove it for a few particular figures whence we can conclude the same thing, by induction, for all the other figures.[53]

And we understand Euler's remarking, in another connection, that 'it seems impossible that the law which has been discovered to hold for 20 terms . . . would not be observed in the terms that follow.'[54] Hence there must be some way of accounting for the propriety of such language. Its propriety, and the propriety of Polya's account as well, will appear — and the paradox will be explained — if, so to speak, we ask for a change of venue. It is the propositional idiom, the coupling of plausibility talk with *propositions*, which is at the root of the paradox. By moving from talk of propositions to talk of verbal expressions the paradox will be dissolved, which is another way of saying it will be understood.

To illustrate, consider the *proposition* expressed by the sentence '57 is factorable', and suppose I say I believe it to be false. Then it cannot be the proposition that 57 is factorable that I believe to be false, for no proposition which is or could be false can be that proposition. However, and this is important to note, there is no paradox whatever in saying one believes that the sentence '57 is factorable' says what is false or that '57' denotes a prime number, for this is merely to have a false belief. Speculation is possible about whether a given *sentence* expresses an *a priori* proposition, for this is speculation on an empirical matter.

To return now to the fact that the sentence of the form 'All f's are g's' expresses something *a priori* true is equivalent to the fact that the sentence '"g" applies to what "f" applies to' expresses an empirical truth about language. Let us call '"g" applies, in point of usage, to what "f" applies to' the verbal counterpart of the necessary proposition that all f's are g's. The singular necessary proposition of the form $fa.ga$ which instantiates the generalisation will have as its verbal counterpart, '"f" and "g" apply jointly to a in virtue of the rules governing their use'. We can now put what Polya wants to say without paradox. Suppose we find a number of cases a, b, c to which 'f' and 'g' apply in virtue of the rules governing these terms. For example, suppose that the rules for the use of 'being of the form $n^2 - n + 41$' and 'prime' dictate their joint application to 41 ($n = 1$). Finding a number of cases to which these expressions apply makes it likely that the rules governing them will continue to dictate their application. That is, they will make it likely that the sentence of the form 'All f's are g's' expresses a necessary truth. When we find that the rules governing the expressions 'being of the form $n^2 - n + 41$ and not prime' has a use, the likelihood that 'All numbers of the form $n^2 - n + 41$ are prime' expresses a necessity drops to 0.

A mathematician who turns to an examination of cases does so in default of having a demonstration. If he finds singular propositions instantiating the generalisation, he may, like Euler, hazard the guess that the law holds for all other instances — that 'it seems impossible' that it should not. This is an ontologically formulated way of asserting something to which such talk is appropriate, namely, statements about terminology. Plausibility talk is appropriate to the verbal counterparts of entailment propositions, for these are empirical. It is a mere matter of fact whether or not certain combinations of terms have a use in mathematical language, that is, whether the sentences in which the combination occurs expresses something true in virtue of linguistic rules. The important difference between establishing that a sentence of the form 'All f's are g's' expresses a law of nature and establishing that it expresses a mathematical law is that in the first case the procedure is to turn to confirming fact and in the second the procedure is comparable to a calculation — a calculation in accordance with the rules for using appropriately related words. The use of the word 'law' in the two phrases 'law of nature' and 'mathematical law' conceals this difference ('holds our mind rigidly in one position'). In consequence, we speak of being convinced of the truth of both sorts of proposition, of their being made plausible, etc. 'Conjecture', 'belief', 'plausibility' are appropriately used in connection with contingent propositions. And since it is an empirical matter whether the sentence we believe to a express a necessary truth does so, there are no paradoxical consequences involved in speculating on this. Paradox arises from describing the non-verbal face necessary propositions present in a way that is proper only to their verbal counterparts. That there is something right about what Polya says rests on the fact that his talk is entirely appropriate to the verbal counterpart which an *a priori* proposition has. The fact that in non-philosophical contexts we do not engage in cumbersome talk about sentences rather than about propositions creates no problem.

Notes

1. G. Polya, *How to Solve It* (1945), Princeton, NJ.: Princeton University Press, pp. 103–6.

2. L. Wittgenstein, *Remarks on the Foundations of Mathematics* (1956), New York: Macmillan, p. 117.

3. G. H. Hardy's description of Ramanujan (1921), *Proceedings of the London Mathematical Society* (2), XIX, p. lviii.

4. From R. Courant and H. Robbins (1941), *What is Mathematics?*, London: Oxford University Press, p. 30.

5. P. E. B. Jourdain (1912), *The Nature of Mathematics*, Edinburgh. See James R. Newman (1956), *The World of Mathematics*, New York: Simon & Schuster, vol. 1, p. 68.

6. My lecture notes, 1933–34, taken preceding dictation of *The Blue Book*.

7. *Philosophical Investigations* (1953), Oxford: Basil Blackwell, p. 43.

8. Lecture notes 1939.

9. *The Blue Book* (1958), Oxford: Basil Blackwell, p. 28.

10. *Philosophical Investigations*, p. 48.

11. The Yellow Book. Notes taken by Alice Ambrose and Margaret Masterman in the intervals between dictation of *The Blue Book*. See *Wittgenstein's Lectures, Cambridge 1932–1935* (1979, 1982), Oxford: Basil Blackwell, p. 69.

12. *Philosophical Investigations*, p. 91.

13. Ibid., p. 51.

14. Ibid., p. 91.

15. See 'Wittgenstein on Universals' (1966), *Essays in Analysis*, London: Allen & Unwin, where I develop this thesis for a related problem.

16. *The Blue Book*, p. 57.

17. Edward Kasner and James Newman (1940), *Mathematics and the Imagination*, New York: Simon & Schuster, p. 359.

18. Lectures (1939).

19. Ibid.

20. *Philosophische Bemerkungen* (1964), Oxford: Basil Blackwell, p. 152; my translation.

21. Ibid.

22. Ibid., p. 190.

23. *Philosophical Investigations*, p. 224.

24. *Tractatus Logico-Philosophicus*, 3.031 (1922), New York: Harcourt, Brace, trans. C. K. Ogden.

25. *Zettel* (1967), Oxford: Basil Blackwell, p. 73, trans. G. E. M. Anscombe, with slight revision.

26. Ibid., p. 121.

27. Wittgenstein's example, taken from a manuscript entitled 'Grundlagen der Mathematik'.

28. *How to Solve It*, p. 152.

29. Cf. *Philosophische Bemerkungen*, p. 145: 'A generality cannot be at the same time empirical and demonstrable.'

30. G. Polya, 'Heuristic Reasoning and the Theory of Probability', *American Mathematical Monthly*, vol. 48, p. 457.

31. Ibid., p. 464.

32. *Philosophical Investigations*, p. 224.

33. *Tractatus Logico-Philosophicus*, 6.112.

34. J. S. Mill, *A System of Logic* (1856), New York: Harper, pp. 167–8.

35. Ibid., p. 164.

36. Ibid., p. 167.

37. Ibid., p. 163.

38. Polya, 'Heuristic Reasoning and the Theory of Probability', p. 450.

39. Mill, *A System of Logic*, p. 149.

40. Ibid., pp. 164–7.

41. My lecture notes, 1934–35.

42. *Zettel*, p. 66e.

43. *Philosophical Papers* (1959), London: Allen & Unwin, pp. 275–6.

44. *The Blue Book*, p. 59.

45. For these distinctions, see M. Lazerowitz, 'Necessity and Language'.

46. *Sophist*, sec. 238, trans. Jowett.

47. *Republic*, Book VI, sec. 511, trans. Jowett.

48. *The Blue Book*, p. 1. The reading originally dictated: 'we try to find a substance for a substantive'.

49. Ibid., p. 47.

50. Ibid., p. 43.

51. *Zettel*, p. 61e.

52. My lecture notes, 1934–35.

53. *Oeuvres* (1901), vol. 10, p. 390, ed. Adam and Tannery, trans. G. Polya.

54. From a schematic abstract given by G. Polya, *American Mathematical Monthly*, vol. 48, p. 454.

7 THE INFINITE IN MATHEMATICS

In their everyday, popular use, the words 'finite' and 'infinite' are connected with the idea of quantity — the first with the idea of a limited quantity or amount, the second with the idea of the unlimited and the vast. Thus, in everyday talk something is said to be infinitely far from us (e.g. a remote galaxy) when it is a vast distance away, in contrast to something which is said to be far but not infinitely far; and infinite wealth, as against limited assets, is understood to be enormous wealth. If we were told that Jones had infinite credit at the bank, we should naturally infer that he had more credit than people who had only limited credit.

The words 'finite' and 'infinite' are not used in their popular senses in mathematics, but the ideas of the huge and the less than huge seem, nevertheless, to be behind the thinking of at least some mathematicians, one of whom inadvertently revealed this in the lapse shown in the following words: 'Representation of a complex variable on a plane is obviously more effective at a finite distance from the origin than it is at a very great distance.'[1] This brings to mind a description in a brochure about a marshland in Ohio, as 'almost endless'.

Wittgenstein is said to have remarked that 'The idea of the infinite as something huge does fascinate some people, and their interest is due solely to that association, though they probably would not admit it.'[2] There is reason for thinking that this remark applies to many mathematicians who adopt Cantor's notion of the 'consummated infinite', the notion that, for example, the series of numbers 1, 2, 3, 4, 5 . . . form a completed totality of elements, just as the first 40-odd numbers form an entire set of numbers, or just as the chimney-pots in Bloomsbury make up a whole class of objects in London. He is also reported as having said,

When someone uses the expression 'plus 1' we get the picture of 1 being added to something. If I speak of 'the cardinal number of all the cardinal numbers' all sorts of expressions come to mind — such as the expression 'the number of chairs in this room'. The phrase conjures up a picture of an enormous, colossal number. And this picture has charm.[3]

Wittgenstein declared, as did Gauss, that infinity has nothing to do with size, and there is reason to think that transfinite arithmetic is primarily a semantic creation for representing the mathematical infinite as the colossal. It may turn out that despite its containing solid mathematics, the discipline which Hilbert described as the paradise created by Cantor and which Poincaré characterised as a disease from which mathematics will eventually recover is at bottom a semantic contrivance for the production of an illusion.

Many people take the view that all numbers are *finite* numbers. Russell gives one explanation as to why this is so. The phrase 'finite number' means, according to him,

> 0 and 1 and 2 and 3 and so on, forever — in other words, any number that can be obtained by successively adding ones. This includes all the numbers that can be expressed by means of our ordinary numerals, and since such numbers can be made greater and greater, without ever reaching an unsurpassable maximum, it is easy to suppose that there are no other numbers. But this supposition, natural as it is, is mistaken.[4]

Russell is suggesting that it is natural to think the finite numbers are the only numbers, and Zeno gives an argument for this notion. One thesis of *Fragment 3* states: 'If there is a multiplicity of things, they necessarily are as many as they are, and not more or fewer. If they are exactly as many as they are, then they will be finite in number.' The counter-thesis is that they must also be infinite in number, but that is not to the point here. Zeno's argument amounts to the contention that a number of things must be a definite number (though we may not know what it is) and therefore finite, i.e. a number expressible by one of our 'ordinary' numerals.

In Russell's opinion the weak point in Zeno's thesis that 'if they are just as many as they are, they will be finite in number' is that it is based on the assumption that definite infinite numbers are impossible.[5] It is by no means clear what is meant by the phrase 'definite infinite number'. The idea of a *definite* infinite number would seem to be that of a number that is like one denoted by an 'ordinary' numeral, but greater than any such number. This may well strike one as being a number that is finite or 'terminate' (Galileo's word), but too great to be finite, a *finite infinite* number. The phrase 'the consummated infinite' also suggests the notion of an infinity of elements whose number is made definite and thus finite. Be this as it may, Russell's objection brings to our attention an important point about the words 'All numbers are finite': this is that if the word 'finite' has a correct application to numbers, then its associated antithetical word 'infinite' must also have a correct application to numbers. It *may* be that in fact the application of 'finite' to numbers does not represent a correct use of the word: it *may* be that the sentences '5 is a finite number' and 'a thousand billion is a finite number' do not represent a correct use of the word. But if they do, then 'infinite' must also have a correct application to *some* numbers. For otherwise 'finite' would not have a use to distinguish between numbers set off some from others, as do the terms 'prime number' and 'proper fraction'. Without its antithesis 'infinite number', the expression 'finite number' would contain a word which serves no function, and 'finite number' would have no use different from that of the word 'number'. It is a curious feature of the view that all numbers are finite that it rests on a distinction which at the same time it obliterates. Without a distinction between finite and infinite numbers, Zeno's putative demonstration could not have been formulated. But if his first thesis is in fact demonstrated, there could *in principle* be no infinite numbers, which would imply that there is *no distinction between finite and infinite numbers*.

Wittgenstein has pointed out that in philosophy words are often used without an antithesis, in what he describes as a 'typically metaphysical way'.[6] He conceived his task as being 'to bring words back from their metaphysical to their everyday usage'.[7] If, allowing that 'finite' has a correct application to numbers, we preserve the distinction implied by its use, we have to 'bring back' into usage the application of 'infinite' to numbers. Doing this upsets the thesis that *all* numbers are finite, and would seem to open the way to the claim that there are numbers which are not expressible by any of the 'ordinary' numerals. Russell remarked:

> When infinite numbers are first introduced to people, they are apt to refuse the name of numbers to them, because their behaviour is so different from that of finite numbers that it seems a wilful misuse of terms to call them numbers at all.[8]

But if it is not a misuse of terminology to call 5 a finite number, it cannot be a misuse of terminology to call an infinite number a number, regardless of how it may differ from finite numbers. And, of course, it would be a wilful misuse of terminology to deny that the number of primes is infinite.

It is a curious and striking thing about the idea of the infinite that in some connections it would be considered unnatural to deny that 'infinite number' has a correct application, while in other and comparable connections it is natural to deny this. There would be no temptation to deny that there is an infinite number of numbers after 1. But it seems entirely natural to state (as the cosmological argument does) that it is, in principle, impossible for there to be an infinite series of causes. No one could take exception to the statement that the geometric series $1 + \frac{1}{2} + \frac{1}{4} + \ldots$ is an infinite series, as against one of its parts, e.g. $1 + \frac{1}{2} + \frac{1}{4}$; but many would take exception to the claim that an infinite series forms a whole. Again, no one would say that $\frac{1}{2}$, $\frac{3}{4}$, $\frac{7}{8}$, $\frac{15}{16}$ is the entire series generated by $(2^n - 1)/2^n$. But many people would, nevertheless, deny that there is such a thing as an entire unending series, and therefore would deny that '1 is *beyond*[9] the whole of the infinite series $\frac{1}{2}$, $\frac{3}{4}$, $\frac{7}{8}$, $\frac{15}{16}$, . . .'.[10] Russell asserted that the first infinite number is 'beyond the whole unending series of finite numbers',[11] and went on to remark that it will be objected that there cannot be anything beyond the whole of a series that is endless. What is the difference between speaking of an infinite series and speaking of the whole infinite series, which makes people accept the one and dispute the other? No one would be tempted to reject the statement that there is an infinite number of natural numbers or that there is an infinite number of primes; and it is mystifying that people who are introduced to infinite numbers may well refuse to apply the word 'number' to them. What, we may ask, is the difference between allowing that there is an infinite number of natural numbers and allowing that there is a number which is infinite?

Russell offers the following explanation:

the number of inductive numbers is a new number, different from all of them, not possessing all inductive properties. It may happen that 0 has a certain property, and that if n has it so has $n + 1$, and yet that this new number does not have it. The difficulties that so long delayed the theory of infinite numbers were largely due to the fact that some, at least, of the inductive properties were wrongly judged to be such as *must* belong to all numbers; indeed it was thought that they could not be denied without contradiction. The first step in understanding infinite numbers consists in realising the mistakenness of this view.[12]

In philosophy we are not strangers to 'mistakes' which have the quality of elusiveness: they strongly impress some people as being mistakes, while making no such impression on others. The 'mistake' of thinking that certain of the inductive properties, such as that $n + 1$ is greater than n, are properties of all numbers, would not be accepted as a mistake by all who are competent to express an opinion. Russell remarked that the 'astonishing difference' between any number occurring in the sequence $1, 2, 3, \ldots$ and the number of all the numbers in it is that

> this new number is unchanged by adding 1 or subtracting 1 or doubling or halving or any of a number of other operations which we think of as necessarily making a number larger or smaller. The fact of being unchanged by the addition of 1 is used by Cantor for the definition of what he calls 'transfinite' cardinal numbers.[13]

And one mathematician has spoken of the 'crude miracle' which 'stares us in the face that *a part of a set may have the same cardinal number as the entire set*'.[14]

As is known, Leibniz was not unaware of the miracle which Cantor later performed, except that he called it a contradiction. 'The number of all numbers', he declared, 'implies a contradiction, which I show thus: To any number there is a corresponding number equal to its double. Therefore, the number of all numbers is not greater than the number of even numbers, i.e. the whole is not greater than its part.'[15] What Russell calls a 'new' number with astonishing properties Leibniz calls an impossible number because of these astonishing properties. And the fact of being unchanged by the addition of 1, or the fact of the whole not being greater than its part, which Cantor used to define the term 'transfinite number', was used by Leibniz to deny there could be such a number. If he had been shown Cantor's symbol for the first transfinite number, '$\aleph_0$', it is fair to suppose he would have said that it is not the name of a possible number, and thus that it is not actually the name of a number. It will be remembered that Gauss protested against the use of the actual or completed infinite as something which is 'never permissible in mathematics'. The important thing to notice about this disagreement is that it is not the result of incomplete knowledge of the facts on the part of anyone. If it is a fact that $n + 1$ is greater than n for *any* number, then all the parties to the disagreement know this; and if it is not a fact, then this too is known. There is no disagreement over whether every number n has a double, $2n$, or over whether every number n has a square, n^2, but there is disagreement over whether facts like these show that there is a contradiction in the idea of an infinite totality of numbers or whether it brings to light a characteristic of such a totality. And nothing new can be brought in to help us decide one way or the other.

Galileo gives a different answer to the question concerning infinite numbers. Leibniz and others thought that infinite numbers are impossible, the implication being that there are none. Cantor and others thought that there are such numbers and that, unlike finite numbers, an infinite number can be equal to a proper part of itself, and also that some infinite numbers are greater than other infinite numbers. Galileo's position is that such terms as 'greater than', 'equal to' and 'less than' are not applicable to infinite numbers. From the fact that there cannot be fewer squares than there are numbers of which they are the squares, i.e. than 'all the Numbers taken together', he does not conclude that there can be no infinite numbers or that infinite numbers have paradoxical properties which defeat our understanding. In the first of his *Dialogues on Motion*, Salʾiati asserts:

> These are some of those Difficulties which arise from Discourses which our finite understanding makes about Infinities, by ascribing to them Attributes which we give to Things finite and determinate, which I think most improper, because those Attributes of Majority, Minority, and Equality, agree not with Infinities, of which we cannot say that one is greater than, less than, or equal to another.[16]

Against Galileo's solution Russell has the following to say: 'It is actually the case that the number of square (finite) numbers is the same as the number of (finite) numbers'.[17] What makes this 'actually the case', we are entitled to ask, as against Galileo's conclusion that 'equal to' is not applicable to the number of numbers and the number of squares?

According to some philosophical mathematicians, commonsense thinkers (as well as mathematicians who might side with either Leibniz or with Galileo) have been taken in by the maxim that if the elements of one set, α, are some only of all the elements of another set, β, then α has fewer elements than β, and β more elements than α.

Russell writes:

> This maxim is true of finite numbers. For example, Englishmen are only some among Europeans, and there are fewer Englishmen than Europeans. But when we come to infinite numbers this is no longer true. This breakdown of the maxim gives us the precise definition of infinity. A collection of terms is infinite when it contains as parts other collections which have just as many terms as it has. If you can take away some of the terms of a collection, without diminishing the number of terms, then there are an infinite number of terms in the collection. For example, there are just as many even numbers as there are numbers altogether, since every number can be doubled. This may be seen by putting odd and even numbers in one row, and even numbers alone in a row below:—
>
> 1, 2, 3, 4, 5, *ad infinitum*
>
> 2, 4, 6, 8, 10, *ad infinitum*.
>
> There are obviously just as many numbers in the row below as in the row above, because there is one below for each one above. This property which was formerly thought to be self-contradictory, is now transformed into a harmless definition of infinity, and shows, in the above case, that the number of finite numbers is infinite.[18]

The idea this passage tends to produce is that a popular belief is being exposed as nothing more than a superstition, that a plain fact is being stated, that something is being shown. Thus the phrases 'breakdown of a maxim', 'there are obviously just as many even numbers as both odd and even numbers', 'shows that the number of finite numbers is infinite' create the impression that a proposition is being upset and that a truth about infinite sets is being supported.

Parenthetically, it is worth noticing that Galileo's claim that 'equal to' does not apply to infinities is pushed aside with the words 'there are obviously just as many . . .'. Galileo certainly was not unaware of the obvious fact that every number has a square, in the face of which he held his own view. If we can ward off the hypnotic effect of Russell's words, supported as they appear to be by the actual transfinite arithmetic developed by Cantor and others, what we see is not that a position is being shown true and rival positions false. What we see, at first glance at least, is that one position is being arbitrarily embraced and that rival positions, rather than being shown false, are simply dismissed. What is called the 'breakdown' of a commonly accepted maxim turns out to be merely a rejection. And we may wonder what the nature of the 'transformation' is which consists of changing a property that is thought by some to be self-contradictory into 'a harmless definition of infinity'.

Russell speaks of 'those who cling obstinately to the prejudices instilled by the arithmetic learnt in childhood'.[19] And R. L. Wilder tries to reassure those who may feel uneasy about the notion of actual infinite numbers that the symbol '$\aleph_0$' for the first transfinite number will, with practice, come to have 'the same significance for us as the number 15, for example'.[20] If we take into account the difference between numbers and the numerals which denote them, or between symbols and their meanings (to which Wilder himself calls attention[21]), then what we are being assured about is that, with practice, we shall think of '$\aleph_0$' as the name of a number or, better, that along with '15' we shall come to think of '$\aleph_0$' as a numeral. The idea which cannot fail to cross one's mind is that Cantor 'christened' the infinite and that followers of his are trying to assure us that there really is an infant. The question is whether $\aleph_0$ *is* a cardinal number, one which gives the *size* of a collection, and whether the *actual use* of '$\aleph_0$' is to denote a number which in any way is comparable to the number 15.

As is known, not all mathematicians accept the notion of a consummated infinite. One mathematician has described an opposing position in the following way: 'Some intuitionists would say that arbitrarily large numbers can perhaps be constructed by pure intuition, but not the set of all natural numbers.'[22] A metaphysical haze surrounds talk of 'constructing numbers in pure intuition', but undoubtedly what it comes down to is talk about the ability to think of various numbers. Some people are able to think of greater numbers of objects than are others. Some arithmetical prodigies are able to do enormous multiplications in their head, and probably can consciously and all at once entertain a large array of natural numbers. But no one, according to the intuitionist claim, has the capacity for presenting to himself the set of all natural numbers. Wilder writes:

If we analyze the psychology of the 'intuitive meaning' of the number 2, we shall probably conclude that '2 apples' brings up to the mind of the hearer an image of a *pair*, here a pair of apples. A similar remark might hold for the phrase '20 apples'; but it would hardly hold for '200 apples'. From the psychological viewpoint, it seems probable that 200 is simply one of the numbers one ultimately gets at by starting with the numbers whose mental images are distinct — 1, 2, 3, — and applying consecutively the operation of adding 1, as taught in the elementary schools. (This is certainly the case with a number like 3,762,147; it is conceivable that, owing to some special circumstances of our occupation, our experience with 200 may induce a special intuitive knowledge of 200.) But numbers such as $\aleph_0$ and c are hardly to be attained in any such manner (by adding 1, that is).[23]

The number for the consummated infinity of natural numbers cannot be attained by the successive operation of adding 1. However astronomically vast a number may be, and however out of the question physically it may be to reach it by the successive addition of 1, a natural number can, in principle, be reached by the operation of addition. Aleph-null, however, cannot in principle be arrived at by starting with *any* natural number and continuing to add 1 to it. Furthermore, the cardinal number supposedly named by the symbol '$\aleph_0$' cannot in principle be conceived, or be an 'object of thought'. It is psychologically impossible to imagine a trillion coins spreading out before us, although we have some idea of what this would be like. But we have no idea of what it would be like to have in view an infinite number of coins. This is because it is logically, not psychologically, impossible to view or imagine an infinite array of objects. The expression 'sees an infinite number of farthings arrayed before him' does not have a descriptive use in the language, unless 'infinite' is used in its popular meaning.

The set of natural numbers 1, 2, 3, 4, . . . is said to be countable, but it cannot be run through, as it forms a non-terminating series. It has been argued that it is only physically impossible, not logically impossible, to run through the terms of an infinite series, because it is in principle possible to count off each successive number in half the time it takes to count off its predecessor: supposing 1 takes half a minute, 2 takes half of half a minute, etc., then at the end of a minute *all* of the numbers of the infinite series will have been counted off, and the number of the natural numbers, $\aleph_0$, will have been reached.[24] Without going into a detailed examination of this argument, it can be seen that since the natural numbers are endless, counting them off would be a task that could not come to an end — *after* which another task might be started. A curious consequence of this argument is that if a minute were composed of an infinite geometric series of time intervals, $\frac{1}{2} + \frac{1}{4} + \frac{1}{8} + \ldots$, then since the series has no end, a minute could come to no end. Furthermore, the entire array of natural numbers cannot be given all at once (as an extension) for if it could be, then in principle it would be possible to run through the entire set of numbers. It is just as impossible to think of all the numbers at once as it is to finish running through them. If the series 1, 2, 3, 4, . . . were a 'consummated' series of numbers, then it would be possible to run through them — as it is, in theory, possible to run through the series of numbers up to 73,583,197,773. And if they could be viewed all at once, as a whole, they could be run through.

It has been maintained that a collection the elements of which can neither be run through nor displayed all at once, may nevertheless exist as a complete totality, and in a sense be given. According to this thesis, the succession of natural numbers covered by the expression '. . . etc. *ad infinitum*' form a completed set just as do the numbers up to the expression, and are given along with them but in a different manner. Thus, Russell:

> it is not essential to the existence of a collection, or even to knowledge and reasoning concerning it, that we should be able to pass its terms in review one by one. This may be seen in the case of finite collections; we can speak of 'mankind' or 'the human race', though many of the individuals in this collection are not personally known to us. We can do this because we know of characteristics which every individual has if he belongs to the collection, and not if he does not. And exactly the same happens in the case of infinite collections: they may be known by their characteristics although their terms cannot be enumerated. In this sense, an unending series may nevertheless form a whole, and there may be new terms beyond the whole of it.[25]

And:

> Classes which are infinite are given all at once by the defining property of their members.[26]

Aristotle held the theory of the concrete universal, according to which 'no universal exists apart from its individuals',[27] the Parmenidean implication being that whatever we can think of exists. But this is a philosophical view and has nothing to do with fact. It *is* an everyday fact, hardly worth mentioning, that we can — and often do — think of what does not exist: it is possible to entertain a concept to which nothing answers, for example, the concept of a cat with five heads; and it is possible to entertain a defining property of a class which happens to be empty, for example, the property of being a pterodactyl. A class that is determined by a given defining property ø may be null, and entertaining a concept is no guarantee that there is anything answering to it. To say that a class is *given* by its defining property is to say only that its defining property is given; and to say that an infinite set is 'given all at once' by the defining property of its members is to say only that the defining property is given. The impression created is that more than this is being said, but this impression is delusive. Furthermore, to argue that an infinite collection can be known by its characteristics and that 'in this sense' an unending series may form a whole is merely to assign a sense to the phrase 'unending series which forms a whole': the phrase is arbitrarily made to mean the same as 'series which is known by its characteristic'. For example, saying that the series 1, 4, 9, 16, . . . forms a whole *in the sense* that its terms are characterised by being values of n^2 is to create by fiat a semantic identity: '1, 4, 9, 16, . . . form a consummated series' means the same as '1, 4, 9, 16, . . . are successive values of n^2'.

There is a further consideration in support of the proposition that an infinity of elements can form an actual class. The idea that there cannot be a completed infinite series is connected with the idea that there cannot be anything beyond an infinite series. The idea behind this would seem to be that there can only be something after, or beyond, a series which forms a whole, and that since a series which comes to no end cannot form a whole series, nothing can come after it. Russell's answer to this is that 1 is beyond the infinite series $\frac{1}{2}$, $\frac{3}{4}$, $\frac{7}{8}$, $\frac{15}{16}$, . . ., the implication being that an unending series can be consummated and form a whole class.[28] About the series of natural numbers he wrote:

> every number to which we are accustomed, except 0, has another immediately before it, from which it results by adding 1; but the first infinite number does not have this property. The numbers before it form an infinite series, containing ordinary finite numbers, having no maximum, no last finite number, after which one little step would plunge us into the infinite. If it is assumed that the first infinite number is reached by a succession of small steps, it is easy to show that it is self-contradictory. The first

infinite number is, in fact, beyond the whole unending series of finite numbers.[29]

As in the case of the infinite series $\frac{1}{2}, \frac{3}{4}, \frac{7}{8}, \frac{15}{16}, \ldots$, with regard to which Russell states that 1 lies beyond the *whole* series, so in the case of the natural numbers he states that $\aleph_0$ lies beyond the *whole* series. Since the possibility of an unending series being a whole is at issue, Russell appears to beg the question. Undoubtedly what he wished to say was that the fact that 1 lies beyond the series $\frac{1}{2}, \frac{3}{4}, \frac{7}{8}, \frac{15}{16}, \ldots$ shows that the series is a whole; and the fact that $\aleph_0$ lies beyond the series of natural numbers shows that $1, 2, 3, 4, \ldots$ is a whole, or a consummated series.

It is not clear what is meant by 'is beyond' or 'comes after' the whole of an infinite series. It is natural to say that 5 lies beyond $1, 2, 3, 4$; but 1 is not beyond the series $\frac{1}{2}, \frac{3}{4}, \frac{7}{8}, \frac{15}{16}, \ldots$ in this sense. The only sense in which 1 might be said to be beyond the series is that it is the *limit* of the series in the mathematical sense. We may be puzzled to know why the word 'beyond' rather than the more usual term is used, until we realise that 'beyond' suggests the idea of something finished which is followed by something else, i.e. the idea of one thing coming after another. The term 'limit' does not carry with it this suggestion, although there is a tendency sometimes to think of the limit of an infinite geometric series like $\frac{1}{2} + \frac{1}{4} + \frac{1}{8} + \frac{1}{16} + \ldots$ as being its arithmetical sum, which also suggests the idea of a completed series. But no series has an arithmetical sum whose terms cannot *in principle* be summed up; and this is not the case with regard to an unending series. Expressed somewhat differently, the series $\frac{1}{2} + \frac{1}{4} + \frac{1}{8} + \frac{1}{16} + \ldots$ has no sum because the sequence $\frac{1}{2}, \frac{1}{4}, \frac{3}{4}, \frac{7}{8}, \frac{15}{16}, \ldots$ has no last term; and this means that neither array of terms is a completed whole. Putting this aside, it can be seen that to contend against the view that 'there cannot be anything beyond the whole of an infinite series' by stating that '1 is beyond the whole of the infinite series $\frac{1}{2}, \frac{3}{4}, \frac{7}{8}, \frac{15}{16}, \ldots$'[30] is not to show that an infinite series is a whole, any more than to demonstrate that a given infinite series has a limit is to show that the series is a whole.

Similarly, to say that $\aleph_0$ is 'beyond the whole unending series of finite numbers' is not to show that the series exists as a completed whole. The series $1, 2, 3, 4, \ldots$ is said to increase without limit, but Russell states that $\aleph_0$ is the limit of the series. He writes:

The cardinal number $\aleph_0$ is the limit (in the order of magnitude) of the cardinal numbers $1, 2, 3, \ldots n, \ldots$, although the numerical difference between $\aleph_0$ and a finite cardinal is constant and infinite; from a quantitative point of view, finite numbers get no nearer to $\aleph_0$ as they grow larger. What makes $\aleph_0$ the limit of the finite numbers is the fact that, in the series, it comes immediately after them, which is an *ordinal* fact, not a quantitative fact.[31]

One impression a close reading of this passage is liable to create is that a fast and loose game is being played with terminology: a series which increases without limit is said to have a limit, but in an *ordinal* sense; and $\aleph_0$ is said to come *immediately* after the series, although the series has no last term. The number 5 comes immediately after the series of numbers $1, 2, 3, 4$. But if we stop to think about it, if we get behind the words so to speak, we find that we have no idea of what it is for something to come *immediately* after a series which increases without limit. Light is thrown on the passage if we connect it with the assertion that '1 is beyond the whole of the infinite series $\frac{1}{2}, \frac{3}{4}, \frac{7}{8}, \frac{15}{16}, \ldots$'. What comes through is that the series $1, 2, 3, 4, 5,$ $\ldots$ is represented as being like the geometric series:

$\aleph_0$ is the limit of (and is beyond) $1, 2, 3, 4, \ldots n, \ldots$
1 is the limit of (and is beyond) $\frac{1}{2}, \frac{3}{4}, \frac{7}{8}, \frac{15}{16}, \ldots (2^n - 1)/2^n, \ldots$

To say that the series $1, 2, 3, 4, \ldots$ has a limit which lies beyond the whole of it, and that $\aleph_0$ comes immediately after it, induces one to think of the series as consummated. But this is not the same as showing that it is. We might say that this way of talking about the series shows nothing about it, but it does produce a change in the atmosphere.

The symbol '1' denotes a number which is the limit of the series $\frac{1}{2}$, $\frac{3}{4}, \frac{7}{8}, \frac{15}{16}, \ldots$; and the symbol '$\aleph_0$' is represented as denoting a cardinal number which is the limit of the series of natural numbers $1, 2, 3, 4, \ldots$ The question is whether '$\aleph_0$' in fact has a use to denote a number, or whether we become dupes when, with practice, we reach a state of mind in which we think of '$\aleph_0$' as a numeral like '15'. It has been seen that there is no way in which an infinite number of objects can be given. It is impossible to finish passing in review an infinity of entities, or to arrive at an infinite totality by counting. It is also impossible to envisage an infinity of objects spread out as a whole before us. The impossibility of counting the elements of an infinite set and of arriving at their number by adding them up is theoretical, as is the impossibility of viewing an infinite array and noting its number, rather than entertaining the defining property of its members.

The impossibility is logical, not one which is due to a psychological or a 'medical'[32] shortcoming. Any shortcoming which makes it impossible for us to carry out a task could in theory, if not in fact, be made good and the task brought within our reach. We know what it would be like to do things that are immeasurably beyond our actual abilities, like snuffing out the sun or jumping to Neptune, but we have no idea of what it would be to finish running through an infinite series or to see it as a completed totality. This is because the expressions 'comes to the end of an endless task' and 'sees an infinite totality before him' describe nothing whatever: the terms 'consummated infinite series' and 'actual infinite collection' have been given no application. Their actual use, regardless of the talk surrounding them, is neither to describe a series nor to describe a collection. If the phrase 'the infinite series of natural numbers' described a consummated series, it would describe what in theory, if not in fact, we could run through. The phrase 'finished running through the series $1, 2, 3, 4, \ldots n, \ldots$' would then have descriptive sense, which it does not.

There is no number which is the number of the totality of natural numbers, because there is no such logically possible totality. Russell asserted that 'It cannot be said to be certain that there are any infinite collections in the world'.[33] This observation carries with it the suggestion that the question whether there are infinite collections in the world is factual, to be investigated by empirical procedures. It should now be clear that the question is not a request for empirical information, and the statement that the series of natural numbers is not a totality of numbers is not an empirical statement. It follows that the statement that there is no number which is the number of the totality of natural numbers is not empirical: the phrase 'the number of the totality of natural numbers' does not describe or refer to a number. And the symbol '$\aleph_0$', which supposedly denotes the number referred to by the descriptive phrase, is, unlike the numeral '15', not only not an 'ordinary' numeral, it is not the name of a number at all.

It need hardly be pointed out that we do speak of the existence of an infinite number of natural numbers and of the existence of an infinite number of rational numbers; and it would be foolish to deny that sentences declaring the existence of an infinite number of terms and the existence of an infinite series, etc. are perfectly intelligible.

How is this fact to be brought into line with what has just been said about '$\aleph_0$', which is represented as denoting the number of their terms? Consider the proposition that there exists an infinite number of prime numbers. Proving it is the same as proving that the hypothesis that there is a greatest prime number is self-contradictory: supposing P to be the greatest prime, then P! + 1 either is itself prime or contains a prime factor which is greater than P. That is, the proof of the proposition that there is an infinite number of primes consists of showing that the concept of a greatest prime implies a contradiction, and thus that no number answers to it — just as no number answers to the concept of an integer between 5 and 6. This means that any expression whose meaning is the concept (in the English language the expression 'greatest prime number') has no use to describe a number. Restated in verbal terms, demonstrating the proposition expressed by the sentence 'There is an infinite number of primes' is nothing in addition to demonstrating that the proposition expressed by the sentence 'There is a greatest prime' is self-contradictory, and this in turn is the same as showing that the phrase 'greatest prime number' has no use to describe or to refer to a number.

The important point to grasp is that a sentence which declares the existence of an *infinite number* of terms in a mathematical series means nothing different from a sentence which declares the *non-existence* of a term answering to a putative description, 'the last number' or 'the least number' or 'the greatest number', and the like. Undoubtedly it was a kind of recognition of this fact that was responsible for John Locke's observation that we have no *positive idea* of the infinite.[34] The sentence 'There exists an infinite number of natural numbers' says the same thing as does the sentence 'There is no greatest natural number'. And the sentence 'There is no greatest number' conveys, without *expressing* what it conveys, the verbal fact that the expression 'greatest natural number' has no use to refer to a number. In other words, the *implicit* import of the sentence 'There exists an infinite number of natural numbers' is wholly verbal and negative, to the effect that a certain expression has no application in the language of mathematics.

It can now be seen why it implies no contradiction to say that an infinite number is not a number, and we can understand why 'when infinite numbers are first introduced to people, they are apt to refuse them the name of numbers'. If we give a moment's thought to

Locke's remark that 'there is nothing yet more evident than the absurdity of the actual idea of an infinite number'[35] and consult the workings of the language of the infinite, we shall see that talk of the consummated infinite is bogus. Wittgenstein made the remark that what the bedmaker says is all right, but what the philosopher says is all wrong, and we might now be inclined to think that what the mathematician shows about infinite series, denumerable, non-denumerable, etc. is all right, but that what the philosophical mathematician says about the actual infinite is all wrong. Instead of declaring that what the philosophical mathematician says is wrong, that he is making mistakes, it is more enlightening to think of him as making up a special language game, in which '$\aleph_0$' and other symbols, e.g. 'c', are treated *as if* they are the names of numbers, for the special aura doing this provides for a certain part of mathematics. It is a secure maxim that philosophers do not make mistakes, mistakes to which they are incorrigibly attached. Instead, they play games with language for whatever subterranean value they may have. A mathematician who surrounds his work with a dramatic language game undoubtedly derives hidden satisfaction from it.[36]

The assertion that an unending series forms a whole, or a completed extension, 'in the sense' that the characteristic of the series is known is an imaginative way of speaking about a rule (whether explicitly formulated or not) for generating terms in serial order, no term being the last that is constructible by the rule. This is what is meant, and all that is meant, by saying that a series is infinite. The *substance* behind talk of the completed infinite, the actual mathematics behind it, is just the explication of the characteristics of formulae for constructing series. To revert to Russell's talk about finite and infinite numbers, the terms 'finite' and 'infinite' have actual applications only to series, not to numbers: the number 7 is not a 'finite' number, it is a number. A series is said to be finite when a number applies to the set of its terms, as in the case of an arithmetic series, and it is said to be infinite when it is linked with a rule which implies the logical (not physical or psychological) impossibility of any term being the last of the series constructible by it. In its actual use 'infinite number of terms' does not refer to a *number* of terms. And to say that a series contains an infinite number of terms is not to make a statement about the number of terms in the series: 'series which contains an infinite number of terms' means the same as 'infinite series', which in turn means the same as 'series that is generated by a formula with regard to which it is *senseless* to say that it generates a last term'. The likeness between such expressions as 'the number 37', 'huge number', and the term 'infinite number' lies in their grammar, to use a word made popular by Wittgenstein: like them it is, grammatically, a substantive expression, but unlike them it neither describes nor names a number.

The grammatical likeness between the term 'infinite number' and terms like 'large number' and 'small number', as well as the grammatical likeness between 'infinite series' and 'finite series', creates possibilities of playing exciting games with language. The idea that this is what mathematical philosophers of the infinite are doing helps us understand the import of the remark that with practice $\aleph_0$ will acquire 'the same significance for us as the number 15'. The underlying meaning plainly is that in time people will enter into the language game and will come to *feel* about '$\aleph_0$' much as they feel about numerals, especially numerals which denote prodigious numbers. The idea that philosophical mathematicians who are concerned to provide a 'theoretical' background for their actual mathematics, who, in other words, wish to have one or another philosophical 'centre piece'[37] for mathematics, gives us insight into the mysterious and continuing dispute between finitists and Cantorians. No mathematical statement or demonstration is actually in dispute. And it gives an improved understanding of the divergence of opinions represented by Galileo, Leibniz and Cantor.

To go to the matter directly, a philosophical mathematician like Leibniz (and a person to whom 'infinite numbers are first introduced') seems to be impressed by the semantic dissimilarity, i.e. the difference in use between 'infinite number', 'huge number' and like expressions, and unimpressed by the similarity of their grammar. In his opinion, it would seem, the grammatical similarity tends to cover up an important difference in the actual use of terminology. And in play, if not in fact, he 'corrects' this shortcoming in language. He declares infinite numbers to be self-contradictory, which, like the greatest prime and a rational number whose square is equal to 2, do not exist. His argument is that no whole number can be equal to a fraction of itself, and since a whole infinite number would be equal to a fraction of itself, e.g., $\aleph_0/2 = \aleph_0$, it is impossible for there to be an infinite number.

Galileo, it would seem, was intrigued by the grammar of the term 'infinite number' and came out in favour of treating the term *as if* its use was to refer to a number. Like Locke, he was aware of the fact that 'nothing is plainer than the absurdity of the actual idea of an infinite number', which is a non-verbal way of stating the verbal fact that 'infinite number', unlike the expressions 'vast number' and 'the first prime number greater than 1,000,000', does not function in the language to refer to or to describe a number. Nevertheless, he chose to group it artificially without changing its actual use, with what might be called substantive number expressions. (Parenthetically, it is worth remarking that although Leibniz and Galileo give opposing answers to the question, 'Is an infinite number a number?', their answers are not the result of any difference in their knowledge of numbers, which would be inexplicable if the question were a request for information about them.) To put it in John Wisdom's way, the question is not a request for mathematical information; it is a request for a redecision with regard to the term 'infinite number', as to whether to classify it with substantive number expressions. The answers represent opposing linguistic decisions, which make no difference to the doing of mathematics and thus can be argued interminably. Treating 'infinite number' as if it is a substantive number expression which gives the number of terms in the series 1, 2, 3, 4, . . . generates the paradoxical property of an infinite set that some only out of all of its elements are no fewer than all of the elements. Leibniz claimed that the property was self-contradictory, and thus that the idea of an infinite number was self-contradictory. Galileo took a different view of what the paradoxical property showed about infinite numbers: its possession is *proof* that 'the Attributes or Terms of Equality, Majority, and Minority, have no place in Infinities, but are confin'd to terminate quantities'. What, according to Leibniz, demonstrates the impossibility of infinite numbers, according to Galileo demonstrates that, unlike 7 and 23, infinite numbers are not comparable: the number denoted by '$\aleph_0/2$' cannot be said to be either less than or equal to the number denoted by '$\aleph_0$'. What can be seen here are not different opinions regarding what is *entailed* by the possession of a certain property, but different ways of marking the unlikeness between 'infinite number' and substantive number expressions. Galileo classifies the term with substantive number expressions, and marks the difference between them by stating that infinite numbers are mysterious, elusive numbers which cannot be compared with each other, numbers over which our 'finite understanding' creates difficulties. No actual entailment claim is in question. Only a way of marking the difference between the actual use of terminology is being put forward.

Cantor, who according to Russell transformed a property

formerly thought to be self-contradictory into a 'harmless definition' of infinity, goes against both Leibniz and Galileo. In his view, infinite numbers are not self-contradictory nor are they mysteriously different from 7 and 23 and $3^3 - 2^2$ in not being comparable in terms of less than, equal to, and greater than. Two sets are said to have the same cardinal number (Cantor's term was 'Mächtigkeit'), or to be equal, if there exists a $(1-1)$-correspondence between their elements. In E. T. Bell's words, 'Two sets are said to have the same *cardinal number* when all the things in the sets can be *paired off* one-to-one. After the pairing there are to be no unpaired things in either set'.[38] He states that 'Cantor proved that the set of all rational numbers contains precisely as many members as the (infinitely more inclusive) set of *all* algebraic numbers'.[39] He might also have said that Galileo *proved* that the set of all rational numbers contains precisely as many members as the infinitely less inclusive set of all the squares of the rational numbers.

There is no reason for thinking that Galileo would have agreed about what he had *proved*. Russell stated that the property of having no more terms than does a proper subset of itself shows a set to be infinite, and that it shows that the number of natural numbers is infinite. There is no reason for thinking that Russell's words would have made Leibniz admit to being mistaken. This is because there is no true opinion and no false opinion about whether infinite sets exist as wholes, and about whether the conceptions of *equal to*, *less than* and *greater than* apply to them. What can be seen is that 'transforming' a supposedly self-contradictory property into a 'harmless definition' of the term 'infinite number' comes down to marking the difference between the use of 'infinite number' and that of substantive number expressions. Like Galileo, Cantor classifies 'infinite number' with substantive expressions like 'large number', but instead of marking the unlikeness between them as Galileo does, he marks it differently. Galileo's conclusion that infinities are not comparable (which is a hidden way of stating that 'infinite number' does not refer to a number) results in one kind of mystification. The Cantorian conclusion that a fraction of an infinite number can be equal to the whole number (which is also a hidden way of stating that 'infinite number' is not a substantive number expression) results in another kind of mystification. Nevertheless, the claim that the terms 'equal to', 'less than' and 'greater than' apply not only to the natural numbers, but also to infinite numbers, brings the term 'infinite number' into line with substantive number expressions — which makes it possible with practice to come to think of '$\aleph_0$' as having a use like that of '15'.

In the theory of infinite sets some sets are said to be equal to each other or to have the same cardinal number, namely those whose elements are (1–1)-correlatable, as are, for example, the terms of the sets of natural numbers, their squares, and the squares of their squares:

$$1, 2, 3, 4, \ldots$$
$$1^2, 2^2, 3^2, 4^2, \ldots$$
$$1^{2^2}, 2^{2^2}, 3^{2^2}, 4^{2^2}, \ldots$$

Some infinite sets are said not to be equal to each other and thus to have different cardinal numbers. Cantor showed that the real numbers (roughly, numbers which can be represented by unending decimals) are not (1–1)-correlatable with the natural numbers, the conclusion being that c, the number of the totality of the real numbers, is not equal to $\aleph_0$. Not to go into the actual demonstration, he showed that assuming the totality of real numbers to be in an array, it is possible to produce real numbers which are not in the array. Hence, there can be no (1–1)-matching of the real numbers with the natural numbers. Imitating the language of E. T. Bell, *after* the pairings of the reals with the natural numbers there will be unpaired terms left in the set of cardinal number c. The fact that the natural numbers cannot be matched (1–1) with the real numbers is taken to imply that there are *more* real numbers than there are natural numbers, and thus that c is a *greater* cardinal number than $\aleph_0$ just as 9 is greater than 7. The reason is that since c is not equal to $\aleph_0$ it must be greater: $c > \aleph_0$, in contrast to $\aleph_0^2 = \aleph_0$. The assimilation of transfinite cardinal arithmetic to the natural number arithmetic, which is characterised by the concepts *equal to*, *greater than* and *less than*, is impressive. The infinite and the super-infinite to all appearances are tamed to the harness of the 'finite' numbers.

The theory of the actual infinite creates the 'crude miracle' of a proper part of a set being no less than the whole set, and to this it adds the further miracle of an infinity that is greater than other infinities, an inexhaustible that is more inexhaustible than an infinitely inexhaustible. Bell writes: 'try to imagine the set of *all* positive rational integers $1, 2, 3, \ldots$, and ask yourself whether, with Cantor, you can hold this totality — which is a "class" — in your mind as a definite object of thought, as easily apprehended as the class x, y, z of three letters. Cantor requires us to do just this thing in order to reach the *transfinite* numbers which he created.'[40] It will be plain that just as we cannot hold the set of all positive rational integers in our mind as an object of thought (not only not as easily as we can hold a set of three elements, but because it is logically out of the question), so we cannot envisage the set of real numbers as a whole. Just as we have no idea of what it would be to apprehend *all* the terms of an unending set, so we have no idea of what it would be to entertain all the terms of a set that has more terms than an unending set. The transfinite numbers which Cantor 'created' are creations of a different kind from what it is natural to take them to be: '$\aleph_0$' and 'c' are *als ob* names of numbers.

There can be no doubt that '$\aleph_0$' and 'c' do have a use in mathematics, although their use, except in semantic appearance, is not to refer to numbers. What their actual use is, as against their apparent use, can now be seen: '$\aleph_0$' refers to rules or formulae for constructing series of terms, no term of which is the last constructible by the formula, and 'c' refers to rules for constructing from sets of terms new terms which are not in the original sets, however large those sets are made. There is no hint of a miracle or of paradox in the fact that for every term constructible by n^2 a uniquely related term is constructible by n^{2^2}, but exciting paradox makes its appearance when we state that there are just as many natural numbers of the form n^{2^2} as there are natural numbers of the form n^2, or that some only out of all the members of a certain collection are no fewer in number than all of the members. It is interesting, but not strange, to be shown, by the so-called diagonal method, that from any array of real numbers a new real number can be constructed which is not in the array, and thus that terms constructed by n^2 cannot be exactly matched with those constructed by the diagonal rule. But there is excitement and strangeness in being told that there is an infinity which is greater than the infinity of natural numbers. The excitement and the appearance of the miraculous are produced not by what is said but by the way it is said. Stating that the real numbers are not (1–1)-correlatable with the natural numbers stirs up no thoughts of the miraculous, but saying that the set of real numbers is more huge than the infinite set of natural numbers creates in some people awe and wonder, although what is being said is the same. One way of speaking opens the gate to paradise for some mathematicians, although to other mathematicians it looks like a disease-ridden land. The actual mathematics is the same for all. It is the surrounding philosophical talk, the mathematical theatre, which attracts some and repels others; but the philosophical talk has no effect on the actual mathematics in transfinite number theory.

Notes

1. Cited by P. E. B. Jourdain (1918), *The Philosophy of Mr B*RT*ND R*SS*-LL*, London: Allen & Unwin, p. 63.

2. Lecture notes 1939.

3. Ibid.

4. *Our Knowledge of the External World* (1914), Chicago, Ill.: Open Court, pp. 160–1.

5. Ibid., p. 170.

6. *The Blue Book*, pp. 45–6.

7. *Philosophical Investigations*, p. 48.

8. *Our Knowledge of the External World*, p. 199.

9. My emphasis.

10. Bertrand Russell, *Our Knowledge of the External World*, p. 173.

11. Ibid., p. 181.

12. *Introduction to Mathematical Philosophy* (1920), London: Allen & Unwin, pp. 78–9, 2nd edn.

13. Ibid., p. 79.

14. E. T. Bell (1937), *Men of Mathematics*, New York: Simon & Schuster, p. 567.

15. Leibniz, *Philosophische Schriften* (1875–90), Berlin, Gerhardt's edn, vol. I, p. 338.

16. See Tobins Dantzis, *Number, the Language of Science* (1930), New York: Macmillan, pp. 208–9.

17. *Our Knowledge of the External World*, p. 194.

18. 'Mathematics and the Mathematicians' (1917), in *Mysticism and Logic*, London: Allen & Unwin, p. 86, 2nd edn.

19. *Our Knowledge of the External World*, p. 182.

20. *Introduction to the Foundations of Mathematics* (1965), New York: Wiley, p. 87, 2nd edn.

21. Ibid., p. 81.

22. Hans Hahn (1956), 'Infinity', in James R. Newman, *The World of Mathematics*, New York: Simon & Schuster, vol. 3, p. 1602.

23. *Introductions to the Foundations of Mathematics*, p. 101.

24. See Russell, 'The Limits of Empiricism', *Proceedings of the Aristotelian Society*, vol. 36. This paper is a critique of Alice Ambrose's papers on finitism in mathematics. For her reply, see her *Essays in Analysis* (1966), London: Allen & Unwin, Ch. 4.

25. *Our Knowledge of the External World*, pp. 191–2.

26. Ibid., p. 156.

27. *Metaphysics*, in *The Works of Aristotle* (1928), trans. and ed. W. D. Ross, Oxford: The Clarendon Press, vol. VIII, Book Z, 2nd edn.

28. *Our Knowledge of the External World*, p. 173.

29. Ibid., p. 181.

30. Ibid., p. 173.

31. *Introduction to Mathematical Philosophy*, p. 97.

32. Bertrand Russell, 'The Limits of Empiricism', *Proceedings of the Aristotelian Society*, vol. 36, p. 143.

33. *Introduction to Mathematical Philosophy*, p. 77.

34. See *An Essay Concerning Human Understanding*, Book II, Ch. 17, sec. 13.

35. Ibid., sec. 8.

36. I may allow myself a conjecture as to one component of the hidden satisfaction. Maimonides said that to study nature is to study God, and this certainly is implied in Spinoza's philosophy. The idea that cannot fail to cross one's mind in connection with Cantor is that to study mathematics is also to study God. It should be remembered that Kronecker declared that God made the integers. It is hard to think that the idea of the consummated infinite is not in some way unconsciously linked with the idea of God as the consummation of infinite greatness.

37. Taken from Freud's well-known observation, 'Putnam's philosophy is like a beautiful table centre; everyone admires it but nobody touches it', in Ernest Jones (1959), *Free Associations. Memories of a Psychoanalyst*, New York: Basic Books, p. 189. Wittgenstein observed that the philosopher's labour 'is, as it were, an idleness in mathematics', in *Remarks on the Foundations of Mathematics*, p. 157.

38. *Men of Mathematics*, p. 566.

39. Ibid., p. 565.

40. Ibid., p. 567.

8 THE METAPHYSICAL CONCEPT OF SPACE

It is not a rare thing in metaphysics to meet a theory, and for that matter a whole constellation of theories, which makes the arresting claim that what we take to be a solid, assured reality is self-contradictory and does not exist. To give a small number of instances: Parmenides, and many philosophers after him up to our own day, held that it is logically impossible to think of what does not exist, a proposition which is in flagrant contradiction to what undeniably occurs with the greatest frequency; Locke and others have maintained that objects like flowers and rainbows cannot have colour, that not only is the lady's cheek under the rouge not red but the rouge itself has no colour; and separated by more than 2000 years, Zeno and F. H. Bradley took the position that space is self-contradictory and does not really exist. If we stop to think about it, we find that we do not understand how such views could possibly win the credence of anyone, and yet it is not to be doubted that they have been and are held. It would seem that they are surrounded by a special atmosphere which induces a kind of somnambulant state and so prevents their being looked at properly. Whether we reject such views as demonstrably false, accept them as established truths, or remain undecided about their truth-value, we are under a spell which blinds us to the semantic curiosities they in fact are, a spell of the intellect which blinds us to their perplexing features, or if we see them, makes us incurious about their explanation.

What will help us dispel the distorting conditions and enable us to reach a vantage point from which to look properly at them?

It has become a commonplace that small matters of detail, detail which seems too trivial to deserve our attention, often turn out to be windows through which important things may be seen. The reaction of some intellectuals to the more flamboyant metaphysical propositions is such a minor detail, which it seems to me should receive our special notice; certainly it deserves more than the first quick assessment and shrug it receives. These individuals are shocked and repelled, and they also appear to divine that the fabric of such views is the fabric from which the whole of metaphysics is woven. In consequence, they turn away from metaphysics as from something which is arid, a verbal wasteland from which they have nothing to learn but erudite deception. Turning away from metaphysics is not, of course, a procedure which holds within itself the promise of furthering our understanding of it. Nor can it lead us to discern more clearly what about it so often prompts the question, 'Is there nothing else more worth your labour?'[1] But sympathetic identification with such people and, instead of 'answering' them, trying to see metaphysical views through their eyes, might possibly lead to insight.

In this study I wish to consider the philosophical view that space is self-contradictory and does not really exist. As is well known, this view has been the subject of barren controversy for more than 20 centuries, and has won scornful dismissal from many intelligent people. It could hardly be considered a waste of time, therefore, if we followed the injunction to deploy our mental energies in the interests of furthering our understanding of a puzzling state of affairs.

There are several things to notice immediately about the view that space is self-contradictory and does not, therefore, really exist. For one thing, a contradiction is purportedly demonstrated in a common concept, the concept of space. For another, from this contradiction it is deduced that what everyone takes to be the phenomenon answering to the concept does not exist. Third, to protect his position against those who protest that their senses unmistakably attest to the existence of space, the metaphysician invokes the impressive, if mystifying, distinction between appearance and reality. He allows that it sensibly looks as if space exists but maintains that the contradiction elicited by his demonstration shows clearly and conclusively that space does not exist. The position can be given in three short statements:

(1) The concept *space* is self-contradictory.
(2) Space does not exist.
(3) There is the sensible appearance of space.

Statement (2) is entailed by statement (1). And those who reject or are inclined to reject (2) on the testimony of their senses are either stalemated or pacified by (3).

The famous exhortation of Parmenides comes to mind here: 'Let not the habit ingrained by manifold experience force you along this path, to make an instrument of the blind eye, the echoing ear, and the tongue, but test by reason my contribution to the great debate.'

The metaphysician supports his proposition that space does not exist with powerful *a priori* arguments, and he protects it with the distinction between appearance and reality. Briefly put, the nuclear argument, taken from Bradley's *Appearance and Reality*, is the following. An analysis of the concept *space* shows that 'space is endless, while an end is essential to its being. Space cannot come to a final limit, either within itself or on the outside. And yet, so long as it remains something always passing away, internally or beyond itself, it is not space at all'.[2] The concept of space is that of 'a thing, or substance, or quality (call it what you please), which is clearly as solid as its parts'.[3] But the parts which it unites consist of extended parts each of which is divisible into further parts, and this implies either of two alternatives, both self-contradictory. One, the final parts of space are points, entities 'which have no parts'.[4] That is, they are entities which lack extension and, therefore, are not spaces. And this entails the self-contradictory proposition that an extended thing or a magnitude is built out of entities which have no extension, that something which has height, width and depth is made up of parts which have no height, width or depth: 'if the parts are not spaces, the whole is not space'.[5] Two, every part of space has extension and is itself a space, in which case space is throughout composite, i.e. relational, and 'is nothing but a relation of spaces'.[6] And this entails the self-contradictory proposition that space consists of relations which cannot have solid terms to relate. In sum, 'Space is a relation — which it cannot be; and it is a quality or substance — which again it cannot be'.[7]

Still a further contradiction derives from the concept of space as a whole, a cosmic receptacle which is a totality of extended parts or spaces. Every space, it is maintained, must be in a greater space. In Bradley's words, 'Space to be space must have a space outside it'.[8] Thus, the notion of a whole of space is the inconsistent notion of a whole which is less than the whole; or better, the notion of space is the self-contradictory idea of something which is a whole and at the same time not the whole. In pictorial language, space is a cosmic box 'with no sides to it'.[9] To sum up the contradictions in the concept of space: 'We have seen that space vanishes internally into relations between units which never can exist. But, on the other side, when taken itself as a unit, it passes away into the search for an illusory whole.'[10]

It must, in all fairness, be admitted that the metaphysician of the unreality of space has gone about his intellectual task with what looks like scientific circumspection. However frivolous his view may seem, he does not neglect the evidence. He is, indeed, consciously faced with the problem of having to choose between two pieces of evidence, an *a priori* argument, in which no incontrovertible mistake has been found for an impressive length of time, and what his senses tell him. And his decision in favour of the evidence of reason as against the evidence of his eyes can hardly be characterised as irrational, particularly as he gives an explanation of how we come to believe that there is such a thing as space. His procedure must impress one as being irreproachable. It is, to all appearances, like that of a mathematician who by his exact calculations upsets what has hitherto been taken as fact. We may disagree with him, but it is hard to see how we could be on firmer ground than he is, if indeed we are on as firm ground. For we perceive nothing which he fails to perceive and, therefore, are not in a position to discount or correct his perceptions. Furthermore, he has a long-standing unrefuted argument for his position.

It would seem that resistance to his view can with plausibility be explained as being due to a person's placing greater reliance on his senses than on reason, which, of course, can be delusive. The metaphysician's decision can be explained as being due to his placing greater reliance on reason than on the senses, which also, of course, can be delusive. The undecided person can, with seeming plausibility, be described as a person who is uncertain about which to place his reliance on, the argument or the deliverance of his senses. But what is puzzling is how to explain in a satisfactory way the reaction of a person who turns away from the view as from a piece of trickery. What has he divined which the others have not divined? Asking him is of little help. For he is unable to put his insight into words, except to say that the argument and the view are verbal and not to be taken seriously.

Bertrand Russsell has said that,

to us, with our methods of experiment and observation, our knowledge of the long history of *a priori* errors refuted by empirical science, it has become natural to suspect a fallacy in any deduction which contradicts patent fact. It is easy to carry such suspicion too far, and it is very desirable, if possible, actually to discover the exact nature of the error when it exists. But there is no doubt that what we may call the empirical outlook has become part of most people's habit of mind; and it is this, rather than any definite argument, that has diminished the hold of the classical tradition upon students of philosophy and the instructed public generally.[11]

Is this the explanation of what it is about the view which puts off some people, namely, that it is an *a priori* conclusion which 'contradicts patent fact' and engenders suspicion in the minds of those who have acquired 'the empirical outlook'? This explanation has obvious appeal, and one hears it given frequently; but in fact it is altogether unsatisfactory. So to speak, it is a *misplaced* explanation made possible by a pun on the word '*a priori*'.

Russell's explanation can without difficulty be seen as an account, not of why metaphysics has come to be viewed with suspicion, but why a *different* intellectual practice has fallen into disrepute. Russell thinks he has given an explanation of one thing while giving a familiar explanation of something else. What he refers to by '*a priori* errors refuted by empirical science' are popularly accepted false *empirical* propositions such as that the earth is flat, that heavy bodies fall with a greater velocity than lighter bodies, and that perpetual motion machines are physically possible, namely propositions which it may be natural to believe and which could only be established or refuted by observation or experiment. To say that such propositions are *a priori* is to say that they are believed without the support of evidence. They are *a priori* in the sense of being empirical speculations which are taken for fact either without evidence or on the flimsiest evidence. But a philosopher who professes to have demonstrated a contradiction in a concept makes an *a priori* statement in a wholly different sense of '*a priori*'. He is not making an unsupported *empirical* claim; he is, instead, maintaining a kind of proposition which cannot, by its very nature, be supported or disconfirmed by empirical evidence. He is stating a non-empirical proposition, with regard to which empirical procedures, experiments and the closest examination of objects, can show nothing whatever about its truth-value. This, perhaps, needs further comment, but it must be evident that neither making an examination of the nature of things nor taking an inventory of what exists nor carrying out scientifically controlled experiments could demonstrate that a concept contains a contradiction. These procedures cannot, therefore, show that a concept is *not* self-contradictory. And it requires no special instruction to see that the metaphysical proposition that the concept *space* is self-contradictory is not empirical and not open to investigation by empirical procedures. The deduced proposition that space does not exist is, therefore, not a proposition with regard to which observation or experiment could possibly be of use and is not an empirical speculation. Apart from its deductive connection with the claim that the concept space is self-contradictory, it is clear that the *metaphysical* proposition that space does not exist, unlike the proposition that heavy objects fall with a greater velocity than lighter ones, is such that no experiment could be described which, if it could be made, would in the least tend to show that space does or does not exist. No observation could conceivably be imagined which, if made, would reveal to the metaphysician what so far has eluded his observation. This makes plain the fact that in the case of the metaphysical proposition looking is not to the point: we know *in advance* that we could point to nothing with regard to spatial phenomena which the metaphysician is not already aware of.

It is not that the instructed person who turns away from the metaphysical utterance as an idle curiosity thinks it an unwarranted empirical speculation which, in violation of the demands laid down by experimental science, is taken for fact. Rather, it would seem that he has a perception of its nature which makes him resist being made dupe to a special kind of verbal trumpery. This certainly is the impression he creates. And one thing which may make us receptive to this impression is noticing an odd kind of consequence which obtains if the utterance is taken in a straightforward way as denying the existence of something. Careful scrutiny of the metaphysical claims with regard to space will bring this consequence to light.

The metaphysical assertion that space does not exist does not lend itself to examination in isolation from the other two assertions with which it is made, namely, (1) that the concept *space* is self-contradictory, and (3) that space sensibly appears to exist. And it turns out that if the three assertions are taken at face value as stating claims of the sort they seem to be stating, the triad involves a contradiction from which an odd and inadmissible consequence about what the metaphysician must believe follows. The contradiction itself is remarkable enough to merit special examination on its own account; for it is as flagrant and glaring as any contradiction could be. Yet it has the mystifying property of making itself so effectively invisible as to have gone unnoticed for centuries. That it has gone undetected so long is made all the more remarkable by the fact that metaphysicians are among the ablest of reasoners and, moreover, are especially practised in ferreting out contradictions. Obviously the attribute of inconspicuousness behind which a glaring contradiction can hide should cause us to wonder, and in the present case should at least provoke curiosity since there is the possibility, however slight it may seem, that the contradiction in the metaphysical position is not of the everyday, run-of-the-mill variety.

More important, perhaps, for immediate consideration is the odd and unacceptable consequence which the contradiction forces on us about the beliefs of anyone who adopts the position. This is that he believes that people constantly imagine themselves to be having certain perceptions and constantly behave as if they are having them while in fact they have no such perceptions, and also that he believes himself to have no such perceptions while he has them. What could be more strange than beliefs such as these? And yet they have to be attributed to the metaphysician, if the words with which he states his theory about space are taken literally. We should not believe our ears if we heard our friend say that he actually had the belief that we never perceived the colour green, not in winter nor in summer nor even in our imagination, despite our assurances to the contrary, and also went on to confess that although he knew perfectly well that he had perceptions of green he nevertheless believed himself to have no such perceptions. And perhaps we should not believe our eyes when we read words which imply the existence of comparably fantastic beliefs in the mind of the metaphysician. To put the metaphysician in a somewhat less unfavourable light, it is to be realised that we are in fact presented with two alternatives, and not just one: either the metaphysician actually holds the beliefs his words imply or his words bear a different interpretation from the one it is natural to place on them. It has, of course, to be shown that the odd proposition about his beliefs obtains in consequence of the normal interpretation of his words, but before this can be done, the contradiction in the position they apparently express has to be brought to light.

It will help to restate briefly the set of metaphysical claims about space. An argument is presented in ostensible demonstration of the proposition (1) that the concept *space* is self-contradictory. From (1) the metaphysician proceeds deductively to (2), the proposition that space does not exist; and (2) he protects against the evidence of our senses with the admission (3), that space appears sensibly to exist. The first of this set of assertions (1), cannot be empirical and, as its putative truth is guaranteed by an analytical argument, must be construed as making an *a priori* claim. And since (2) is deduced from (1) as an immediate consequence, we must suppose that (2), despite its air of having the logical character of the empirical assertion that the river Styx does not exist, is also *a priori*. It is patent that an empirical proposition, one which can in principle have a truth-value other than the truth-value it actually has, cannot logically be a deductive consequence of an *a priori* true proposition. For since the apodosis of an entailment cannot be false and its protasis true, if the protasis is *a priori* true, such that under no conceivable condition could it be false, there will be no conceivable circumstance given which the apodosis would be false. That is to say, if a given proposition p entails a further proposition q, which rules out as a logical impossibility the propositional combination $p \cdot \sim q$,

$$\sim\!\Diamond(p \cdot \sim q),$$

then q could be empirical and have falsehood as one of its possible truth-values only if p is theoretically open to falsification, i.e. is empirical. But if p is true *a priori*, which means that it is not open, in principle, to falsification, then q will have to be *a priori*. In short, either q is not a logical consequence of an *a priori* true proposition or it is itself *a priori* true. Despite appearances sometimes being to the contrary, as in the case of a rationalist like Spinoza, no one could imagine himself to be deducing the truth of a proposition which could logically be false from one which could only be true, any more than he could imagine himself to be standing on his own shoulders. And with regard to statements (1) and (2), if (1) is *a priori* true and (2) is a consequence of (1), (2) must also be *a priori*. Anyone who in fact, and not just in appearance, thinks that a contradiction has been established in the concept *space* and that (1) is true *a priori* and, furthermore, thinks that (2) is a logically necessary consequence of (1), must think that (2) has its truth-value by logical necessity. We cannot, thus, without attributing the grossest of errors to him, suppose him to think that (2) is about a phenomenon whose existence equally with its non-existence is theoretically conceivable.

This is one conclusion we are led to about the nature of (2) and about how the metaphysician must view the proposition — on the premise, of course, that (1) is taken to be logically necessary and (2) its consequent. We are, however, also led to precisely the opposite conclusion. For considered from the other end of the triad of propositions which together compose the position about space, (2) must be taken to be empirical, not *a priori*; and the metaphysician must be supposed to think that (2) is not *a priori*. It is clear that (3) — namely, the proposition that space sensibly appears to exist,

whether the appearance it declares to exist is delusive or not —
implies that (2) is empirical, about a phenomenon whose existence is
equally conceivable with its non-existence. That is to say, if (3)
declares in fact what it seems to declare, the existence of the
appearance of space, then (2) must declare the non-existence of the
corresponding reality, which even though it does not exist could
possibly exist. In general, a proposition of the form '. . . appears to
exist' is compatible with the associated proposition '. . . does not
exist', and implies the possible truth of '. . . exists'. And if (3) is a
proposition which states the existence of an appearance, whether
actual or only possible, it implies that the appearance might
conceivably not be delusive, or that the corresponding reality could
conceivably exist. It, therefore, implies that (2) has either of two
possible truth-values with each of which it is compatible. Considered
with respect to (1), the proposition that space does not exist is
logically necessary and its denial, *viz.* that space exists, is logically
impossible. Considered with respect to (3), the proposition that
space does not exist is not logically necessary and its denial is in
principle a possible truth. Hence, just as the metaphysician must be
supposed to be believing that (2) is *a priori* and its falsifiability a
conceptual impossibility, so he must be supposed to be believing
that (2) is empirical and its falsifiability a conceptual possibility. By
protecting (2) non-analytically with (3), the function of which is
primarily to pacify those who rely on their senses, he acknowledges
his belief that (2) is empirical.

   The contradictory consequences with respect to (2) can be seen to
derive from the fact that (1) and (3), taken at face value as making
the claims they seem to be making, are inconsistent with each other.
There cannot, in principle, exist a sensible appearance of what is
logically impossible any more than there can exist a logically impossible state of affairs. Thus, for example, just as there cannot be a
state of affairs in which one church spire is in two different places at
once, so there cannot be the optical illusion of the same spire being
simultaneously in two separate places, although there can, of
course, be the illusion of there being two exactly similar spires when
in fact there is only one. What can be represented or pictured by a
perceptual appearance or an image or a painting could exist, at least
in principle, and what is prevented from existing by logic is
prevented by logic from appearing to exist. For to be presented with
the appearance of there being a certain state of affairs is to know
what it would be like for there to be that state of affairs, and this

implies the conceivable or theoretical existence of the state of affairs. And since a logically impossible state of affairs is not open to conception we cannot know what it would be like for it to obtain, which implies that there cannot, conceivably, be an appearance of its existence.

The matter might be put in still a different way. Quite in general and without the possibility of there being an exception, an appearance which is delusive is one which in principle might not be delusive. Being delusive is a contingent property of any sensible appearance ϕ, and whether the reality corresponding to ϕ exists or does not exist is, consequently, an empirical matter. The non-existence of the corresponding reality makes ϕ delusive and the existence of ϕ implies the possible existence of the reality. Hence if (3) states the existence of a sensible appearance, (2) makes an empirical claim about a phenomenon the existence of which is conceivable. It might, in this connection, be contended that it is possible to imagine or picture a state of affairs without being able to imagine or picture it *as existing* and similarly, that there could be an appearance of something whose existence is inconceivable. You can, it may be maintained, conceive one thing being in two places at once, but you cannot think of there *existing* a thing which is simul-taneously in two places. But to imagine or picture anything is to imagine or picture it as it would be if it existed, i.e. as existing; and to be the appearance of anything is to be the appearance of it as existing. To put this in Kantian terms, to attribute existence to anything is not to add in any way to our conception of its nature; and to attribute non-delusiveness to an appearance is not to say anything about the conception of the reality.

All this must be as plain as it is elementary, and it therefore comes as something of a disconcerting surprise to hear it disputed. Usually, if not always, those who contest the claim that what cannot logically be the case, cannot logically be represented in appearance, contest it only as holding for logical impossibilities in metaphysics. They grant that an ordinary logical impossibility, such as the impossibility of a billiard ball being in two places at once or the impossibility of there being a collection of only three pennies four of which are copper, cannot be pictured or be presented in an appearance. But they deny that demonstrating the logical impossibility of anything in metaphysics at the same time demonstrates the logical impossibility of there being an appearance of the thing. This would seem as unintelligible as it would be to say that 2 plus 2 equals 4 ordinarily but not in metaphysics. If 2 plus 2 did not equal 4 in metaphysics it would not be the 2 plus 2 of arithmetic. And if in metaphysics being a self-contradictory or logically impossible state of affairs precludes it but not its perceptual appearance from conceivable existence it would not be the kind of self-contradiction or logical impossibility we are familiar with in non-metaphysical *a priori* reasoning. If the logical impossibility of space existing does not preclude the possibility of space appearing to our senses to exist and the logical impossibility of a thing existing which is uniformly blue and also orange all over does preclude the possible existence of the visual appearance of a thing being blue at the same time that it is orange in every part, the first logical impossibility must be different in some important respect from the second. But what the difference is remains obscure. It may in the end turn out that the logical impossibility of metaphysics is not what we take it to be, and this is something which will have to be investigated.

If we say that a contradiction is a contradiction regardless of the concept in which it is established and that a logical impossibility is a logical impossibility regardless of the proposition to which it applies, we cannot avoid concluding that the metaphysician states a triad of propositions two of which are inconsistent with each other, (1) and (3), and one of which, (3), is self-contradictory. It is puzzling then to know how to account for the contradictions remaining invisible so long. But more troubling than this is the odd consequence about the beliefs a metaphysician must have who adopts the triad of propositions. He must have the extraordinary belief that people generally imagine themselves to be having perceptions, whether or not verid-ical, which they cannot be having, and he must have the further extraordinary belief that he himself does not have perceptions which he in fact has. For in thinking, whether rightly or wrongly, that the concept *space* is self-contradictory and that the existence of space is logically impossible he must believe that there can be no spatial appearances and, therefore, no perceptions of a sort everyone takes for granted he constantly has. While protecting (2) with (3) he plainly shows that he is aware of the existence of spatial appearances and has space perceptions which, in maintaining (1) and (2), he must deny. He is, it has to be concluded, under the intellectual delusion that he is not having perceptions which he knows he has, and he believes that mankind has suffered from the delusion that it has perceptions of a certain kind which it does not have.

But how could anyone have such grotesque opinions as these?

Certainly, the human mind is capable of the most bizarre fantasies, and these it turns out have their sources in unconscious needs. But plainly it would be unrealistic to imagine that the fantasies attributed to him by the standard interpretation of his position are the expression of an unconscious wish in the mind of the metaphysician. Moreover, apart from the evidence afforded by the standard, and admittedly natural, construction to which his position lends itself, there is no evidence whatever for thinking that he has these fantastic ideas. The metaphysician would be astonished to be told that he has them, and his behaviour and usual talk, and even the talk in which he embeds his philosophical utterances, constitute convincing evidence against supposing that he has them, quite apart from the fact that he would reject them if questioned. They are beliefs which never betray themselves and are only inferentially arrived at from his position alone.

It is tempting at this point to think that the metaphysician has embraced his position without seeing that it is self-contradictory and without realising what the consequences of holding it are. It is not a rare or uncommon thing for people to accept propositions which are later discovered to be self-contradictory or to accept propositions which have unexpected consequences; and it is hard not to succumb to the temptation to assimilate the metaphysical case to the ordinary kind of case. But to do this is wholly unsatisfactory. It is nothing more than a refusal to face disconcerting facts and it hides behind two screens: one a superficial resemblance between the metaphysician's failure to discern contradictions and the more ordinary failure in mathematics or elsewhere, and the other a confusion. The confusion is that between not seeing the consequences of holding the metaphysical view and the consequences not following from holding the view, which are of course entirely different. Not perceiving that a consequence follows shows nothing with regard to the validity of the consequence, and we can and, indeed, do know propositions without knowing what they imply, as in mathematics, to give an obvious example. The fact that the metaphysician is unaware of the proposition about his beliefs which is implied by his holding the view about space does not mean that the truth of the proposition is not consequent on his holding the view; and if its truth is consequent on his holding the view, then it states a fact about the beliefs of the metaphysician who adopts the view, regardless of whether he is intellectually aware of the connection between his beliefs and holding his theory. If holding the view implies, as it clearly does, the proposition that he is convinced that he does not have perceptions which he in fact has and also that everyone believes himself to have perceptions which are impossible to have, then regardless of whether he realises that the proposition is implied, his holding the view makes the proposition true, and he has these absurd convictions. It is only to confuse things (perhaps not without motivation) to argue that since the metaphysician fails to see intellectually the consequence of holding his view, the consequence does not truly state a fact about him or that since he fails to see the consequence he does not have the absurd convictions.

We have been brought back to the place where a decision is forced on us. We are presented with the alternatives of holding fast to the first and obvious interpretation of the metaphysician's utterances and accepting its odd consequence, or of rejecting the consequence and with it relinquishing the interpretation. And the tendency now will be to *minimise the importance* of the consequence, to allow that it holds for the metaphysician but to urge that the beliefs it attributes to him, though odd, are deserving of passing notice only. But they most certainly are deserving of more than a cursory glance. For if we face with sufficient curiosity the idea of his having them we are compelled, in all sobriety, to agree that the idea is incredible. Only mental pathology could account for anyone's actually believing that the world's population has through the centuries laboured under the delusive conviction that it has sense perceptions which it could not even in theory have; and only a mental split, a Janus mind, could account for anyone's actually believing that he is not having perceptions which he does constantly have. This *could* be someone's mental state, but the likelihood of this being the metaphysician's state of mind is less than impressive. On the contrary, the probability of its not being his state of mind and of his having no such dumbfounding beliefs is too great to be discounted. It is certainly impressive enough to make us explore carefully the possibility that the first interpretation of his utterances is mistaken. But before we can proceed to this, there is the further point to be considered, namely, the claim that the metaphysical triad of statements is the self-contradictory set of propositions it seems to be and that those who embrace it simply fail to see the contradictions.

It is natural to assimilate these contradictions to those established in propositions by *reductio ad absurdum* proofs in mathematics and logic. They look like the familiar kind which have the form $p \cdot \sim p$ or imply propositions of this form; and it would seem foolish to deny

that they are contradictions. It would seem silly to say that the assertion, 'It is logically impossible for space to exist', is not really inconsistent with the assertion, 'Space sensibly appears to exist', and
maintain that the assertion, 'It is logically impossible for a thing to be
in two places at one time', is inconsistent with the assertion, 'The
same thing sensibly appears to be in two places at once'. If, however,
we assimilate metaphysical contradictions to the class of logical
contradictions, which means that we take metaphysical 'contradictions' to be contradictions, we are faced with a perplexing
occurrence for which there is no satisfactory explanation. We might
put the difference between ordinary contradictions and those found
in metaphysics in the following way. An ordinary contradiction
which eludes detection for a considerable period of time is subtle
and can be seen only after going through a more or less complicated
chain of reasoning. So to speak, it is invisible because it is not
glaring. The metaphysical contradictions, by contrast, are gross and
glaring, and what has to be explained is how they have managed to
make themselves so inconspicuous as to avoid detection by the most
subtle reasoners for a vast period of time. Metaphysics is full of such
'inconspicuous' contradictions, contradictions which, furthermore,
have the curious property of not deterring a philosopher from
holding his view when he is made aware of the fact that his view
entails one of them; and it might be instructive to make a brief
excursion and glance at several instances.

Plato and Hume are examples of philosophers who were aware of
contradictions in their positions and were not troubled by their
knowledge, certainly not troubled enough to give up their views.
Hume was aware of the fact that the considerations which led him to
reject traditional views about the self, 'continu'd and independent'
objects, and causation entailed the contradiction that he looked for
what he could not, theoretically, have been looking for.[12] And
strangely enough, after going through the motions of showing that
we have no idea (e.g. of continued and independent things) he
proceeded to explain how we come to form such an idea. And to
compound an intellectual felony, on his own accounting he could not
have failed to realise that his search for the 'originals' of the ideas
was no more than the caricature of a search for something. We might
well be filled with wonder by an unusually gifted reasoner who is not
at all disturbed by a contradiction he sees in his described procedure[13] and who fails altogether to see the contradiction in proffering
an explanation of how we come to form an idea which we do not

have. Plato, as is well known, did not give up his Ideal Theory about the nature of universals, a theory which he used as the basis of some of his most important views, despite being aware of the argument of the third man.[14]

Parmenides, as well as his intellectual descendants up to the present, offers a particularly instructive example of an acute thinker with a practised eye for recognising contradictions overlooking an 'inconspicuous' contradiction in his own position. This is a type of contradiction which in the history of philosophy has repeatedly occurred and gone unnoticed. Once seen, we realise it is in fact a glaring contradiction which has the mysterious quality of making itself inconspicuous. Parmenides, like Bradley in *Appearance and Reality*, erected his system on the rationalistic premise that the self-contradictory, or the inconceivable, is equivalent to the non-existent, and the conceivable to the existent. As is well known, he claimed to have demonstrated the non-existence of multiplicity by an argument which professed to establish a contradiction in the notion of multiplicity. Like the metaphysician who argues against space while allowing its apparent existence, Parmenides relegated the multiplicy of things encountered in sense experience to the limbo of delusive appearance. But unaccountably he failed to notice that there appearing to be a multiplicity of things — apples, stars, houses, and the like — entails the conceivability of there being a number of things. Obviously, if a state of affairs visually seems to someone to exist, he must have the idea of there being such a state of affairs. Hence, by Parmenides' own basic premise multiplicity must exist in fact. That is, Parmenides' position implied the non-existence of multiplicity, because of the claimed self-contradictoriness of the concept of multiplicity; and it also implied that multiplicity must exist, because the appearance of there being a multiplicity of things implied the idea of multiplicity.

An interesting sidelight is provided by Zeno's defence of Parmenides' view about the nature of Being, namely, that it is a single, continuous, spherical body which fills all of space.[15] Ostensibly against the pluralists of his day and to protect his master's position, Zeno gave an argument which professed to show that space does not exist. What he and subsequent commentators and historians failed to see was that this argument undermined the view it was designed to protect. Could anything be more plain than that if space does not exist, a spherical body does not exist? To argue that reality must be a single sphere because space does not exist is like arguing that a cherry must be red because it is not coloured, and the mistake is equally obvious in each. Parmenidean Being, which according to the theory was a plenum filling all of space, could not exist without space for it to fill. This is so evident that it becomes a real problem to explain its oversight, not only by one acute reasoner but by a long succession of reasoners. Rip van Winkle can beguile us in our fantasy life, but anyone who in actual life claimed to be a Rip van Winkle would not win our credence. Rip slept longer than is humanly possible; and, if the contradictions we have noted are indeed the contradictions they appear on the surface to be, then our intelligence has slept longer than an intelligence educated to perceive contradictions can be expected to sleep. Either we have to accept an abnormal intellectual somnolence or else we have to suppose that the 'contradictions' are not the contradictions they seem to be.

It must be clear that there is no satisfactory way of explaining the odd features attaching to the metaphysical view about space, if the view is taken for what at first glance it seems to us to be. The bizarre consequence of holding the three propositions, namely, that the metaphysician would be thinking that people believe themselves to have perceptions which they could not have and also that he has the belief that he does not have certain perceptions which he in fact does have, is an unavoidable consequence which cannot be dismissed as unimportant nor be given a reasonable explanation. And of course we are perplexed by the curious inconspicuousness of the contradictions in the view. If we suppose the metaphysician to be actually holding what his words appear to make him hold, then there is no escaping the fact that we are presented with the intrinsically inexplicable. But if we are sceptical about the proposition which attributes the queer beliefs to the metaphysician and if, furthermore, we wish genuinely to discover what it is about the contradictions which has made them invisible, we can discern a new possibility. The possibility emerges that the view is not what it seems to be and the contradictions are not the straightforward contradictions they seem to be. And if we succeed in identifying ourselves with the disappointed intellectual who turns away from metaphysics as from something which is 'just verbal', something which is a kind of linguistic trumpery, our investigation of the possibility that the three statements are not about what they seem to be about will be made with special attention to how language is being employed. The idea which forces itself on our attention is that language is being used delusively to create the semblance of a theory being expressed and held, and this is the idea which I propose to investigate, with the primary object of explaining the perplexing features attaching to the metaphysical position.

Consider again the three statements:

(1) The concept *space* is self-contradictory.
(2) Space does not exist.
(3) Space sensibly appears to exist.

Statement (1) is a claim which, whether it is true or not, implies that the concept *space*, like the concept *greatest prime number*, is not open to exemplification. If (1) is true it is not the case that nothing in fact answers to the concept, but rather that nothing could theoretically answer to it. The difference between, say, the idea of a strawberry ripening in sub-zero temperature and the idea of a spire which is taller than itself is that the first is in principle open to exemplification, has a hypothetical realisation, while the second is not. The words 'strawberry which is ripening at 30° below zero' describes something which, if it occurred, would be counted a miracle, whereas the words 'church spire which is taller than itself' describes nothing at all. To put the matter yet another way, it is proper to say, 'The probability of a strawberry ripening at 30° below zero is negligible', but there is a linguistic inappropriateness in saying, 'The probability of there being a church spire which is taller than itself is negligible'. For the improbable could be imagined as happening; we know what it is like for the improbable to occur, but we do not know what it is like for a self-contradictory state of affairs to obtain. As Wittgenstein has said, 'we could not *say* of an "unlogical" world how it would look'.[16]

The fact that a self-contradictory concept cannot logically have an exemplification implies that any term which expresses it will fail to have application, not because, as in the case of the term 'winged horse', there is in fact nothing to which the term applies, but because it has been given no application, no descriptive use. Nothing in theory could answer to a self-contradictory concept, ϕ, for if something did answer to it there would exist a self-contradictory state of affairs, which is absurd. Hence, since ϕ can have no imaginable instance, i.e. no instance which could without self-contradiction be described, any term *t* which expresses ϕ will have to lack application. The fact of being self-contradictory, which prevents φ from having instances, prevents *t* from having either an ostensive definition or descriptive use. To put it somewhat differently, it is obviously impossible for a concept to be incapable in principle of having exemplifications while a word which denotes it applies, whether in fact or in fiction, to instances; for that would imply that the word has application to either actual or conceivable instances of a concept which has no conceivable instances. Thus, for example, the expression 'spire taller than itself' has no imaginable application and thus no descriptive use, because the concept *spire which is taller than itself* is self-contradictory and in principle not open to exemplification.

It will be clear that a metaphysician who makes the claim (1) that the concept *space* is self-contradictory, and literally means what he says, implies that any term which denotes the concept *space* has been given no use. If his claim is true, then it will be a fact with regard to the English language that the word 'space' and space-denoting expressions lack use: they will be in a class with terms like 'bachelor husband' and 'greatest prime number'. And even if the claim is not true it is plain that anyone who *thinks* it is true and expresses his claim in English must believe that the word 'space' and space-denoting expressions have no use in sentences to describe states of affairs. For in general, correlated with a true proposition expressed by the form of words, 'Concept φ is self-contradictory', there will be a true proposition expressed by the form of words, 'The term "φ" has no descriptive use'. This is not to say that an *a priori* proposition implies an empirical proposition about the use of an expression. but it is clear that anyone who declares that φ is self-contradictory implies that the word he uses for φ has no application in fact or in theory. For the empirical proposition that the *sentence*, 'The concept φ is self-contradictory', expresses a true *a priori* proposition entails the empirical proposition that the term 'φ' does not function descriptively in the language in which it occurs. To illustrate, the true empirical proposition that the English sentence, 'The concept *three-legged biped* is self-contradictory', makes a true *a priori* claim entails the true verbal proposition that the term 'three-legged biped' does not function descriptively in the English language. To every fact about a sentence which states truly that a mentioned concept is internally inconsistent there corresponds the fact that the word used in the sentence to mention the concept is devoid of descriptive sense.

To come back now to (1), it will be clear that a metaphysician who states in English the claim made by (1) implies that the word 'space' is a contradictory term and is not used in sentences which convey information about states of affairs. That is to say, if his sentence, 'The concept *space* is self-contradictory', expresses a true *a priori* proposition, then it will be a fact about actual usage that 'space' is a word which is not used in descriptive expressions although its grammar seems to imply that it belongs to the class of terms which function descriptively. To be sure, the sentence, 'The concept *space* is self-contradictory', does not *say* that the word 'space' lacks descriptive use; it could not say this and also make an *a priori* claim. We might say that the two sentences, 'The concept *space* is self-contradictory' and 'The term "space" is a word which usage informs us has no descriptive sense', have the same import (to stretch the word 'import') but do not *say* the same, or do not express the same proposition. They are prevented from saying the same thing by the different idioms in which they occur, in the one case the ontological idiom and in the other the verbal idiom, just as the two sentences, 'A chanticleer is a male chicken' and '"Chanticleer" means male chicken', are prevented from saying the same thing by their difference in idiom. In answer to the question, 'What is a chanticleer?', we say *either* 'A chanticleer is a male chicken' *or* '"Chanticleer" means male chicken'; and these are also answers to the question, 'What does "chanticleer" mean?' This makes clear the fact that we convey the same information with either sentence to anyone who asks the question, although the two sentences do not say the same. We might say the two sentences have the same *import*, and, of course, to say this is to stretch a word in order to bring out a point of likeness between the two types of sentence.

It can now be seen why if the sentence (1a), 'The concept *space* is self-contradictory', expressed an *a priori* true proposition, the sentence (2a), 'Space does not exist', would express an *a priori* proposition, and why (2a) could not be construed as making any sort of claim about the non-existence of anything. If the proposition (1) expressed by (1a) implied the proposition expressed by (2a), the second proposition, like the first, would have to be *a priori*. And we should have to construe (2a) as coming to the same thing as does the sentence (2b), 'It is logically impossible for space to exist'. It may be urged that (2a) does not mean the same as (2b), that the proposition expressed by the second is implied by, but is not identical with, the proposition expressed by the first. And it may be urged, further, that (2a) does make a factual claim about space, comparable to the claim made by 'Angels do not exist'. It may be maintained at this point that the metaphysical position should have been stated in four sentences, not three, namely, (1a), (2b), (2a), and the sentence (3a), i.e. 'Space sensibly appears to exist', where the claim expressed by (1a) entails the claim expressed by (2b), which in turn entails the claim expressed by (2a). Thus, if it is true to say 'The concept *space* is self-contradictory', then it will be true to say 'It is logically impossible for space to exist' and, hence, true to say 'Space does not exist'. It is frequently held that what is logically impossible does in fact not exist, that a proposition which declares a state of affairs, ψ, to be logically impossible entails a proposition which declares the factual non-existence of ψ, although the entailment does not go the other way. If this is correct it will have to be supposed that (2a) makes a weaker claim than does (2b), where to say that the first claim is weaker than the second is to say that the first is not to the effect that the existence of space is logically impossible but only to the effect that space does not exist. This makes it look as if the first claim is a factual proposition to which sense experience is relevant; and in deducing it from the second it looks as if an empirical proposition is being deduced from one which is *a priori*. Distinguishing between (2a) and (2b) in terms of the different propositions they supposedly express would seem to imply the view that a proposition which gives information about the physical universe is deducible from a proposition which, since it is *a priori* and cannot have its truth value determined by what the world is like, is not about the physical world. But this view, as has already been seen, is a mistake, and furthermore is the kind of 'inconspicuous' mistake which requires an explanation.

We have now at hand a further and more enlightening way of seeing why if (2) follows from (1), or why if the proposition expressed by (2a) is entailed by the proposition expressed by (2b), (2) cannot be about the world and the sentence (2a) can in the English language state nothing about the existence of anything. For if in saying 'The concept *space* is self-contradictory' it is implied that the word 'space' is not applicable to anything, then the sentence, 'It is logically impossible for space to exist', cannot be using the word 'space' to mention or describe something the existence of which the sentence declares to be impossible. And the proposition expressed by the sentence (2a), 'Space does not exist', taken as a deductive consequence of the proposition expressed by (2b), cannot be to the effect that something does not exist. Nor can the sentence (2a) assert the existence or non-existence of anything. For if the proposition that space does not exist denied the existence of something, in the way in which the proposition that angels to not exist does, the word 'space' in (2a), would have to function descriptively, that is, be used to mention something whose actual existence the sentence denies. Thus the word 'space', if used in this way, would have a theoretical application, and this would imply that the proposition expressed by (2a) could not be a consequence, mediate or immediate, of the proposition expressed by (1a).

Perhaps the following consideration will bring out the point more clearly. The assertion that 'The concept *space* is self-contradictory', makes a true *a priori* claim implies that the term 'space' has been assigned no application. Hence the sentence 'It is logically impossible for space to exist' does not use 'space' to mention anything which, if it existed, would be an instance of the concept *space*. Consequently, the sentence 'Space does not exist' does not use 'space' to refer to anything the existence of which it denies, despite its verbally appearing to do so. To generalise, no sentence expressing a proposition which is deduced from an *a priori* truth expressed by a sentence of the form 'Concept φ is self-contradictory' uses the word which denotes φ descriptively. The *import* of the first sentence in the above sequence is verbal, and the import of the other two sentences cannot thus be other than verbal. This, of course, is not to imply that the sentences express verbal propositions. But it can be seen that no proposition about the existence or nature of a state of affairs is deducible from a proposition which is expressed by a non-verbal sentence the *import* of which is verbal, i.e. about the use of an expression.

The reason why there cannot be a sensible appearance of what is self-contradictory, or why there cannot be self-contradictory sensible appearances, emerges now with greater clarity. It is relevant to observe that a point when made in the ontological form of speech, that is, in the form of words in which we describe the nature of and state the existence of things, can be argued interminably, while the same point made in words which are explicitly about usage is less likely to become the subject of enduring disagreement. The durability of philosophical disagreements, which has troubled so many people, is in some measure due to the fact that verbal points are hidden by non-verbal modes of expression and that contested claims embodying verbal points are expressed in such a way as to have the air of being statements of material fact. Thus, for example, compare 'It is impossible for a soap bubble to support an elephant' with 'It is impossible for a soap bubble to be on top of itself'. The second sentence looks as if it is making a claim about soap bubbles comparable to the claim made by the first. But whereas the first does assert something about soap bubbles, the second says nothing with regard to them, although it has the semantic air of doing so. And this is an air which it is not always easy to dispel.

Before considering (1) in relation to (3), let us look at a non-controversial instance of a proposition that a given concept is self-contradictory in relation to the corresponding statement that there is the sensible appearance of there being something that falls under the concept. Specifically, let us consider the proposition expressed by the sentence 'The concept *four-legged biped* is self-contradictory', in relation to the proposition expressed by the corresponding appearance sentence, 'There visually appears to be a four-legged biped'. It is tempting to say that the first proposition is true and the second false. It is tempting to think this with regard to every such pair of propositions, and furthermore to suppose that this marks the difference between a non-metaphysical pair and a metaphysical pair. But if there is such a difference between the metaphysical and non-metaphysical case, it is a difference we cannot hope to understand. The existence of such a difference cannot, of course, be granted. The sentence, 'There appears to be a four-legged biped', does not say what is false, i.e. does not falsely declare the existence of an appearance, as does the sentence, 'There appear to be two moons in the night sky in October'. Rather, unlike the second sentence, the first sentence expresses a self-contradictory proposition, not one which is as a matter of fact false. For the fact that 'The concept *four-legged biped* is self-contradictory' states a true proposition implies that the term 'four-legged biped' is not used in sentences to describe anything. Clearly, then, since 'four-legged biped' is a term barren of descriptive sense, the corresponding appearance expression, 'appearance of there being a four-legged biped', has no application to any appearance, actual or theoretical. Such phrases as 'appearance of a billiard ball colliding with itself', 'appearance of a spire which is in two places at once', etc. apply to no theoretical appearances because the self-contradictory terms they involve have been given no application.

In general, the expression 'appearance of there being a ϕ' functions descriptively only in those cases in which the value of 'ϕ' is a term which has a range of application. Expressed in the ontological mode of speech, the point is that a concept which cannot logically have instances cannot logically have apparent instances; there can no more be the sensible appearance of there being an instance of a self-contradictory concept than there can be the instance itself. Put verbally, a word, '*w*', which denotes a concept that is not open to exemplification cannot function to describe exemplifications, and therefore cannot function descriptively in such a phrase as 'appearance of there being a *w*'. For if it functioned descriptively in the appearance phrase it would have a conceivable range of application. And if it does not function descriptively in the appearance phrase, the phrase cannot describe an appearance. The sentence, 'There sensibly appears to be a four-legged biped', expresses a self-contradictory proposition, as does the sentence, 'There is a four-legged biped'. And the sentence, 'The appearance of a four-legged biped does not exist', is not to be construed as being about an appearance which in fact does not exist but could be conceived to exist. It expresses an *a priori* truth which is not different from that expressed by 'It is logically impossible for there to be the appearance of a four-legged biped'.

To come back to the view about space, if the metaphysician has established a contradiction in the concept *space*, he has shown in one idiom what in the other idiom amounts to showing that the word 'space' lacks application. If he has shown this then he has also shown that the word 'space' and space-denoting expressions do not function descriptively in appearance expressions. Such an expression as 'It looks as if there is a tall church spire in the distance' makes no more sense than does the expression 'It looks as if there is a druld on the table'. And even if the metaphysician mistakenly thinks that he has established a contradiction in the concept, he must have the idea that space-denoting expressions cannot function descriptively in appearance phrases.

It will be plain that on this construction of what the theory comes to, a construction which makes it out to be about actual usage, it is possible to give an explanation of the curious features attaching to the view. For one thing the metaphysician's position comes to the claim that space-denoting expressions are barren of application, and for another, it comes to the claim that they only seem to have a use: the first claim is the verbal import of (2), and the second claim is perhaps the reasonable construction to be placed on (3). Holding this view plainly does not imply that the metaphysician has the curious belief that people fancy themselves to be having perceptions which it is impossible for them to have nor that he himself believes that he does not have perceptions which he in fact has. And on the present construction the view does not contain obvious contradictions which somehow go unnoticed: there is no contradiction between an expression's having no application and yet seeming to have one. Furthermore, the present construction has the virtue of giving us a possible explanation of the reaction of the informed non-philosopher to the view. It may be that he has turned away from a subject in which it is possible to make such outrageous verbal claims and be taken seriously by one's colleagues. In this connection it may be observed that some philosophers are now ready to say that the metaphysician's view about space is linguistic in substance and reduces to nothing more than a mistaken claim with regard to the actual use of space-denoting expressions.

The present construction has considerable appeal, but nevertheless it too is unsatisfactory. For on it, as on the previous construction, impossible beliefs have to be imputed to the metaphysician, beliefs which are nearly if not quite as bizarre as the earlier ones attributed to him. If the present interpretation of the position is the right one, then if the claim it makes about usage is true, it will be the case that vast numbers of people over a long period of time and in all languages use a variety of expressions under the impression that they are making intelligible statements, asking sensible questions to which appropriate responses are made in words and behaviour, while in fact all this is nothing more than illusion. It follows that in using space-denoting expressions they make themselves understood no more than would a person who said, 'Open the open window', or who said, 'The British coin in my hand is of no denomination', or 'This piece of metal has no properties in virtue of which a thing is a piece of metal'. But it certainly cannot be a *fact* that this sort of situation actually obtains. Every culture has its mythology, but it cannot be true that with regard to all languages and all people it is a myth that space-denoting expressions have an everyday use. This would indeed be a strange semantic phenomenon; and of course it does not exist. The proposition declaring it is a consequence of the second construction, which itself therefore must be rejected. And obviously with its rejection must also go the notion that it gives the metaphysician's view. For if this is his view it follows that he has outlandish beliefs which, apart from the construction which we ourselves have placed on his words, there is no evidence whatever that he has. It is no less incredible for him to have such beliefs than it would be for us, and it would seem reasonable to think that he, no more than ourselves, has them. The inescapable conclusion is that the second construction, like the first, is unacceptable as an account of what the metaphysician actually holds.

The metaphysician's words cannot reasonably be interpreted as making declarations with regard to the apparent existence of phenomena of a certain kind, nor can they be interpreted as making declarations about the actual or accepted use of expressions of a certain class. The second version is no more satisfactory than the first, but unquestionably it does bring us nearer to the character of the view. To confine our attention to the first statement of the triad, regardless of its semantically appearing to make a claim about a concept, and regardless of the *a priori* proof adduced for the claim, we cannot suppose that the metaphysician really believes the word 'space' and concrete space-denoting expressions are, as they are actually used, senseless. But no obstacle, except a strong feeling of resistance, stands in the way of supposing that he is indulging in some sort of semantic pretence with his words, that he plays a game with the word 'space' and *makes* it self-contradictory even though he is not consciously aware of the nature of his activity. This is a hypothesis which goes against the dignity that attaches to the time-honoured subject of metaphysics, but that this hypothesis demands investigation cannot now be denied. For on either of the two constructions so far considered, obviously unacceptable consequences obtain. It will have been noticed that the two interpretations have one thing in common, which is that each implies that the metaphysical utterances have truth-values. And if because of their wild consequences we refuse to accept either of the interpretations, we must give up the notion that the metaphysician's utterances make truth-value claims.

No statement has a truth-value which is neither *a priori* nor empirical. *A priori* and empirical statements between them exhaust the class of truth-value statements. Hence, if we are not prepared to dismiss the metaphysical position as being unintelligible gibberish, we must grant the possibility that the metaphysician's utterances have no truth-value while being intelligible. The alternatives are plainly before us: we can choose either the first construction, the second construction, the contemporary view that the position is a piece of literal nonsense, or the hypothesis that it constitutes a deceptive use of language. The first two alternatives have already been dealt with. The third need not detain us, especially if we consider the position on space in relation to the demonstration which *leads* to it. There can be no real question as to whether the utterances (1) to (3) are perfectly intelligible and understood. And if we stop to consider the last possibility dispassionately, we can realise that these utterances are a special kind of semantic creation, which in order to flourish require a special kind of academic atmosphere. They could not for a moment survive in the hard sunlight of the street. It is one thing to argue the question of the reality of space with our colleagues; it is an altogether different thing to say to a police officer, 'It is logically impossible for me to have made the left turn you charge me with, because space does not exist, as my argument shows'. Apart from the practical consequences saying this would involve, there is an obvious *inappropriateness* about saying it which would deter even the most ardent metaphysician. This shows it is not meant for everyday talk, that the words do not bear their everyday meaning.

Consider again the first of the set of statements composing the metaphysical position about space, namely, the statement that the concept *space* is self-contradictory. If the concept *space*, like the concepts *greatest prime number* and *colourless blue*, were self-contradictory, it would be a linguistic fact that any word, and thus any English word, used to denote the concept has no descriptive sense. The term 'space' and space-denoting expressions do, of course, have descriptive use: it makes perfectly good descriptive sense to say, 'The spaces separating the stars are vast' and 'Jones is a head taller than Smith'. This is known, and it would seem less than plausible to suppose that a philosopher who makes the metaphysical statement has a series of lapses of memory. Nevertheless, the metaphysician does *appear* to make a claim that space-denoting expressions are in their everyday use terminological contradictions and have no descriptive function. Since it can no longer seriously be entertained that he in fact makes the claim he appears to be making, it is entirely reasonable to think that *in some way* he *imports* a contradiction into the concept *space* and into the space-denoting terminology in the language in which he expresses himself. How he imports a contradiction into contradiction-free-descriptive terminology remains to be seen, but it cannot reasonably be doubted that a contradiction has been *manufactured* by the demonstration. A kind of semantic 'frame-up' has been unconsciously perpetrated. As will be seen, the metaphysical contradiction is different from a contradiction of the familiar, everyday kind. And it has an unusual job to perform. This is to deprive space-denoting expressions of their descriptive sense in sentences which declare the existence of what they are normally taken to describe, although, it is to be noticed, it does not deprive them of their descriptive sense in sentences which declare the existence of appearances of what they describe.

If we consider the claimed contradiction, i.e. (1) by itself, without regard to the other utterances in the set, we are led to the hypothesis that the metaphysician of the unreality of space in unconscious fantasy cancels out the descriptiveness of space terminology by importing a contradiction into it. He voids it of its descriptive sense by *making* it self-contradictory, though the manner in which he expresses himself creates the impression that he adduces an argument which *establishes* a contradiction in a concept. He then proceeds to strengthen this impression by creating the illusion of scientifically establishing a fact, i.e. by demonstrating deductively the proposition that space does not exist. The deductive progression of statements, whether explicitly pronounced or not, is: (1) The concept of space is self-contradictory; therefore, (2a) it is logically impossible for space to exist; therefore (2) space does not exist. The last of this triad of assertions is in the factual indicative. It has the grammatical form of statements which deny the existence of possible things they describe. What has happened becomes transparent. The metaphysician has unconsciously taken advantage of a grammatical fact to heighten the air that he is demonstrating something about a familiar phenomenon. It is a fact that, for example, in the language of mathematics the two forms of speech, the factual indicative and the modal indicative, are used interchangeably. Thus, we can say either that $2 + 1$ *is not* less than 3 or that $2 + 1$ *cannot* be less than 3, and we can also say either that $2 + 2$ equals 4 or $2 + 2$ must equal 4. Or again, the same information precisely is conveyed by the use of either form of speech, 'A red thing has colour' and 'A red thing necessarily has colour'. This would seem to be obvious, but perhaps the following consideration will be a useful piece of evidence. Understanding a sentence for a logically necessary, or *a priori* true, proposition comes to knowing a fact about the functioning of expressions, although, to be sure, this fact is not what is *expressed* by the sentence. For example, in order to understand the sentence, 'A chanticleer is a male chicken', a person must know that 'chanticleer' means male chicken, and that is all that he does know in understanding it. Expressed more carefully, understanding the sentence, 'A chanticleer is a male chicken', is the same as knowing that the sentence, '"Chanticleer" means male chicken', says what is true. Now, in understanding '2 + 2 necessarily equals 4', what we know is a fact about the functioning of '2 + 2' and '4'. And since '2 + 2 necessarily equals 4' cannot express a logically necessary proposition and '2 + 2 equals 4' not, what we know in understanding the second sentence is also a fact about the functioning of '2 + 2' and '4'. That is, what is known in understanding either sentence is the *same* fact. And if 'It is logically impossible for space to exist' expressed an *a priori* truth, then to pass from this sentence to 'Space does not exist' would be no more than to pass from one way of expressing a proposition to an equivalent way of expressing the same proposition. What creates the illusion of deducing a matter of fact from a logical necessity is that although all sentences in the modal indicative can be reformulated in the factual, non-modal indicative, not all sentences in the factual indicative can be reformulated in the modal indicative. This makes it look as if in reformulating a modal sentence in the factual indicative we have made an irreversible deduction.

According to the construction arrived at so far, all that has happened behind the screen of a professed demonstration of an astonishing fact about space, is that space-denoting expressions have in unconscious semantic pretence been made self-contradictory and deprived of the use they have in everyday speech. This construction of what the metaphysical position comes to semantically has yet to be brought into relation with (3), the statement that space is a delusive appearance. This interpretation has the not inconsiderable merit of avoiding the consequence of the previous interpretation: the consequence that the metaphysician has wild beliefs about common terminology and about what people think about it. For the hypothesis that the metaphysician's view is nothing more than a *make-believe* revision of language which withdraws space terminology from currency does not imply that he thinks the terminology of space is senseless. Nor does it imply that he thinks that people constantly talk self-contradictory gibberish under the strange illusion that they are making perfectly good sense and are responding to each other with understanding.

How is (3), i.e. the statement that space sensibly appears to exist, to be taken? It cannot, now, be understood as making an empirical claim comparable to that made by a person who states that there are water mirages in the Great Salt Lake Desert in Utah. For the metaphysician is not denying the existence of space, and he has no need to protect his position by taking into account the testimony of the senses. The two statements, (2) that space does not exist and (3) that space appears to exist, combine into the single statement that space only appears to exist, or that it is 'mere appearance'. And it is plain that a philosopher who states that space is mere appearance could not be making a claim about an appearance if in pronouncing (2) he was not making a factual claim about the non-existence of the corresponding reality. Further, if the assertion that space is mere appearance is not to be construed as implying that a certain kind of appearance is delusive, (3) is not to be understood as declaring the existence of a sensible appearance. Neither is (3) open to the former construction placed on it, according to which it makes a declaration about an entire class of expressions; for since the metaphysician is not denying that space-denoting expressions have descriptive use in ordinary speech, he has no need to try to explain their frequent occurrence in everyday talk. On the linguistic interpretation of (3), (2) and (3) combine into the assertion that space-denoting expressions merely seem to have descriptive use. If (2) is no longer open to the verbal interpretation that space terminology lacks descriptive use, then clearly the statement that space-denoting expressions only seem to have descriptive sense cannot say what it appears to be saying, namely, that space terminology does not have descriptive sense in ordinary sentences. Hence, since it is not to the effect that a verbal appearance is delusive, (3) is not open to a construction according to which it states the existence of a linguistic appearance.

The problem at this point is to bring (3) into line with the interpretation reached of (1), or into line with an interpretation not far removed from it. The problem, that is to say, is to bring (3) and (1) into unity under a single interpretation. It seems plain that if the correct interpretation of (1) is that it declares, in a veiled form, a playful language change, (3) must also herald an academic language alteration. For the propositions of the metaphysician combine into a position and must be cut from the same cloth. What gives us a clue to the solution of our problem is the middle assertion, (2), that space does not exist. Considered in conjunction with the metaphysician's granting the existence of the 'self-contradictory appearance'[17] of space, (2) suggests a unitary interpretation. It is hardly necessary to remark again that demonstrating a contradiction in what is taken to be a descriptive term, t, shows not only that t has no descriptive sense but also that appearance expressions the descriptive part of which is t, i.e. an expression like 'appearance of there being a t', has no descriptive function. Thus, for example, 'appearance of there being a blue thing which is everywhere yellow' describes no appearance because 'blue thing which is everywhere yellow' describes no theoretical reality, just as 'there looks to be a druld' has no sense because 'druld' has been given none. And one may wonder why a metaphysical contradiction does not behave in the same way, what it is about its nature which allows it to do only part of its expected work. But the fact that it does only part of the work of a contradiction throws some light on the connection between (2) and (3) and, furthermore, suggests a modification of the present interpretation of (1) which relates to (2) and (3) under a unified interpretation.

As will be remembered, the metaphysician gives an argument which professedly establishes a contradiction in the concept *space*. He then proceeds to the statement that space does not exist and concludes that space is 'mere appearance'. The construction finally placed on the first of the three assertions was that it announces, in the non-verbal form of speech, a pretence casting-out of space-denoting expressions. But on this construction (1) cannot be brought into unity with (3), which requires the retention of space-terminology for use in appearance expressions. Taken by itself, the claim that the concept *space* is self-contradictory lends itself to a rendering according to which it eliminates an entire class of expressions. This rendering can be brought into harmony with (2) but not with (3), and must be modified in such a way as to bring it into harmony with both. Taken in conjunction with (2), the rendering of (1) tells us that space terms have no descriptive use in what, for convenience, may be called reality-sentences, i.e. sentences of the form 'There is . . .' or '. . . exists', in which the descriptive parts do not denote appearances. The modification of the rendering required by the fact that the word 'space' and space-denoting expressions are not, as is made evident by (3), barred from occurring in the descriptive parts of appearance sentences presents itself naturally: the work of the metaphysical contradiction is not to strip space expressions of their descriptive sense but, rather, to *confine* their use to a class of sentences. Its work is to rule out their occurrence in reality sentences but not to rule out their occurrence in appearance sentences. In the academically revised language of the metaphysician, surreptitiously announced by (2) and (3), such sentences as 'There is a rugged mountain in the distance' and 'Elephants are bigger than horses' are shelved, or to make it stronger, have no place in it. So to say, they are grammatically ostracised. His 'contradiction', unlike an orthodox contradiction, does not expose an expression, or a class of expressions, as being devoid of application, but *makes* inadmissable their occurrence in certain forms of sentence.

On the surface the metaphysician creates the idea that he imagines himself, rightly or not, to have established a contradiction in a basic concept and thus to have reduced what everyone takes to be solid reality to the ghostly stuff of 'bare appearance'. But on closer inspection this idea proved unacceptable, because of the curious consequences to which it gave rise. The further idea that he was indirectly making claims with regard to terminology in everyday use also had to be discarded because of its curious consequences. And it is an indisputable merit of the present construction that it does not involve our having to project fantastic beliefs into the metaphysician's mind, beliefs which, apart from his philosophical utterances, he gives no evidence whatever of having. The explanation of such oversights as those of Parmenides and Zeno now becomes possible. It will, no doubt, be objected that the construction we are proposing requires us to think the metaphysician is indulging in an activity no less strange than are the beliefs imputed to him by either of the other interpretations, an activity the metaphysician would certainly and emphatically disavow.[18] His *conscious* disavowal is not, however, to be considered a decisive piece of evidence against the construction placed on his words. We need take it no more seriously than the denial by a person who had made an embarrassing slip of the tongue that his slip was motivated. For apart from his disavowal, which stands on the same footing with the construction placed on his utterance, he is required to give *evidence* against the construction. He is, at the conscious level of his mind, no less a spectator of his own linguistic work of art than we are.

We do not yet have insight into the structure, the mechanics, of the demonstration which exhibits the contradiction in the concept *space*. But the demonstration can hardly be expected to turn out to be the straightforward analytical argument it looks to be, since the contradiction brought to light is, as the job assigned to it clearly shows, not a contradiction of the familiar logical type. The metaphysician, indeed, gives evidence of having an inkling of the unorthodox nature of the contradiction he produces, as his own words would seem to show:

There is only one way to get rid of contradiction, and that is by dissolution. Instead of one subject distracted, we get a larger subject with distinctions, and so the tension is removed. We have at first A, which possesses the qualities *c* and *b*, inconsistent adjectives which collide; and we go on to produce harmony by making a distinction within this subject. That was really not mere A, but either a complex within A or (rather here) a wider whole in which A is included. The real subject is A + D; and this contains the contradiction made harmless by division, since A is *c* and D is *b*.[19]

And also,

We have only loosened 'what' from 'that', and so have made appearance; but we have in each case then bestowed the 'what' on a wrong quality within the real subject. We have crossed the threads of the connection between our 'whats' and our 'thats' and have thus caused collision, a collision which disappears when things are taken as a whole.[20]

What kind of contradiction is it, one may well ask, which is capable of 'dissolution' and of being made 'harmless by division'. An ordinary contradiction such as 'greatest prime number' or 'billiard ball which is in two places at once' does not have a dissolution; it cannot be made 'harmless by division' nor does it constitute 'a collision which disappears when things are taken as a whole'. Only an apparent contradiction could have a dissolution and only if a piece of reasoning is spurious could it give rise to a contradiction which can be made 'harmless by division'.

But a metaphysician does not think that his argument contains a mistake or that it does not back the conclusion he draws from it. Indeed, he gives every sign of thinking that his demonstration is not fallacious and that the contradiction it brings to light is not the bogus contradiction in, e.g. the statement, 'Jones is in New York now and also Jones is now in Aberystwyth, 3000 miles from New York', where 'Jones' is used to name two different people. Obviously, if his contradiction were bogus in this way, if it were a deception comparable to a kind of verbal trickery used in folk conundrums, he would not take his contradiction seriously, something it would be absurd to imagine. Nor would he think that his demonstration had any worth or that it showed anything about the concept *space*. He behaves as if his contradiction is the real article, to be taken with the utmost seriousness, and he describes it as if it were a fake, a spurious contradiction which is resolved by correcting a verbal deception or by untangling a verbal mistake. This is a dual attitude which can only be understood if we interpret it as expressing the metaphysician's intuitive perception of the esoteric nature of the contradiction, the two sides of which are separately indicated by the two parts of the attitude. The metaphysician seems to show veiled awareness of the fact that the contradiction is synthetic or manufactured, and not the logical contradiction it is represented as being; and it also recognises the importance of the invention of the metaphysician. It is recognised as a contradiction which has a dissolution, one which can be made harmless by division; a claim which when *read in reverse* shows it to mean that the contradiction is 'put together'. Unlike an ordinary trumped-up contradiction, however, it is important and not just a quibble. It is a serious fake; and it is this which the metaphysician divines and expresses in his misrepresentation, a misrepresentation which makes use not only of the techniques of distorted description, but also the technique of intellectual fragmentation, i.e. of separating factors which belong together.

At this point, it will probably be objected that the process of elucidation used here *explains away* contradictions and mistaken notions about how contradictions are resolved rather than explains what the metaphysician seeks to prove and where his mistakes and oversights lie. Undoubtedly it has been noticed that throughout this study the attempt has been to discover an explanation which avoids the implication that the metaphysician has wild beliefs or that he embraces contradictions the character of which he is prevented from seeing by an incorrectible myopia. In protest against the apparent artificiality of this procedure it may be contended that the demonstration *is* what it professes to be, but contains a mistake, and that the metaphysician's account of how actual contradictions are resolved is simply wrong and not a distorted description of a contrived contradiction. It may also be argued that on the present account of the position on space, no less than on each of the preceding interpretations, the position involves an absurdity, and can hardly be accorded preferential status over the others.

It is entirely obvious that the concept *sensible appearance* is so connected with the concept *real* that the logical possibility of there being a sensible appearance of a state of affairs φ entails the logical possibility of there being the corresponding reality: an appearance which is delusive, however fantastic it may be, is such that it could, logically, be non-delusive. To put the matter in terms of language, an expression of the form 'sensible appearance of φ existing' has descriptive sense only if 'φ exists' has descriptive sense. This means that a sentence of the form, 'There is the sensible appearance of φ existing', declares the existence of an appearance only if the corresponding sentence 'φ is real' or 'φ exists' declares, whether truly or falsely, the existence of a state of affairs denoted by 'φ'. But if, as according to the present construction, the metaphysician shelves existence sentences using space-denoting expressions while retaining existence sentences using space-appearance expressions, he embraces a class of expressions which he has stripped of their sense under the illusion that they have retained their sense — a remarkable illusion indeed.

It is no longer certain whether there are any philosophers who hold that the utterances of metaphysics are pieces of literal nonsense, although not so long ago it would have been quite certain that some philosophers would have characterised the view as mere nonsense, which indeed it now appears to be. But the contemplation of mere nonsense cannot be granted the durable value which the contemplation of the view has had for philosophers from Zeno to our own day. And, of course, the view is connected with an argument which is perfectly intelligible, an argument such that anyone who grasps it would be able to go on independently and pronounce the view as its conclusion. The old positivist claim with regard to metaphysics could give only a frivolous account of the durable interest metaphysical utterances had for many philosophers and it could give no explanation of the connection between utterance and relevant argument, i.e. it could give no satisfactory account of how an intelligible piece of reasoning could in a relevant way support a string of words which made no literal sense. It is indeed reasonable to think that the positivistic 'nonsense!' is no more than an emotional dismissal. It is also hard to doubt that metaphysics was dismissed with simplistic considerations, for fear that insight into the nature of metaphysics might well lead to the same upsetting insight into a cherished philosophical activity, so-called logical analysis. The indefiniteness and ambiguity of one positivist's description of what can be achieved by analysis is fair evidence for this:

> those who have taken, or accepted the title of phenomenalists have thought that they were doing more than extending their patronage to a word.

Yes, but what more? What is the point of introducing the sense-datum vocabulary? The idea is that it helps you to learn something about the nature of physical objects, not indeed in the way that doing science does, but that you come to understand better what is meant by propositions about physical objects, what these propositions amount to, what their 'cash value' is, by restating them in terms of sense-data. That is, the fact that you *can* restate them in this way, *if* you can, tells you something important about them. Furthermore, it is claimed that if you talk in terms of sense-data you are somehow getting deeper than if you are content to talk, as we all do in everyday life, in terms of physical objects.[21]

(Parenthetically, it may be observed that analysis as a technique of investigation in other parts of philosophy has been no more successful in obtaining solid, uncontested results than have the techniques used in metaphysics.)

On the hypothesis that the metaphysician is playing a game with language for its fantasy value, it is possible, despite the former difficulty, to give a sober and plausible account of the nature of the view. The plausibility of this account will be strengthened if the argument turns out to lend itself to an analysis which makes it fit in with the account of the nature of the position. The metaphysician cannot reasonably be imagined to be holding a view which implies his believing either that people are constantly being deluded by vivid appearances of spatial states of affairs or that they are chronically mistaken about space-denoting expressions. Neither do we obtain a clear and satisfactory picture of him, if his position is made out to be a distorted description of a revised non-workaday form of everyday speech, a revision which banishes sentences stating the existence of situations answering to space-denoting expressions while retaining sentences declaring the existence of circumstances answering to expressions descriptive of spatial appearances. For, as has already been remarked, sentences of the second class are so connected by *rules of usage* to sentences of the first class that if the language does not provide the possibility of formulating sentences of the first class or for some way of saying what they now say in the language of common speech, sentences of the second class lose their function, and become literally unintelligible. Thus, the ordinary sentence, 'There appears to be a high mountain in the distance', asserts the existence of a sensible appearance because the corresponding sentence, 'There is a high mountain in the distance', is descriptively intelligible and says something which could conceivably be true. But if in a language in which the first sentence occurred there were no way of saying what the second sentence says, the first sentence would be empty of descriptive content.

It is of some interest in this connection to notice that the *philosophical* distinction between primary and secondary qualities, according to which it would be *logically* impossible for physical objects to have colour, apparently would not leave room for the possibility of things seeming to have colours, of grass looking green and buttercups yellow. And if any philosopher did actually hold, as e.g. Descartes seems to have held, that things could not logically have colour, while allowing that they do sensibly appear to have colour, we should be constrained to think that he had two obviously incompatible beliefs which he persistently failed to notice were incompatible. But the distinction may not be the one it seems to the uncritical glance to be; it may, instead, be a fantasied revision of terminology made, for one thing, with the object of creating an intellectual illusion.

The hypothesis that the metaphysical theory is, so to say, a holiday revamping of language cannot easily be dismissed, since a moment's reflection shows that no other explanatory hypothesis exists which can compete with it. The difficulty mentioned above arises only if the revamped philosophical language is taken to be a substitute for ordinary language, designed to do the kind of work ordinary language does. Metaphysical appearance sentences would do the work of everyday appearance sentences, if, like the latter, they had associated reality sentences, and lacking which they have no descriptive function. The metaphysician of the unreality of space banishes an entire class of reality sentences without making linguistic replacement; and this makes it clear that the revised language does no practical work, that in fact it is only a *dummy* language. Unconsciously, no doubt, the metaphysician does not wish them to do their accustomed work, and he contrives this by failing to make good for what he has cast out. It is not that he fails to see that his appearance-sentences will not do their ordinary work; rather, we may conjecture with good reason, he wishes them to do unusual, out of the ordinary work for him. If, now, we attend to the impression his dummy use of terminology as well as his arguments create, and also to the talk with which he surrounds them, we cannot help but discover the task assigned to it. His language creates the delusive idea that it announces an upsetting and fundamental fact about a kind of phenomenon, and it must be the engendering of this idea which the revision of language is designed to bring about. The effect produced by the new terminology, which otherwise is useless for the purpose of communication, must be the point and intent of the new terminology. The purpose must be the intellectual deception it perpetrates, an illusion which must connect with deeper materials in our minds.

With his utterances, namely, that the concept *space* is self-contradictory and that space only deceptively appears to exist, the metaphysician gives the impression that he is making a remarkable pronouncement about space, a pronouncement comparable to the astronomical statement that the dome of the sky is actually an optical illusion. The colourful idea is created that he is stating an impressive finding of a special science, a science which attempts to discover facts of a more fundamental sort than those investigated by the ordinary, empirical sciences. To many people metaphysics looks like a superior science which attempts by *a priori* methods to take us to the realities behind the cosmic curtain of appearances. It can easily be seen that this grandiose idea would be dissipated if the metaphysician introduced into his fantasied language sentences which did the linguistic work of those he deleted. For his language would then do the same work that is done by ordinary language, which perpetrates no such dramatic deception on us. The creation and maintenance of the intellectual illusion that his words, 'Space is self-contradictory and is mere appearance', describe a discovery about the universe, rather than announce an empty language revision, *require* that the philosophical space appearance-sentences be linguistic frauds, while in the ordinary language we use for everyday communication their originals together with the banished sentences retain their usual descriptive function.

Without unaltered everyday speech as a backdrop the dummy sentences cannot produce their strange effect, nor could they do this if made descriptive by the introduction of linguistic compensation for the discarded forms of speech. For the production of the metaphysical magic the metaphysician requires both the linguistic dummies and the language of common discourse in which space existence-sentences retain their normal use. This fact explains why the metaphysician is not the language reformer he is sometimes represented as being. It also throws light on the mystifying distinction which he makes between existence and reality, and on the claim that 'Nothing is actually removed from existence by being labelled "appearance"'.[22] The admission that space exists is an oblique way of calling attention to the occurrence of space existence-sentences in ordinary language, and the claim that space is not real is a distorted way of saying that sentences of this form have been banished from his fantasied re-edited language.

We may describe the metaphysician as someone who knows how to daydream with language, although he is not aware of the nature of what he indulges himself in. And by communicating his daydream to other intellectuals, who may agree or disagree with him, accept or reject his position, he creates a public semantic diversion. He is a verbal entrepreneur who is adept in the production of a remarkable, highly abstract kind of theatre, the semantic imitation of deep and reasoned speculation about the universe. It is this which the intellectual, who turns away from philosophy in disappointment, dimly perceives and which makes him characterise philosophy as verbal and arid. He comes to philosophy for lore about the world and, instead of the knowledge he thirsts for, has palmed off on him a verbal bubble, a piece of semantic necromancy which masquerades as pronouncements about existence.

It is hardly to be imagined that producing the semblance of a striking theory about a phenomenon or group of phenomena is the sole work of the metaphysical *leger de main* with language. The delusive impression that language is being used to announce a theory is the production of work unconsciously done with words, and the metaphysician is as much a diverted spectator as is anyone else. An uneasy feeling about the nature of his work undoubtedly sometimes enters his mind, but the feeling is relatively formless, the whisper of a suspicion which fails to bear fruit. The fact that the feeling is never permitted to become strong enough to lead to a serious investigation of the many unsatisfactory features of philosophical theories and disagreements is revealing, and helps us arrive at an understanding of the great value placed on the illusion of metaphysics. What inhibits curiosity to a remarkable degree and enhances the importance of the illusion created by the game the metaphysician plays with the words 'space', 'real' and 'exists' must have deeper sources in the mind than the obvious wish to be a scientist without having to do the empirical drudge work of the real scientist. If the only work of the metaphysical language game were the production of an intellectual deception, it is hard to see how it could have endured without exposure for so long a time. It would thus seem entirely reasonable to assume that deeper satisfactions are involved, satisfactions which deflect our curiosity.

It would seem reasonable to think that the metaphysical pronouncement not only creates a vivid deception by the language it introduces, but at the same time actually expresses thoughts which are unconsciously grasped. The words of one important philosopher, known particularly for his meticulous and exact use of English, can be construed as indicating something of this sort, not, to be sure, that he wished to indicate this. He wrote:

> Mr Lazerowitz concludes that when, for instance, I tried to shew that time is not unreal, all that I was doing was to recommend that we should not use certain expressions in a different way from the way in which we do! If that is all I was doing, I was certainly making a huge mistake, for I certainly did not think it was all. And I do not think so now.[23]

He should have said that it was *not at all* what he was doing, not denied it was all that he was doing. His verbal lapse, if regarded as an unconsciously determined slip rather than an instance of mere carelessness, is quite revealing. It covertly admits the substantial correctness of the claim about the nature of his philosophical refutations, and implies that there is more to it than just that. What else can the *more* be except unconscious fantasies philosophical utterances are made to express? And only psychoanalysis is able to unearth these. Semantic analysis can tell us what 'Space is an unreal appearance' does not say. Only psychoanalysis can discover for us what it does say.

Let us turn now to the considerations by which the metaphysician professes to demonstrate the self-contradictoriness of the concept *space*. Several different, although related, contradictions are to all appearances shown to infect the concept, contradictions which are a logical obstacle to the existence of anything answering to the concept but are not an obstacle to the existence of the sensible appearance of there being something answering to it. One contradiction is that the concept *space* is the concept of a thing which cannot logically exist as a whole, i.e. a thing which cannot exist in part only and yet cannot exist in entirety either. Another contradiction is that the concept is that of a composite substance which has no substantial parts, a kind of thing which is composed of parts but which, nevertheless, has no parts. These two contradictions are summed up in the statement that 'space is endless while an end is essential to its nature. Space cannot come to a final limit, either within itself or on the outside. And yet, so long as it remains something always passing away, either internally or beyond itself, it is not space at all'.[24] According to the showing of the arguments, the proposition that space exists has the contradictory consequence that a thing exists the magnitude of which is not its whole magnitude, and it has the further contradictory consequence that a thing having magnitude exists, the final parts of which have no magnitude and which therefore cannot be parts of which a magnitude is composed. The second of the contradictions, which obtains from the infinite divisibility of space, leads to a third contradiction. This is that space consists of relations which can have no terms to relate. The argument for this conclusion is that as every space is a relation of spaces, there can be no infinitesimals of space which are not themselves relations and there can therefore be no possible terms for the relations to relate: 'space = relations of spaces' yields a vicious regression.

The first two contradictions lead to the conclusion that the concept *space* is the concept of a logically impossible thing, 'a quality or substance, which it cannot be' and the third contradiction leads to the conclusion that the concept of space is the concept of a logically impossible relation, that 'space is a relation, which it cannot be'.[25] According to the natural reading of the metaphysician's words, an analysis of the concept *space* brings to light three baffling contradictions, contradictions which make an intellectual enigma out of a concept in common use, one that normally puzzles no one and does not even puzzle the metaphysician when he is not doing metaphysics. St Augustine's famous words about time come to mind here: 'What, then, is time? If no one asks of me, I know; if I wish to explain to him who asks, I know not.'

The metaphysical claim about the concept *space* is paralleled by the proposition, whether explicitly asserted or not, that any word which denotes the concept is a terminological contradiction. And in the case of a metaphysician who expresses his arguments and their conclusion in the English language, he can be taken to be tacitly making the claim that the word 'space' is a contradiction in terms. Thus, the claim that the concept *space* is the concept of a self-contradictory *thing* has, so to speak, its cash value in the associated verbal proposition that the word 'space' is a self-contradictory *noun*. The concealed assertion behind the philosophical assertion is that 'space' is a substantive which is not the name of a substance. This is true. It is a fact that 'space' is a noun which is not the name of a kind of thing; and the philosopher appears to show this by his analysis. It cannot be admitted that he actually demonstrates a contradiction in the concept *space* or that he shows the word 'space', as it is commonly used, to be a terminological contradiction. But it might be the case that taken as a noun which *is* the name of a kind of thing, i.e. as denoting a cosmic receptacle, as the word 'box' denotes a container, a contradiction can be generated. It will be plain that a contradiction generated in this way and attributed to the ordinary use of the word 'space', so to speak, projected into the concept *space*, constitutes a kind of linguistic frame-up. It is manufactured evidence with a special mission assigned to it. And what that mission is has already been stated; it is to justify an academic change of language, a change which very likely enables the metaphysician to express unconscious fantasies.

It is easy to see that the standard contradictions discovered by philosophers in the concept *space* obtain only if space is regarded as a thing, in particular as a kind of chamber. Viewed in this way, the idea of space becomes transformed into the idea of space as itself a spatial thing, as a thing having magnitude, i.e. as a thing which is itself *in space*. The three contradictions can then be readily elicited: space is a thing which cannot exist as a whole; it is a composite which nevertheless has no parts; and it is no more than a relation with no possible terms to relate. Viewed as an object, space becomes a box without sides, a magnitude which is built out of parts which have no magnitude, and also a nest of impossible relations. With regard to the word 'space', if it is taken to be the name of a kind of thing, it becomes a terminological contradiction. The word is, of course, a substantive. Furthermore, it is used in phrases which make it look as if it is a noun which names a thing, i.e. it is used in phrases which bear an outward resemblance to phrases about rooms, containers, and the like. This fact, if attended to carefully, sheds light on how the metaphysical contradiction is manufactured and also on its motivation, at least at the linguistic level.

It is a natural form of speech to say of bodies such as the planet Uranus and the stars that they are far out *in space*. This is only another, if more intriguing way, of saying that they are far from the earth or that they are immense distances from us. And it is, apparently, not an unnatural extension of language to speak of things, i.e. bodies such as chairs, houses, mountains, the earth, as being *in* space. Thus, for example, Kant and G. E. Moore speak of such objects as being things of the kind 'to be met with in space'.[26] We say that there is a sofa in the living-room, and by a natural extension of language we speak of sofas and living-rooms as being kinds of things which are in space. The series of expressions, 'The sofa is in the living-room', 'The living-room is in the house', 'The house is in space', conjures up in our minds the picture of a thing which is a nest of boxes, the outermost box being space itself. But this picture misrepresents the meaning of the last of the series of expressions. The forms of words, 'The sofa is in the living-room', and 'The sofa is in space', are grammatically alike, alike in a respect which makes them look as if they are values of the same function, 'The sofa is in —'. But the difference between them, which is covered up by their outward grammatical similarity, is enormous. It is tempting to say that the difference is as great as the difference between being in a mood and being in a house. The phrase 'in the living-room' is so used that with regard to anything about which it makes literal sense to say that it is in the living-room it also makes perfectly good sense to say that it is not in the living-room or that it is being moved out of the living-room: it makes literal sense to say 'The sofa is no longer in the living-room; it has been put in the attic'. But the phrase 'in space' is so used that it makes no literal sense whatever to say, 'The sofa has been taken out of space and put somewhere else' or 'The sofa still exists but it is no longer in space'. To make the point non-verbally, it is possible to take a sofa out of a living room, it is physically impossible but logically possible to hull out the fiery centre of the earth and deposit the contents elsewhere, but it is *logically* impossible to take the sofa out of space. As against the sentence 'Sofas are things which are normally found in living-rooms', which expresses an empirical proposition, the sentence, 'Material bodies are normally met with in space', is an absurdity of language. This is because 'Material bodies exist only in space' expresses a logically necessary proposition: being a material body *entails* being in space. The fact that the words, 'Material bodies, such as sofas and houses, exist only in space', are used to express a logically necessary proposition implies that the expression 'in space' is so used that it applies to whatever 'material body' applies to. Unlike the sentence, 'The sofa is in the living-room', or the sentence, 'You will find the sofa in the living-room', which says *where* a certain thing is, the sentence, 'The sofa is in space', says nothing about where that thing is or is to be found. The expression 'in space' has a use which is altogether different from the use of such

an expression as 'in the house'. And what its use is, what it means, is
not hard to discover. The expressions 'in the house' and 'inside my
body' are used to convey information about the location of objects.
The expression, 'in space', to which there does not correspond an
intelligible expression like 'outside of space', is not used to convey
information with regard to the whereabouts of objects; instead it has
adjectival import, it means 'spatial': x is in space = x is spatial.

It is clear that if to be in space is not to be *in* anything, then space
itself cannot be a kind of thing, a sort of container or, for that matter,
an object in which a thing could, theoretically, be embedded.
Oblique recognition that space is not a thing is to be found in descriptions which appear to make space out to be a thing. Thus, according
to one description space is 'a box without sides'. This is a vivid but
patently self-contradictory description of space as a box: being a box
entails having sides and having no sides entails not being a box.
Hidden behind the contradiction we can discern the denial that
space is a box. Pascal described space as a sphere with its centre
everywhere and its circumference nowhere; and his imaginative
words also tell us that space is not a kind of spherical thing.
Nevertheless, it must be granted that the idea that space is an object
comes naturally to us and is perhaps unavoidable. Even the descriptions which in an oblique way deny that it is an object make it out to
be one. Bradley has observed that the concept of space is that of 'a
thing, or substance, or quality (call it what you please)'.[27]

We *seem* to have the idea that space is a thing, but it cannot be
allowed that there *is* such an idea. For if there were the concept of
space as 'that of a thing, or substance', there would be the concept of
space as a thing which other things enter and from which they could
leave; and there is no such concept. We cannot conceive or imagine
anything answering to the words 'entered space, remained there for
a time, then left', which is to say that they express nothing
conceivable and have no descriptive sense. Hence, we are unable to
imagine or conceive anything answering to the words, 'space is a
thing, or substance', which amounts to the fact that 'space is a thing,
or substance' is an expression which has no descriptive use. We do
not have an *idea* of space as a substance in the sense of knowing what
it would be like for space to be a substance. At most we can say that
we have the delusive notion that the words 'space is a thing, or
substance' express an idea about the nature of space, actual or
theoretically possible. We do not have the false idea that space is a
kind of thing; we have, instead, the false idea that the expression

'space is a thing' stands for a conception. The source of this false idea must be in language, in the word 'space' and its equivalents. For there is nothing else to give rise to this illusion. The word 'space' is a substantive, and to say that space is a thing or substance is in the non-verbal idiom to give expression to this linguistic fact. The 'idea' that space is a thing is nothing more esoteric than the fact that the word 'space' is a substantive; but when this fact is expressed in the ontological idiom it gives rise to the spurious notion that the words 'space is a thing' have descriptive import.

The word 'space' (and its equivalents in other languages) has a use in ordinary speech and is not, of course, a terminological contra-diction: sentences like 'A rocket has been shot far out into space' and 'As distances between stars go, the planets in the solar system are near each other in space', are not self-contradictory. Philosophers are no more ignorant of this than are others, nor do they use space terminology less 'gaily'[28] than ordinary, philosophically uninstructed people do. The word 'space' is, however, a noun which in semantic appearance belongs to the class of substantives that are names of receptacles or containers, without in fact being such a name. Its function in, e.g. the sentence, 'There are myriads of stars in space', is not at all like the function of 'casket' in the sentence, 'There are many jewels in the casket', although it simulates the function of 'casket'. It is a counterfeit substantive which parades in our language along with such words as 'casket', 'drawer', and 'house'; and some philosophers on whose attention this impresses itself will take advantage of the linguistic appearance, engendered by phrases in which the word occurs, to play a special language game with the word. A philosopher who 'discovers' that the concept *space* is riddled with contradictions, and that space therefore exists only as appearance, has made an actual discovery, but not the kind of discovery he fancies himself to have made. What he has discovered is a way of using to advantage the actual and apparent features of the use of the word 'space' to *contrive* the contradictions he supposes himself to find. The contradictions he uses to justify his linguistic move with the word, *viz.* its confinement to appearance-sentences.

The contradictions in the concept *space*, it will be recalled, are the following:

(1) Space is a whole which cannot be a whole: 'Space is endless while an end is essential to its being.'
(2) Space is a magnitude the parts of which are without

magnitude, but 'If the parts are not spaces, the whole is not space'.

(3) Space is a relation which has no terms to relate, it is 'a relation of what vanishes into relations, which seek in vain for their terms'.[29]

To put the matter ontologically, the first two contradictions involve the notion of space as a kind of thing, that is to say, as a spatial entity of some sort. According to the first contradiction, the concept of space is the concept of an object which by its nature can neither exist in part nor in its entirety. According to the second contradiction, the conception of space is that of a thing which is made up of parts of which it cannot be composed. The third contradiction is intimately bound up with the second and indeed in conjunction with it is the second horn of a dilemma. According to it the conception of space is the conception of something which requires parts and has none. The so-called 'parts' of the second contradiction make space impossible, and the absence of parts of the third contradiction also makes space impossible.

In addition to the notion of space as a kind of thing or object, the first two contradictions (and also the third) involve the notion of infinity. A moment's reflection shows that (1) uses the conception of a divergent infinite series; it involves, that is to say, the idea of space as entailing a series of spaces of increasing magnitude none of which is the greatest space. These two ideas, space as a kind of thing and as involving a divergent infinite series of spaces, gives rise in combination to the contradictory idea of a whole thing which cannot be the whole thing. The second contradiction, (2), also uses the notion of an infinite series, this time of a convergent series. It involves the idea that a space, however small or great, is composed of an infinite series of increasingly smaller spaces converging on a point. The underlying thought here (which seems inescapable) is that a point, consciously or unconsciously conceived as a dimensionless *entity*, is the final term of such a series. One metaphysician partially, if also ambiguously, recognised this when he wrote: 'But space and time are thus resolved in the process of their intellectual construction into a *continuous infinite series* of which the terms are spatial or temporal positions or points.'[30] The idea of space as a kind of spatial object, i.e. as something possessing magnitude, together with the notion that space is an infinite series of spaces which converge on a point counted as their terminus, yields the contradictory consequence that space is a thing which has size and yet is made up of parts having zero size. The third contradiction also uses the idea that a space resolves itself into an infinite geometric series of spaces, but with a difference. It calls attention to the fact that such a series can have no final term (and to the fact that every member of the series resolves itself into a series having no final term) to back the claim that space is 'a relation which vanishes into relations'.

The first contradiction, presented in pictorial language, is that space is a box which cannot be less than infinitely large, and being infinite is too large to have sides, top, and bottom and so cannot be a box. Restated in the verbal idiom, this comes, in English, to maintaining that the word 'space' means infinite box or container and therefore that it is a substantive with the self-contradictory meaning, *a container and not a container*. It cannot be repeated too often that the word is not a terminological contradiction, that it does not have a self-contradictory meaning, and thus that its meaning is not given by the phrase 'infinitely large container'. Nor can it be remarked too often that a metaphysician who declares that space is 'a self-contradictory appearance' knows that 'space' is not a contradictory term. He knows, therefore, that its use is not governed by the two defining criteria *infinitely large* and *kind of container*. It is fair to think that what he does is to *make* them defining criteria of the word, though not consciously and not with the practical intent of correcting usage. It is plausible to suppose that he is unconsciously playing a game with the word. Evidence for this is the fact that he chronically misinterprets what he does and the fact that he reserves his language game for special occasions, never letting it intrude into his normal and serious use of language.

The contradiction he professes to have elicited in the language of space by his analytical technique he *imports*, by 'a play of words',[31] into the language which in its ordinary use is, of course, free from contradiction. The question as to why a metaphysician does this, what value the game has for him, is one to which we should like to know the answer. We can surmise that its primary value lies in an unconscious fantasy it enables him to express to himself, and also to many others. The interpretation of the psychological content of the language game played with the word 'space' requires a special knowledge and skill. Fortunately, for the purpose at hand, no more than conjectures are required in the construction of the explanatory hypothesis about what the metaphysician is doing and how he can continue effectively to conceal his game from himself. By far the greater importance attaches to the question as to how the metaphysician creates his 'contradiction', what the tricks of language are by which he produces the semblance of the discovery of contradictions where none exists.

One of Zeno's arguments goes as follows: 'If there is such a thing as space it will be in something, for all being is in something, and that which is in something is in space. So space will be in space, and so *ad infinitum*. Accordingly, there is no such thing as space.'[32] Every space, this argument tells us, is enclosed or contained in a greater space, so that the whole of space will itself have to be contained in a greater space and cannot, therefore, be the whole of space. What has been done to bring this contradiction into being is now discernible. In effect Zeno can be made out to be asserting that:

Space is a kind of physical container.
Physical containers are things of the kind that are in space.
Therefore, space is in space.
Therefore, space is an infinitely large container, which is absurd.

Reformulating these statements linguistically, which makes manifest the verbal point of the apparently *a priori* claims made by them, they become in English,

The word 'space' is the name of a kind of physical container.
It makes literal sense to say, 'Physical containers are in space' and it makes no literal sense to say, 'Some physical containers are not in space'.
Therefore, 'Space is in space' makes literal sense, and 'Space is not in space' makes none.
Therefore, 'space' means *infinitely large container*, and is a terminological absurdity.

If we now bring into consideration the semantic appearance surrounding the use of the word 'space', i.e. the existence of such expressions as 'in space', 'outer space', 'far out in space', and 'far apart in space', and connect up the appearance with the grammatical fact that 'space' is a noun, it becomes a simple matter to see how the contradiction has been manufactured.

It is a linguistic fact that the word 'space', in the use that attracts to it the attention of philosophers, is a noun which is not the name of a spatial object, having height, width and length. It is also a fact that its metaphorical, and not unnatural, use lends it the appearance of being the name of a kind of physical thing, a container. So to speak, 'space' is a noun by grammatical courtesy, a substantive in name only, which if treated as if it were actually the name of a container generates a contradiction. Zeno's form of words, 'Space is in space', shows this clearly. Understood as expressing an *a priori* true proposition, its verbal import is to the effect that the word 'space' denotes a kind of thing to which the phrase 'in space' correctly applies. And *if* the word were in fact used as the name to which the phrase 'in space' did apply correctly, then indeed the metaphysician of the unreality of space would have *proved* a contradiction. What has happened, it is plausible to think, is that the metaphysician has used the semantic appearance surrounding the word to create the semblance of a contradiction in its ordinary use. He constructs the pseudo-contradiction by taking for a reality its appearance of being a substantive which names a kind of extended object. The 'space' of 'Space is in space' does resolve itself into a divergent infinite series; but its occurrence in the metaphysical statement does not give its actual use. It is much as if the metaphysician said, 'If the appearance of "space" being the name of a kind of object is taken for fact, then a terminological contradiction can be shown to obtain. This implies that "space", although a noun, is not the name of a thing.' But instead of expressing himself in this manner he resorts to the dramatic illusion-creating ontological idiom, the form of speech in which words are not mentioned. He says something like the following: 'If there is such a thing as space (or if space is real), then it will be in space, etc. *ad infinitum* (or be a whole thing which cannot be a whole thing); hence there is no such thing as space.'

Freud has shown that the wit of a witticism is lost when its content is restated in the language of the 'secondary process'. A comparable thing takes place when a metaphysical utterance is reformulated in language which brings out its verbal content: the illusion of an argument being brought in to support a theory about a phenomenon is destroyed. In fact, the metaphysician does no more than point out that 'space' is a spurious noun, a noun which is not the name of a kind of thing. And this fact he uses as an academic justification either for banishing it from the language ('There is no such thing as space') or reducing its status, making it into a second-class noun, so to speak ('Space is mere appearance'). Behind the façade of a science of reality erected by the form of discourse he uses, the metaphysician plays a game with the word 'space', a game to which his choice of language makes him as much dupe as it makes others. And undoubtedly the game answers to needs at many levels of his mind.

The first argument, which makes use of the fact that the word 'space' (or its equivalent in any other language in which the argument is expressed) is a noun and that there exists phrases like 'in space', leads to the second argument against the reality of space. According to the second argument, any space, S, resolves itself into an infinite series of spaces converging on a point; and the claimed consequence of this is that S, which has magnitude, must (and cannot) be built out of points, entities having zero, or no, magnitude. The sentence, 'Space is in space', which is a non-verbal way of saying that the words 'in space' apply to the object (supposedly) denoted by 'space', suggests the further form of words, 'Space contains space', which says, non-verbally, that 'contains space' applies to the object (apparently) referred to by 'space'. Like the sentence, 'Space is in space', the sentence, 'Space contains space', generates an infinite series, this time, of course, a convergent series. How ordinary terminology has been manoeuvred is clear. Again, the word 'space' is treated *as if* it is a noun which is the name of a kind of thing, and this together with taking the phrase 'contains space' non-metaphorically, i.e. *as if* its use were like that of 'contains a compartment', generates the evanescent series, $space_1$ contains $space_2$ contains $space_3$ . . . etc.

At this juncture of the argument two further considerations are brought in, considerations centring on the terms 'series' and 'point'. To begin with, it may be observed that the word 'infinite' is linked in our minds with the idea of the huge, and it cannot be doubted that the crude, perhaps unconscious, thoughts in back of even its precise use in mathematics are those of the vast — vast lengths or vast magnitudes. The infinite is thought of as that which is greater than the finite. To put it in a self-contradictory way, which will nevertheless evoke imagery associated with the term, the infinite is thought of as a finite amount greater than that which is finite, a *magnified* finite. In this connection a slip which occurs in the work of an eminent Cambridge mathematician is very revealing:[33] 'Representation of a complex variable on a plane is obviously more effective for points at a finite distance from the origin than for points at a very great distance.' The specific unconscious fantasies with which the term 'infinite' is invested undoubtedly are numerous, and some of them must be connected with 'the oceanic feeling' many people experience. However that may be, it is clear that when the term is connected with the notion of a series the background thought is that of a huge or enormously long series. Thus, the two expressions, 'finite series' and 'infinite series', appear to apply to series which differ from each other in respect of length. The infinite series $1 + \frac{1}{2} + \frac{1}{4} + \frac{1}{8} + \frac{1}{16} + \ldots + \frac{1}{128} + \ldots$ is thought of as being like the series $1 + \frac{1}{2} + \frac{1}{4} + \frac{1}{8} + \frac{1}{16} + \ldots + \frac{1}{128}$, but longer: to use Cantor's word, both series are thought of as 'consummated'.[34] The tendency, that is, is to think that the difference between them is one of degree rather than of kind. In fact the difference between them, in general respects, is just the opposite: it is one of kind rather than of degree. A series having an infinite number of members is not longer than a series having a finite number of members in the way in which one finite series is longer, or has more members, than another finite series. Galileo maintained[35] that infinite sets were not comparable, that e.g. one could not say intelligibly that the set of whole numbers was either equal to or greater than or less than the set of square numbers; and this certainly holds true of infinite series in relation to finite series. A finite series is a series with a last term, whereas an infinite series, either divergent or convergent, can have no final term. There can, therefore, be no whole, or entire, infinite series, whereas a finite series is an entire series. This means that although finite series are comparable with each other in respect of number of members, an infinite series cannot be compared as to length with a finite series. And they cannot be compared, or better, they are intrinsically incomparable, because there is no whole of the one to be compared with the whole of the other. One mathematician has observed that the series $1 + \frac{1}{2} + \frac{1}{4} + \frac{1}{8} + \frac{1}{16} + \ldots + \frac{1}{128} + \ldots$ does not have a sum in the arithmetic sense of 'sum'; it has a sum in the sense of having a limit. But the limit 2 of the series is not the calculated arithmetic sum, and the fact that the series does not have an arithmetic sum means that it is not a complete series. This is to say that it is not a series in the way in which a finite series is a series. Aristotle said that 'nothing is complete which has no end'.[36] To this might be added that a series which has no end cannot exist as a whole, or to put the matter differently, there is no such mathematical entity as an entire infinite series. So-called partial series are not, as their name suggests, parts of a series in the way in which sections of a picket fence are parts of the picket fence.

All this comes to saying that the term 'infinite series' is not the general name of a type of series, in the sense of 'series' in which 'finite series' is the general name of a type of series. The fact that it is logically impossible for an infinite series to be an entire series, or extension, is paralleled by the linguistic fact that the sentence, 'It is impossible for there to be the whole of an infinite series', expresses an *a priori* truth. And this fact about the sentence implies that the expression, 'whole of an infinite series', has no use, is not a phrase which describes a *series*. This quite plainly implies that the word 'series' does not function in its occurrence in the phrase 'infinite series' as it does in the phrase 'finite series'. The words 'finite' and 'infinite' do not *both* function as adjectival modifiers of a noun which preserves the same meaning, as is the case with 'picket fence' which means the same in both phrases, 'long picket fence' and 'short picket fence'. The difference between the uses of the phrases 'finite series' and 'infinite series' may perhaps be summed up by stating that 'An infinite series is not a series' is not a self-contradiction[37] and 'A finite series is a series' is a tautology.

A person who has perception into this linguistic state of affairs will be inclined to do either of two things, and sometimes he will be inclined to do both things. If he is impressed by the outward similarity between the two phrases and also of course by the partial likeness of their actual use, he will be tempted to heighten their likeness by some verbal device or other. If, however, he is influenced by their dissimilarity, he will tend to feel that their outward verbal similarity minimises this, that it covers up a difference that deserves to be made more visible. Sometimes he will be tempted to do both things, one alongside of the other. And whatever he does, whether he tries to bring out their similarity or their dissimilarity, or to do both things, he uses the form of speech in which words are not mentioned and either are or appear to be used to describe objects and their properties.

A philosopher who wishes to enhance the outward similarity between the terms 'infinite series' and 'finite series' will make concealed use of the word 'point'. It is a fact that 'point' is a substantive which, like the word 'space', is made linguistically to look like the name of a kind of object. Thus, Russell wrote,[38] 'The space of geometry and physics consists of an infinite number of points, but no one has even seen or touched a point. If there are points in sensible space, they must be an inference.' The word 'point' is made to look like the name of a geometrical atom too minute to be divisible, to which corresponds a fraction greater than zero and also indivisible, an infinitesimal. And one or the other pseudo-name, 'point' or 'infinitesimal', is treated as if it stands for the final term of a series the first part of which is given by a partial series. Hume's statement that 'whatever is capable of being divided *in infinitum* must consist of an infinite number of parts . . .'[39] gives us a clue to what is done by a mathematical metaphysician to create the semantic deception that 'infinite series' is the general name of a species of series, on a footing with finite series. Each of the infinite number of *parts* of the infinitely divisible is a trumped up terminal member, a point or infinitesimal, of the whole of an infinite series. A philosopher who wishes to lay stress on the dissimilarity between the functioning of 'infinite series' and 'finite series' will make more pronounced the fact that it is not a contradiction to say that an infinite series is not a series (not an extension or an array). To make use of Hume's language, with opposite intent, we may say that what is capable of being divided *in infinitum* cannot consist of an infinite number of parts. No member of an infinite series is a part, itself 'perfectly indivisible, and incapable of being resolved into any lesser unity',[40] which is to say that each member is expressible as a series no member of which is a point. This, when expressed in such words as 'An infinite series is ". . . a relation of what vanishes into relations, which seek in vain for further terms"'[41], in a veiled way describes the refusal to apply 'series' to what is called 'infinite series', and in this way makes more pronounced the linguistic gulf between the use of the two terms.

We are now in a position to see how the remaining contradictions in the concept of space are contrived. By treating 'space' as if it is the name of a spatial object and the expression 'contains space' as if it uses 'contains' in the way in which the word is used in 'contains a compartment', 'space' is *made* to entail the infinite convergent series, 'space contains space which contains space which . . .'. It can readily be seen that if, on the one hand, to this manufactured series we conjoin the first account of the use of 'infinite series' (as an extension with a terminal member), we come out with the result that space is a thing having magnitude but is composed of parts which have no magnitude, i.e. is made up of points. The space series become 'space$_1$ includes space$_2$ which includes . . . point', with the conclusion that 'if the parts are not spaces the whole is not space'. If, on the other hand, the space series is conjoined with the second account of the use of 'infinite series' (as a relation which can have no final terms), we come out with the conclusion that space is an impossible relation, having no terms to relate: 'so long as it remains something always passing away . . . it is not space at all.'[42]

The three arguments professing to demonstrate contradictions in *space* have turned out to be quite different from what they have been taken to be by mathematical metaphysicians for many hundreds of years. One philosopher has plaintively observed that 'We all know from painful experience that it is difficult to think philosophically and so it is difficult to see whether a philosophical argument is valid or not, and this being so, it is easy to understand why people should differ about these matters'.[43] This explanation will undoubtedly be accepted with alacrity by philosophers; but unfortunately it is nothing more substantial than a rationalisation of a painful fact we all have to face, which is that 'people differ about these matters' endlessly and fruitlessly. On the present interpretation of the nature of the arguments and of the position for which they are adduced it is possible to give a realistic account of this painful fact. All three arguments construct contradictions which do no more than bring out the fact that the word 'space' is a noun which is not the name of a kind of physical object. And these arguments are then used as pretexts for banishing its use from existence-sentences and confining it to appearance-sentences. What is being covertly remarked by the statement, 'Space does not exist except in appearance', is that the noun 'space' is not a name, it only appears to be one, and the statement itself embodies a linguistic stricture on the metaphorical, poetic use of the word. If a philosopher does not wish to accept the stricture he will be unimpressed by the contradictions, not think the arguments 'valid'. And if he does wish to accept the stricture, he will think some or all of them 'valid'. What is at issue is a non-practical holiday language change, and since neither validity nor utility is at issue the difference can permanently resist resolution.

When looked at through semantic spectacles the game played with the word 'space' seems too trivial to win the interest it has received from many intellectuals over the years. To be sure, the language in which the verbal game is formulated creates the impression, comparable in its intense vividness to a perfect mirage, that a theory fortified by powerful evidence is being announced. But intriguing as this refined mirage is, it is far from sufficient to account for the enduring interest in the game. Some intellectuals have, as a matter of fact, dimly seen past the mirage to the verbal reality behind it, and have been repelled by their glimmer of insight. It is they who characterise philosophy as a verbal wasteland. To account for the enduring absorption in the piece of verbal theatre it has to be supposed that there is something other than the semblance of a claim about a phenomenon which engages and holds our attention. And this obviously is not something of which we are conscious. Freud somewhere describes a dream as a bench with one leg in our recent past experience and another in the earliest experiences of our life. A philosophical theory may be described in a somewhat similar way: it is a structure with one leg in the adult part of our mind, the educated intellect, and another leg in the archaic part of our mind, the unconscious.

One of the unconscious fantasies with which the words, 'Space does not exist', and 'Space is only an appearance', would seem, quite unmistakably, to be connected centres on the fear of space. Many people labour under some or other variant of agoraphobia; and not only does it take open and direct forms which seriously restrict a person's freedom, it is also capable of manifesting itself in subtle, displaced forms which are difficult to recognize. It should not, then, come to us as a great shock and as altogether surprising to learn that the invisible entrepreneur which backs the theatrical manoeuvring with the word 'space' is the fear of open, unfamiliar, or unprotected expanses *displaced* onto the word. Parmenides and many philosophers after him, including Bertrand Russell, have maintained that empty space is impossible; and it would not be surprising if in the depths of the minds of these thinkers there lurked the fear of finding themselves alone in an otherwise empty expanse, in Parmenides' 'unutterable and inconceivable' place where there is *nothing*. The fear of empty space when intellectualised in the form of a theory and displaced on to the phrase 'empty space' (or its equivalents) can be coped with more easily and with less pain than it can in its original form, and the defences against it may even yield intellectual pleasure. The metaphysician of the cosmic plenum quiets his inner panic in a game he plays with the term 'empty space': he fantasies its exorcism from language, while retaining the expression 'full space', or 'plenum'. A philosopher like Zeno, Bradley or Taylor goes further. He banishes the word 'space' from our vocabulary, again only in play, by riddling it with contradictions. He destroys it semantically. Or else he makes it harmless by confining its use to expressions which describe *mere* appearance. It may be observed parenthetically that Kant, who held, as one of his views about space, that 'space lies within the mind', or is 'in us', was a metaphysical Jonah who reversed the process and swallowed the whale. He made space safe for himself by introjecting it. As is well known, Kant never went more than a few miles from Königsberg, although his interests reached out to remote parts of the world, and even to the solar system, about whose origin he formulated a hypothesis which has recently been revived. Psychologically speaking, he could explore what was safe, within himself.[44] The words, 'Space lies within the mind', do not, as they appear, state a theory about space; instead, they are used as a secret description of a psychological feat.

The view that there is no such thing as space and that it exists only as an appearance has revealed itself to be a remarkable linguistic contrivance, a subterranean language change which does one piece of work at the conscious level of our mind and another piece of work at lower levels of our mind. The sentence, 'Space does not exist', embodies an unheralded, non-workaday alteration in the use of 'space', which produces the deception of making a profound claim about everyday phenomena and at the same time provides us with a highly refined medium for setting up defences against a painful emotion.

Notes

1. F. H. Bradley (1920), *Appearance and Reality*, London: Allen & Unwin, p. 2, 7th impression.

2. Ibid., p. 30.

3. Ibid., p. 37.

4. Euclid's *Elements*.

5. F. H. Bradley, *Appearance and Reality*, p. 37.

6. Ibid.

7. Ibid., p. 36.

8. Ibid., p. 38.

9. C. D. Broad (1927), *Scientific Thought*, New York: Harcourt Brace, p. 27.

10. F. H. Bradley, *Appearance and Reality*, p. 37.

11. Bertrand Russell (1914), *Our Knowledge of the External World*, Chicago: Open Court, pp. 7–8.

12. David Hume (1902), *An Enquiry Concerning Human Understanding*, Oxford: Clarendon Press, sec. VII, Part II, 2nd edn.

13. Ibid.

14. John Burnet (1928), *Greek Philosophy, Thales to Plato*, London: Macmillan, pp. 253 ff.

15. Ibid., p. 68.

16. L. Wittgenstein, *Tractatus Logico-Philosophicus*, 3.031.

17. F. H. Bradley, *Appearance and Reality*, p. 43.

18. See G. E. Moore's 'A Reply to My Critics', in *The Philosophy of G. E. Moore*, ed. P. A. Schilpp', The Library of Living Philosophers, vol. IV, p. 675, Northwestern University.

19. F. H. Bradley, *Appearance and Reality*, pp. 192–3.

20. Ibid., pp. 193–4.

21. A. J. Ayer (1954), *Philosophical Essays*, London: Macmillan, pp. 141–2.

22. F. H. Bradley, *Appearance and Reality*, p. 15.

23. G. E. Moore, 'A Reply to my Critics', p. 675.

24. F. H. Bradley, *Appearance and Reality*, p. 30.

25. Ibid.

26. G. E. Moore (1939), 'Proof of an External World', British Academy Lecture, *Proceedings of the British Academy*, vol. XXVIII. (Also in *Philosophical Papers*.)

27. F. H. Bradley, *Appearance and Reality*, p. 37.

28. C. D. Broad's word in a different philosophical connection, Introduction to *Scientific Thought*.

29. F. H. Bradley, *Appearance and Reality*.

30. A. E. Taylor (1912), *The Elements of Metaphysics* (1912), London: Methuen & Co., p. 250.

31. Taken from Hume (1888), *A Treatise of Human Nature*, Oxford: Clarendon Press, ed. L. A. Selby-Bigge, Part II, sec. 11.

32. Fragment 4. See *Selections from Early Greek Philosophy* (1947) ed. Milton Nahm, New York: F. S. Crofts, p. 122.

33. Cited by P. E. B. Jourdain (1918), *The Philosophy of Mr B*TR*ND R*SS*-LL*, London: Allen & Unwin, p. 63.

34. Georg Cantor (1883), 'On Linear Aggregates'.

35. *Dialogues Concerning the New Sciences* (1636). See Tobias Dantzig (1930), *Number, the Language of Science*, New York: Macmillan, pp. 208–10.

36. *Physica*, in *The Works of Aristotle*, Translated into English under the editorship of W. D. Ross (1930), Oxford: Clarendon Press, vol. II, Book III. 6.

37. This, of course, is a paradoxical thing to say, but it helps bring out a point of contrast.

38. Bertrand Russell, *Our Knowledge of the External World*, p. 121.

39. Hume, *A Treatise of Human Nature*, Bk. I, Part II, sec. 1.

40. Ibid., sec. 2.

41. F. H. Bradley, *Appearance and Reality*, p. 37. Also Hume's formulation, 'as extension is always a number, according to the common sentiment of metaphysicians, and never dissolves itself into any unit or indivisible quantity, it follows that extension can never at all exist.' *A Treatise of Human Nature*, Part II, sec. 11.

42. F. H. Bradley, *Appearance and Reality*, p. 36.

43. A. C. Ewing (1956/57), 'Pseudo-Solutions', *Proceedings of the Aristotelian Society*, p. 32.

44. For an interesting study on the fear of empty space, see Michael Balint's *Thrills and Regressions*.

9 THE PASSING OF AN ILLUSION

A belief that derives its strength from a wish rather than from evidence is an illusion. It sometimes happens that a belief which springs from and is sustained by a wish later turns out to be true, but when this happens the belief does not lose its quality of having been an illusion. The world is indifferent to our wishes, and illusions are seldom realised; the old saying that if wishes were horses beggars would ride, certainly applies to them. As is well known, Freud declared religion to be an illusion. To convince oneself of the correctness of his claim no more need be done than to notice the difference between the demands for evidence a scientist who is also religious places on his scientific propositions and those he places on the propositions laid down for him by his religion.

The thesis to be developed in these pages is that academic, reasoned philosophy, exemplified by the central doctrines of Aristotle, Anselm, Descartes, Hume and G. E. Moore, is an illusion, but an illusion which is different in a remarkable way from that presented by religion. To put it roughly, a set of religious beliefs is about reality and what we can expect from it. A philosophical system, which appears to be a set of propositions about the world, is not at all what it appears to be. Language can be used to express illusions, but things can be done with language to create the deceptive illusion that words are being used to express propositions about things. Philosophy, it turns out, is a linguistically contrived illusion. It is hardly an exaggeration to describe it as an unconscious semantic swindle, by which the swindler is also swindled. If one becomes attentive to a philosopher's defence of his discipline, what stands out is its likeness to the defences of religion, underlying which is a seriously weakened ability to be critical. Thus, a philosopher whose attention is called to the bewildering fact that philosophy, which is by no means a young discipline, has not achieved a single uncontested result will show a remarkably weakened sense of curiosity, coupled with blithe unconcern.

Technical philosophy, which supports its claims with reasoned arguments, holds an ambiguous place amongst the disciplines that profess to give us knowledge of things. It is taken by philosophers, and by many people who have peripheral acquaintance with it, to be a kind of science, but not just one amongst the sciences. It is thought to be more basic than the standard sciences. Not only does it make deeper investigations into the nature of things, it also critically examines the presuppositions on which the special sciences rest. It is also realised, sometimes explicitly, that philosophy makes no use of the modes of verification employed in astronomy, chemistry, biology, or by any of the other natural sciences. It has no laboratories of its own; there is no such thing as a philosophical experiment. And if, as the language of philosophers sometimes suggests, it resorts to observations, it seems to have no need for instruments which extend the reach of our senses. Some philosophers have the notion that an underlying wish of many theoretical physicists is the desire to attain a philosophical understanding of 'the inner nature of reality'.[1] Nevertheless, it is realised by everyone, however indistinctly, that a physicist who embarks on a *philosophical* investigation into the nature of things — the outcome of which are such views as that things are collections of minds and that there are abstract entities — leaves behind him the observational and experimental methods of the sciences. It would seem that a philosophical investigation of things, which probes into their ultimate nature, requires methods more refined than the gross ones of the special sciences, methods which differ from them *in kind*. But what these methods are is shrouded in mystery. One philosopher said: 'Whistling in the dark is not the method of true philosophy.'[2] These words have the ring of a magical reassurance formula. It may well be that a philosopher who thinks 'that philosophical problems are genuine and that they are capable of being solved'[3] is whistling in the dark, and is trying to reassure himself against the failure of philosophy to produce results.

A number of the great figures in philosophy who became sensitive to the total absence of undisputed philosophical propositions have placed the blame for this *malaise* on the absence of a correct method of procedure, and have tried to make good the lack. Names that will immediately come to mind are Descartes, Kant, Bertrand Russell and G. E. Moore. As was to be expected, the riot of claims and counter-claims has continued with abandon and unabated enthusiasm. But there is not the slightest sign that reasoned philosophy will eventually reach a stage when it can begin to boast of ordered progress. Nevertheless, the work of Descartes, whose model of an ordered science was mathematics, and that of other philosophers has tended to bring philosophy out of its obscurity and to make somewhat more visible its inner character.

The picture of the philosopher as the investigator of reality who goes about his work without any of the tools of science demands an explanation. We should not treat anyone with respect who tells us what is in books which he has never opened and into whose pages he has never looked. But the philosopher is, on the surface at least, treated with respect, even though one sometimes gets the impression that it is the word 'philosophy' rather than its special subject-matter that is deferred to. Freud has remarked that philosophy 'is of interest to only a small number even of the top layer of intellectuals and is scarcely intelligible to anyone else'.[4] The philosopher would lose the interest of even the top layer of intellectuals, however, if he could produce no credentials attesting to the validity of his pursuit of cosmic knowledge, no methodology which would support the notion that his pursuit was both sober and responsible. C. D. Broad, who explicitly called attention to the great difference between the method of philosophy and that of the natural sciences, stated, 'Experiments are not made, because they would be utterly useless.'[5] Philosophy resembles pure mathematics 'at least in the respect that neither has any use for experiment'.[6] Broad distinguishes between speculative philosophy and what he calls critical philosophy, which is 'the analysis and definition of our fundamental concepts, and the clear statement and resolute criticism of our fundamental beliefs'.[7] The criticism of a belief is not different from the analysis of a concept or a proposition, and the claim about the method employed by critical philosophy that comes out distinctly is that it is the analytical scrutiny of concepts. Broad does not say what the method is for checking the statements of speculative philosophy, whether it is analysis or experiment, but he does say that critical philosophy performs a task not performed by any of the natural sciences: 'The other sciences *use* the concepts and *assume* the beliefs: Critical Philosophy tries to analyse the former and to criticise the latter. Thus, so long as science and Critical Philosophy keep to their own spheres, there is no possibility of conflict between them, since their subject-matter is quite different.'[8] No one can fail to see the striking similarity between Broad's attempt to reconcile critical philosophy and the natural sciences, and the attempt to reconcile religion with them.

What the analysis of concepts (and of propositions) is, and what it is supposed to achieve for us, is obscure. Some philosophers think that it consists in making explicit the components of the concepts we have of things, that doing this consists in making 'our ideas clear', and thus that it can yield no new information about the nature of the things falling under the concepts. Wittgenstein expressed this notion in the following way: 'A philosophical work consists essentially of elucidations. Philosophy does not result in "philosophical propositions", but rather in the clarification of propositions.'[9] Other philosophers, however, have the idea that the analysis of a concept is capable of yielding new information about the things exemplifying it, that analysis is capable of yielding facts about the inner constitution of things. The underlying suggestion is that analysis is a more refined method of investigation than either experiment or observation, and that it continues at the point where these must leave off. Still other philosophers think that what is called the analysis of concepts is just the analysis of the uses of terminology in a language. This idea represents philosophy as being a kind of linguistic investigation. The picture of the philosopher as the investigator of language seems less mystifying than the picture of the philosopher as probing into concepts, but each presents us with an enigma.

On the view that philosophical analysis is just clarification, whether it articulates concepts or explicates the rules for the use of terms in a language, philosophy cannot be construed as an investigation of the world, an investigation which informs us of the existence of things and of how they operate with respect to each other. Analysis may be preliminary to an ontological investigation but cannot be such an investigation itself. And plainly, if philosophical methodology is confined to analysis, philosophy can tell us nothing about the world and can give the philosopher nothing that he seeks. On the view that the analysis of our concepts is an instrument for obtaining knowledge of the world, we find ourselves in the presence of a riddle. For this view implies that the concept of a thing contains hidden information about the nature of the thing. To see this it need only be realised that the meaning of a word, for example 'planet', is a concept: to say that a general word names a concept is another way of saying it has a meaning. Thus the analysis of a concept is no more than the analysis of the meaning of a general word. Now if the analysis of the meaning of a word is to give us new information about things, we shall have to suppose either that we have given more meaning to our words than we are aware of, or that our words have more meaning than we have assigned to them. Neither alternative is acceptable. Words do not have meanings by nature, meanings they have not been given; and we can hardly suppose that we give to words more meanings than we consciously assign to them. But in either case analysis of the meaning of a word would be of no use. The analysis of a known meaning of a word cannot bring to light an unknown meaning, since the unknown meaning cannot be *part* of the known meaning. It would seem that no inference from concepts to things can be the result of an analysis.

Kant said that we find in nature what we ourselves have put there. Reformulated in terms of concepts, this comes to saying that we find in the meanings of our words what we ourselves have put into them. But sober reflection should make us see that no philosopher actually thinks that we put hidden information about things into the meanings of our words, something we unwittingly do and later *discover*. This idea supposes that we have more knowledge of the nature of things than we actually have, knowledge that we had prior to the investigation of our meanings. The underlying fantasy is that to which Plato gave explicit expression in the *Phaedo*, i.e. his reminiscence theory, the theory that we are born with unremembered knowledge. The other view, *viz.* that philosophical analysis is the analysis of the use of terminology, implies an odd delusion which we cannot really attribute to any philosopher. This is that unknown facts of ontology can be inferred from a scrutiny of words. In sum, the inferential leap from concepts to things, as well as the leap from words to things, cannot be justified by the analysis of either words or concepts. And how anyone could *appear* to think otherwise will have to be explained.

The picture of the philosophical cosmologist is that of someone who obtains knowledge of things by looking more deeply into usage than the lexicographer or by reflecting in a special way on concepts. The reason given in support of a philosophical claim, e.g. that motion does not exist, or that in addition to concrete sense data there are abstract entities, is not a piece of empirical evidence, either observational or experimental. To some philosophers it appears to be the eliciting of the consequences of a concept, while to others it appears to be the explication of the rules for the use of expressions. In either case the philosopher is pictured as trying to obtain knowledge of what there is at a remove from what there is. And to many people the attempt to do this suggests that the philosopher is suffering from some sort of delusion. Thus to Broad, the linguistic philosopher (who behaves as if a philosophical examination of usage will teach him things about the world) seems to be suffering from 'one of the strangest delusions that has ever flourished in academic circles'.[10] But the same words apply to the philosopher who imagines that the analytical examination of concepts will give him new information about things. To suppose that factual information about things is obtainable by studying objects other than the things themselves is to suffer from a bizarre delusion.

The philosopher appears to suffer from this delusion while also being free from it. His talk throws an aura of unreality over his work, while his behaviour is that of the normal man who knows how to live in the world. G. E. Moore has remarked on a paradox which deserves more attention than it has received, namely, that philosophers 'have been able to hold sincerely, as part of their philosophical creed, propositions inconsistent with what they themselves *knew* to be true.'[11] And if, as seems to be the case, a philosopher consults either usage or concepts rather than things in the attempt to discover facts about them, basic or otherwise, Moore's paradox clearly applies to him: philosophers have been able to believe that they can discover facts of ontology by consulting verbal usage or concepts while knowing their belief to be false. To help explain this odd state of affairs, Moore observed that a philosopher is able to hold his unusual beliefs in what he called 'a philosophic moment'. But whatever the bewitchment is that takes over in a philosophic moment, the philosopher's behaviour remains normal. He does not give the impression of being a somnambulist or in any way suffering from an abnormal state of mind.

Philosophical analysis is represented as an ultra-refined scientific instrument which permits the philosopher to determine the nature and structure of reality without leaving his study. But it would indeed take remarkable powers of self-deception to be able to accept this representation at face-value. We have to say that he carries on his work seriously, which certainly implies self-deception of some sort; but we also have to say that *in some way* he is not deceived. To illustrate briefly, a philosopher who seriously says that motion does not exist is in some way deceived and yet is not deceived, as is shown by the rest of his talk and his behaviour. It will be clear that philosophy is in an equivocal position, which would explain its being approached with ambivalence. Philosophy uses reason, which wins our respect, but attempts to obtain knowledge of things without going to the things, which makes it seem ludicrous. Freud exemplified the ambivalence many people feel toward philosophy, as the following passage shows.

Philosophy is not opposed to science, it behaves like a science and works in part by the same methods; it departs from it, however, by clinging to the illusion of being able to present a picture of the universe which is without gaps and is coherent, though one which is bound to collapse with every fresh advance in our knowledge. It goes astray in its method of over-estimating the epistemological value of our logical operations and by accepting other sources of knowledge such as intuition. And it often seems that the poet's derisive comment is not unjustified when he says of the philosopher:

Mit seinen Nachmützen und Schlafrokfetzen
Stopft er die Lücken des Weltenbauc.[12] [13]

It is clear from this passage that Freud had two conflicting ideas about philosophy: it works in part at least by the methods of science but it nevertheless is the target of jibes. The background picture Freud seems to have had of the philosopher is that he is a kind of scientist who cuts a comical figure.

Ernest Jones, who interested himself in philosophy, also had conflicting ideas about it. Sometimes it seemed to him to consist of 'tenuous sophistries that have no real meaning',[14] and at other times it seemed to be a highly abstract and important discipline. Thus, he criticised Jung who postulated a psychic toxin which poisons the brain by remarking that 'his grasp of philosophical principles was so insecure that it was little wonder that they later degenerated into mystical obscurantism'.[15] About Greek science, however, he said: 'It is no chance that when the Greek genius faltered at the threshold of scientific thought by disdaining the experimental method and enmeshing itself in the quandaries of philosophy, it was medical study alone which forced it into some relationship, however strained, with reality.'[16] There can be no question that some perception into the workings of philosophy created in Jones conflicting attitudes to it, which he was able temporarily to resolve only by attributing great mental power to philosophers and disparaging his own ability in 'abstract fields'.[17]

The reasons Freud gave for the condition philosophy finds itself in are that it over-estimates the 'epistemological value of our logical operations', and that it makes use of intuition. It is not clear what Freud had in mind by intuition, nor is it clear what he meant by logical operations. He seems to be alluding to an idea entertained by many philosophers from Leibniz on, the idea expressed by Bertrand

Russell's statement that logic is the essence of philosophy. But the idea that logic is the tool of philosophical investigation is nothing different from the idea, going all the way back to Parmenides, that analysis is capable of uncovering basic truths about reality. As has already been remarked, philosophical analysis is a method which a philosopher can only use at a remove from the phenomena about which he professes to be seeking knowledge. His placing exclusive reliance on philosophical analysis is bound up with a 'disdain' for the experimental method. It succeeds only, to use Jones' words, in enmeshing him in the quandaries of philosophy, or as Wittgenstein graphically put it, in imprisoning the fly in the fly-bottle. If we look again at the passage quoted from Freud, what suggests itself is that the philosopher works under the domination of fantasied omni-science, which is concealed by talk of logic and analysis. Freud's remark that the philosopher over-estimates the epistemological power of logic is a distorted way of saying that the philosopher imagines that he can plumb the secrets of nature by the power of his mind alone. This of course fits in with what *in some way* is known to everyone, that the philosopher does not trouble to go to nature herself in his quest for knowledge of the essential nature of things.

The philosopher indeed whistles in the dark, for fantasied omnipotence of thought is the mainspring of philosophical methodology. Spinoza, who in his *Ethics* lays out the geography of the cosmos, declared that the order and connection of things is the same as the order and connection of ideas. Parmenides held that thought coincides precisely with being; and Hegel laid down as his basic postulate that the real is the rational.

We now have two pictures of the philosopher. One is the familiar picture of the philosopher as the cosmic explorer whose method does not require him to leave his study. The philosopher who naturally comes to mind in this connection is Spinoza: he did not find it necessary to leave his room in The Hague to delineate reality. The other, which is behind the first, is that of someone who has not been able to relinquish his narcissistic attachment to the power of his own thought, in other words, of someone who is still under the domination of mental megalomania. Aborigines speak of time before memory as dream time, and it would seem that a philosopher has found a way of giving satisfaction to a stage of development of his own dream time in the practice of philosophy. Behind the façade provided by philosophical analysis he is able to give gratification to the wish to encompass reality, like divinity, with his mind alone. His wish keeps him at a sufficient distance from the activity to prevent him from seeing what it is, and his activity gives him imagined realisation of his wish. Technical philosophy may truly be described as a sophisticated but delusive way of satisfying a wish which cannot be satisfied in reality. Moore invoked the expression 'philosophical moment' to minimise the strange state of mind that permits a philosopher to say without embarrassment such things as that time is unreal and that things do not exist. We have a possible explanation, at least in part, of what a philosophic moment is, namely, that for the moment he is under the domination of an unconscious wish. This, however, cannot be the entire account. There needs to be a further explanation of philosophical activity which will help us understand why philosophical statements that appear to be about the world can be investigated away from the world.

The narcissism which finds expression in an unconscious belief that one is in possession of stupendous mental powers acts as a sentinel against trespassers who might be led by curiosity to try to obtain a closer view of things. The philosophical investigation of existence can be nothing more than a delusive way of gratifying the wish for omniscience, and the end result of the investigation as well as the investigation itself are protected from our scrutiny by the strength of the narcissistic investment in them. Without protection the philosophical creation would evaporate into thin air and leave behind a semantic residue that could deceive no one. If we can ward off the influence of a philosophic moment and draw sufficiently close to a philosophical theory, e.g. the theory that matter does not exist, what we shall see is a contrived re-edition of familiar terminology the sole function of which, apart from its connection with unconscious material, is to create an intellectual illusion, and not to describe or declare the existence of a kind of object.

To get a preliminary understanding of what goes on in philosophy it is necessary to see clearly the difference between using an expression in a statement about a thing and mentioning that expression in a statement about its use in the language. This distinction is elementary but important to keep in mind. For it is possible to formulate sentences which make no explicit mention of terminology but whose sole content is, nevertheless, verbal; and therein lie the seeds of philosophy. To anticipate, it is by means of the non-verbal façade, i.e. the ontological form of speech, that the philosopher, whose work consists of nothing more than verbal manoeuverings, is able to create the image of himself as a cosmological cartographer.

The sentence 'A cockerel is incapable of doing arithmetic' uses the word 'cockerel' to refer to an object about which it makes an assertion. The sentence '"Cockerel" means a young male fowl' mentions the word 'cockerel' instead of using it. The first sentence may be said to have ontological import: it uses language to state a claim that is not about the use a term has in a language. The second sentence states a claim, true or false, about the use, or the literal meaning, of a term, and clearly has only verbal import. The sentence 'A cockerel is a young male fowl' is unlike the verbal sentence '"Cockerel" means a young male fowl' in that it does not mention the word 'cockerel', and in this respect it is like the non-verbal sentence 'A cockerel is incapable of doing arithmetic'. The content of the sentence 'A cockerel is a young male fowl' is nevertheless verbal, and this tends to be veiled by the non-verbal form of speech in which the sentence is formulated. Understanding it, just as understanding the ontological sentence 'A cockerel is incapable of doing arithmetic', requires knowing the fact expressed by the verbal sentence; but getting to know that what it says is true, unlike learning that what the ontological sentence says is true, requires learning nothing in addition to the fact stated by the verbal sentence. It may be helpful to put the difference[18] between the verbal sentence and the non-verbal one by saying that the verbal sentence records what the non-verbal sentence, which mentions no word, presents. The likeness between the sentence with ontological content and the non-verbal sentence whose content is wholly verbal, lies in the mode of discourse in which they are framed (what I have elsewhere called 'the ontological idiom').

Making perspicuous the likenesses and differences between the three sentences is important because it brings out the fact that the verbal content of an utterance may be obscured by the form of speech in which the utterance is framed. It is possible for an ontologically formulated sentence whose content is verbal to create a delusive idea as to what the sentence is about. To illustrate briefly, the sentence 'A cockerel is a young male fowl' can be rewritten as an entailment sentence: 'Being a cockerel *entails* being a young male fowl.' To many philosophers the entailment sentence presents the appearance of expressing a proposition about essential properties of an object, properties the object cannot fail to have. These, as against non-essential properties which can be learned only by experience, are thought of as being discovered by analytical penetration into the concept under which the object falls. To see that this picture is delusive all we need do is translate the entailment sentence back into 'A cockerel is a young male fowl', the content of which can be seen to be the fact stated by the verbal sentence. Seeing that the ontologically formulated sentence has verbal content evaporates a metaphysical theory.

It is important to notice that not only is a matter of established usage sometimes brought before us in the ontological idiom, but that re-edited terminology is frequently announced in it. Sometimes this is done merely for convenience, to avoid the more clumsy verbal form of locution. But sometimes it is done for the striking effect which presenting a redefinition in the ontological idiom is capable of producing. In a recent address to a Jewish audience the statement was made that assimilation is ethnic genocide. It is quite clear in this case that the word 'genocide' was being redefined, and that the application of the word was being *stretched* by an act of fiat so as to apply to whatever 'assimilation' is used to cover. The verbal sentence corresponding to the ontologically formulated sentence 'Assimilation is ethnic genocide' corresponds to, 'Assimilation should be called "ethnic genocide"'. This certainly lacks the dramatic quality of the ontologically formulated utterance, which can produce the idea that an unsuspected property of assimilation is being disclosed. The way to dispel this idea is to show that the statement has only verbal content, *viz.* an arbitrary redefinition, which fact tends to be hidden by the ontological mode of speech.

According to the thesis to be developed in these pages a philosophical theory resembles in important respects the ontologically formulated statement about assimilation. Its content is verbal and it is capable nevertheless of creating the idea that it expresses a theory about things. The main difference between a philosophical utterance and the statement about assimilation is in the durability of the intellectual illusion it generates, which makes it more difficult to expose the underlying verbal content. In the case of an utterance like 'Motion is self-contradictory and exists only in appearance' or 'Ultimate reality is undifferentiated experience' the philosophic moment in which it is accepted as true or rejected as false undoubtedly has support from subterranean sources. This is to say that philosophical utterances give expression to unconscious clusters of ideas which serve to keep us at a distance from them. Nevertheless, the only way, to use Wittgenstein's word, of 'dissolving' the erroneous impression created by them is to expose the verbal content behind the ontological façade. In the case of the statement that motion is really impossible and exists only in appearance, what needs to be shown is that the word 'motion' is academically deprived of its use. Doing this consists in part of showing the difference between the sentence 'The images on the screen are not really in motion although they appear to be' and the philosophical sentence 'The arrow in flight is really stationary'.

The thesis to be developed here is that a philosophical theory is an illusion which is created by presenting in the ontological mode of speech a gerrymandered piece of terminology. It is a two-layer structure consisting, on the one hand, of re-edited nomenclature, and on the other, of the idea, which is generated by the way the nomenclature is introduced, that words are being used to express a theory instead of to herald a redefinition. Joined to these is a third and less accessible layer, a complex of unconscious fantasies. It will be maintained that unconscious ideas are given expression by a philosophical utterance; it is these which hold the philosopher in bondage to his theory and prevent him from seeing it for the meagre linguistic contrivance that it is. To allude again to Wittgenstein's metaphor of the fly in the fly-bottle, it is the unconscious fantasy that holds the philosopher captive and makes it so difficult to show him the way out. Nevertheless, the only way to lead him out is by laying bare the linguistic content of his philosophical utterances. Once this is done we can be free to conjecture regarding some of the unconscious material on which a philosophical structure rests.

One philosophical problem, which reaches all the way back to Parmenides, is linked in a special way with the notion of analysis as a method of investigating the world of things. It may be usefully considered first in the series of views to be examined. This problem revolves around the rationalistic claim that we cannot think of what does not exist. The two basic traditions in philosophy — empiricism and rationalism — appear to be antithetical, the one to all appearances accepting the senses as a source of knowledge of things, the other placing its reliance on reason alone, or at any rate the weight of its reliance on reason. There are good grounds for thinking that the difference between rationalism and empiricism is not, as it would seem, in their methods of investigation. There is reason to think that behind the scenes empiricism, like rationalism, rejects the employment of the senses in its investigations, and in the words of Plato 'examines existence through concepts'. Parmenides urged that we turn away from the senses and use 'the test of reason' in the investigation of reality; and if we can look behind the empiricists' talk, what we see is that under their semantic skin they are Parmenideans. There are many and very different ways of saying the same thing in philosophy. There is even reason for thinking that the most sober of all philosophers, G. E. Moore, who explicitly protested that analysis was not the only thing he tried to do,[19] nevertheless was confined to the technique of analysis. One philosopher has supported Moore's protest, claiming that it was justified on the grounds that 'Moore also looked to philosophy to determine what kinds of things there were in the universe'.[20] But looking to philosophy to determine what exists is neither to look at things nor to experiment with them: the investigation can only be analytical and completely removed from things.

The claim that the philosophical empiricist is a disguised rationalist[21] cannot be gone into now. The question of present concern is whether it is possible to think of what does not exist. A review[22] of A. N. Prior's *Objects of Thought* contained the following statement: 'in Part II the problems chiefly discussed are those raised by the fact that what we think *about* may be *non-existent.*' It is a curiosity, but one often met with, that what some philosophers declare to be a *fact* other philosophers declare to be impossible. Thus Parmenides, and many other philosophers with him, took the position that it is impossible to think of what does not exist. One formulation of this position is the following: 'It is impossible to think what is not and it is impossible for what cannot be thought to be. The great question, *Is it or is it not?*, is therefore equivalent to the question, *Can it be thought or not?*'[23]

One consideration in support of the proposition that it is impossible to think of what does not exist is that thought must have an object. To think is not to think of nothing, it is to think of something, which therefore must exist, as not to exist is to be nothing. Wittgenstein put the matter in the following way:

> How can we think what is not the case? If I think that King's College is on fire when it is not on fire, the fact of its being on fire does not exist. Then how can I think of it? How can we hang a thief who does not exist? . . . Our answer could be put in this form: 'I can't hang him when he doesn't exist; but I can look for him when he doesn't exist.'[24]

A Parmenidean rejoinder would no doubt be that we cannot *really* look for a thief who does not exist. The object of our search and of our thought equally with the object of our act of hanging him cannot be a thief who does not exist.

Some philosophers who explicitly reject the rationalistic claim of Parmenides seem nevertheless to reinstate it in a more subtle form, under the cover of a puzzling distinction. Thus Russell, who rejected the existential theory of judgement, *viz.* that 'every proposition is concerned with something that exists',[25] wrote:

> Whatever can be thought of has being, and its being is a precondition, not a result, of its being thought of. As regards the existence of an object of thought, however, nothing can be inferred from the fact of its being thought of, since it certainly does not exist in the thought which thinks of it.[26]

He observed that, 'Misled by neglect of being, people have supposed that what does not exist is nothing.'[27]

The term 'being' has two uses which are relevant here. In one it has the meaning of a kind of thing or entity, and in this use it is correct to speak of the Greek gods as beings; in the other, it has the meaning of existence, and in this sense it is, in everyday language, correct to say that the Greek gods have no being, i.e. do not exist. It does not seem too much to suppose, for the present at least, that confounding these two senses of 'being' is responsible for the philosophical distinction between the terms 'has being' and 'has existence', which serves to reinstate in a subtly disguised form a claim that is explicitly rejected. We may say that some things which exist are beings and that other things which exist are not beings (e.g. shadows, sneezes), but that everything that exists has being. Whatever has being (regardless of whether it is a being or a kind of thing) is part of what there is and exists. Hence the claim that whatever can be thought of has being, implies the Parmenidean proposition that whatever can be thought of exists. Russell remarked that 'Everyone except a philosopher can see the difference between a post and my idea of a post',[28] and there is reason for thinking that only a philosopher could see a difference between saying that a thing has being and saying that it exists.

F. H. Bradley, the twentieth-century Oxford Parmenides, appears to have held that we cannot think of the non-existent. The following two remarks suggest this as clearly as anything else he says in his *Appearance and Reality*: 'to suppose that mere thought without facts could either be real, or could reach to truth, is evidently absurd';[29] and 'A mere thought would mean an ideal content held apart from existence. But (as we have learned) to hold a thought is always somehow, even against our will, to refer it to the Real.'[30] Parenthetically, it is worth noting that underlying the so-called consistency theory of truth is the notion that conceivability and existence coincide, i.e. that the existence and nature of things can be derived from our self-consistent thoughts, and the non-existent from our self-contradictory thoughts.

Moore, who rejected the Parmenidean thesis, nevertheless constructed an interesting argument for it.

> 'How' (I imagine he [Bradley] would ask) 'can a thing "appear" or even "be thought of" unless it is there to appear and to be thought of? To say that it appears or is thought of, and yet that there is no such thing, is plainly self-contradictory. A thing cannot have a property, unless it is there to have it, and since unicorns and temporal facts *do* have the property of being thought of, there certainly must be such things. When I think of a unicorn, what I am thinking of is certainly not nothing; if it were nothing, then, when I think of a griffin, I should also be thinking of nothing, and there would be no difference between thinking of a griffin and thinking of a unicorn. But there certainly is a difference; and what can the difference be except that in the one case what I am thinking of is a unicorn, and in the other a griffin? And if the unicorn is what I am thinking of, then there certainly must be a unicorn, in spite of the fact that unicorns are unreal.'[31]

Moore thought it obvious that this argument contained a fallacy, and he suggested that people might even think it 'too gross' for Bradley to have been guilty of it (although he was quite sure that Bradley was guilty of it). An outsider to philosophy, to whom it is represented as a highly rational discipline, one that uses exact analytical tools, might be shocked to witness one known and important philosopher declare the view of another known and important philosopher to be a gross error. He would be even more shocked and astonished to learn that the mistake has been in existence, and never without its adherents, for a truly remarkable number of centuries. In philosophy 'grossly mistaken' claims seem to have an infinite viability: what is a plain falsehood to some people remains a clear and indestructible truth to others for generation after generation.

We are, to be sure, familiar with this kind of situation in religion, where it is not considered to be an enigma. But to discover that it exists everywhere in a discipline which parades as a *demonstrative science* is to be faced with an enigma that challenges our intelligence. To leave this for the moment, however, it is interesting and important to notice that although the Parmenidean–Bradleian 'mistake' is crass, Moore confesses to not being sure what the mistake is in the claim that our being able to think of a unicorn is sufficient to prove that there is one.

It seems to him that the mistake (that is, the main mistake) consists of supposing that the statement 'I am thinking of a unicorn' is of the same form as the statement 'I am hunting a lion', whereas in fact they are different in a crucial way. The second statement is equivalent to 'There are lions (at least one) and I am hunting a lion',

$(\exists x)$ (x is a lion. I am hunting x),

while 'it is obvious enough to common sense' that the first statement has no like equivalent, although 'their grammatical expression shows no trace of the difference'.[32] A philosopher always has a rejoinder (which is perhaps what made Moore not quite certain that the 'mistake' was a mistake), and a Parmenidean would respond that the philosopher of common sense was begging the question in claiming that the statement 'I am thinking of a unicorn' does not entail the statement 'There are unicorns'. It would be urged that instead of meeting the argument, which supports the thesis that the existence of the thought of a thing implies the existence of a thing corresponding to the thought, Moore actually does no more than assume the counter-thesis. It is easy to expand on this defence against Moore and say that if the analysis of 'I am hunting a lion' into a conjunction of statements *is* correct, then that is also the correct analysis of 'I am thinking of a unicorn',

$(\exists x)$ (x is a unicorn. I am thinking of x).

Wittgenstein's remark that although we cannot hang a thief who does not exist, we can look for one who does not exist, which he took to be an *answer* to the Parmenidean claim, would also be rejected as a *petitio*. The rejoinder would be that just as I cannot hang a thief who does not exist, so I cannot look for him nor yet think of him. If I could hang him, he must exist; if I can look for him, he must exist;

and also, if I can think of him, he must exist. The observation that is relevant at this point is that if the words 'It is possible to think of what does not exist' give the correct answer to the question 'Is it possible to think of what does not exist?', then a Parmenidean knows this as well as did Moore and Wittgenstein. The important question to investigate is the nature of the Parmenidean thesis. Do the words 'Whatever can be thought of exists', or the words 'It is impossible to think of what does not exist', express an experiential proposition, or do they express an *a priori* proposition, or are they intelligible but express neither an *a priori* nor an experiential proposition?

There is no question about the kind of claim the words *seem* to express. They give every appearance of making a statement about what we can think and about how things are related to our thoughts. In fact so vivid and lively is this appearance that to deny, or even doubt, that they do make such a statement would seem to indicate an impairment in one's sense of reality. Nor is it to be doubted that, at the conscious level, it is the idea that the words make a factual claim about thoughts and things which wins and holds the attention of philosophers, both those who reject the idea as false as well as those who embrace it as an ontological truth. This idea is as self-evident and compelling as once was the idea that the earth is flat. The strange thing is that the known points of detail which upset the idea about the earth and enabled Aristarchus to calculate the earth's circumference to a remarkable degree of accuracy were thrown into shadow and forgotten. Undoubtedly it was the alarming astronomical picture associated with the new idea which required that it be lost to memory. In philosophy also small known points of detail which, when investigated, lead to disconcerting revelations have continuously remained in the shadow of inattention. One of these is the curious intractability of philosophical disagreements, in the present instance the truly strange intractability of the disagreement over whether it is possible to think of what does not exist. Both Descartes and Kant expressed their dissatisfaction with the total anarchy of opinions in philosophy, but neither turned out to be an Aristarchus.

If we reflect with detachment on the words 'Whatever we think of exists', we will realise that, however a philosopher is using them, he is not using them to state a claim that is founded on experience or to which experience is in any conceivable way relevant. If, like the words 'Whatever we wish comes to be', their use was to describe an alleged state of affairs, the disagreement over whether the state of affairs actually obtains would have been resolved long ago, if indeed it would ever have come into existence. A person who holds that it is impossible to think of what does not exist has not come to his notion as a result of *trying* in a number of instances to think of something that does not exist and failing in each instance. And a philosopher who declares that whatever we think of exists has not been taught by experience that for every thought of a thing there exists a thing. His statement is not an inductive generalisation from observed concomitances of thoughts and things: the thought of an elephant with an actual elephant, the thought of a dolphin with an actual dolphin, the thought of a buttercup with an actual buttercup, etc.

A generalisation which issues from a series of concomitances that experience discovers, such that the dissociation of any of the observed concomitances is possible in principle, is one which, no matter how secure experience shows it to be, is nevertheless a generalisation to which an exception is conceivable. If we look on the claim that every thought has a corresponding real object as an inductive generalisation, we are faced with a bewildering puzzle: what some philosophers cite as confuting instances, as cases which upset the generalisation, other philosophers maintain are *not* confuting instances. A philosopher who cites as an exception his thought of a purely imaginary creature, such as a unicorn or a dragon, finds that his example is rejected as not really going against the general claim. The difference of opinion amongst philosophers over the putative counter-example appears itself to be factual. If, however, we examine it with care we can see that the generalisation is not empirical and neither is the disagreement over the example.

To suppose otherwise — that is, to suppose the difference of opinion about whether an actual unicorn corresponds to the thought of a unicorn is factual — leaves us puzzled about what could possibly resolve the dispute. For the experience of the philosopher who insists that there is a unicorn is not different from that of the philosopher who denies that there is. The one does not have a delusive perception of a creature which does not exist, nor does the other fail to perceive a creature that does exist, although the factual interpretation implies either that the Parmenidean philosopher suffers from something comparable to an hallucination or that the commonsense philosopher suffers from a kind of selective blindness. We can hardly be criticised for being reluctant to accept this implication about the minds of philosophers on either side of the issue. But if we reject the implied consequence of the natural interpretation of the Parmenidean view, we also have to reject the construction it is natural to place on the dispute.

We approach the correct, paradox-free understanding of the words 'You cannot think of a unicorn that does not exist' and of the general statement that it is impossible to think of what does not exist, when we cease confining our attention to a single disputed example. We then realise that *every* instance cited as being a case of someone thinking of what does not exist would be rejected as being such an instance and is instead declared to be a case of thinking of what does exist. If for the sake or argument we allow that we are mistaken in supposing that unicorns do not exist and that dinosaurs no longer exist, and go on to ask our philosophical adversary for a *hypothetical* instance of someone thinking of what does not exist, we shall find him unable to provide us with one. He cannot say what it would be like to think of what does not exist. With regard to an accepted generalisation like Bernoulli's law that an increase in the velocity of a fluid is regularly accompanied by a decrease in the pressure it exerts, it is in principle possible to *describe* an instance which, if it existed, would upset the generalisation. An instance of the velocity of a fluid being increased without the occurrence of a corresponding decrease in its pressure is conceivable even though this never in fact happens. This shows what might be called a logical difference, a difference in kind, between the philosophical generalisation and the scientific one, and it helps us see in an improved light the nature of the disputed instance. It helps us see that a philosopher who insists that unicorns exist is not under the domination of a fanciful imagination.

The fact that the philosopher cannot give us an idea of what he would accept as upsetting his general claim shows that the philosophical claim that whatever we can conceive has real existence, unlike Bernoulli's law, is not open to falsification by any theoretical experience. It is not an experiential proposition, however much the language expressing it suggests. And that it is not a proposition which could be either confuted or supported by observation or by any experiment fits in with the kind of evidence adduced in its support, an argument. The words 'I am thinking of a non-existent unicorn' or 'I am thinking of the highwayman Dick Turpin who no longer exists' are rejected not as presenting false empirical claims, but as stating what is logically inconceivable.

A classical scholar remarked that an ancient view, according to which there was neither motion, change, nor variety of phenomena in the world, flouted all experience and was supported by an argument in which evidence played no role. In his opinion the view is 'a way of thinking about things which is perpetually refuted by actual contact with things'.[33] As is known, Moore has said something similar, to which philosophers have paid no discernible heed.[34] We should indeed think a person was suffering from a deranged state of mind who held beliefs about things which are 'perpetually refuted' by his actual experience of them or who held views about things which he knew to be false. And we should think philosophers a strange breed who were able to believe that one cannot think of what does not exist, of a leprechaun at his writing desk, or a winged hippopotamus, or of a friend who is no more. However, the strangeness surrounding the philosophical view, which is held solely on the basis of an argument regardless of sense evidence, is largely dissipated once we realise that it is not empirical and thus cannot go against any experience, actual or possible. As the philosopher uses the words 'No one can think of what is not', whatever their literal import may turn out to be, they do not express an empirical proposition, one which flies in the face of everyday experience. A philosopher who states that it is impossible to think of what is not the case does not recognise that his statement is perpetually refuted by 'actual contact with things', not because he fails to see a glaring inconsistency with his experience but because it is not the kind of statement that experience could conceivably refute. It cannot be upset (or confirmed) by experience because it is not about a possible experience, about what we can and cannot think. The philosopher does not recognise that his statement is inconsistent with what he knows to be true, namely, that he can and frequently does think of what is not or of what no longer is, because it is not inconsistent with what he knows.

The problem which faces us is how to understand the philosopher's words. Once we give up the notion that they are used to make an empirical claim, to the testing of which experience is relevant, it seems entirely natural to adopt the notion that they make an *a priori* claim about what we can and cannot think. Seen in this way, they appear to state a proposition which is like that expressed by the words 'It is impossible to think of an oblong with no more than three sides' or by the words 'It is impossible to ride a horse that does not exist'. We are accustomed in philosophy to the distinction that is made between the accidental properties of a thing, properties which it could be conceived of as not having, and its essential properties, without which it cannot be conceived. We are also familiar with the philosophical distinction between necessary existence and contingent existence.[35] Leading philosophers have maintained, for example, that a perfect being possesses its existence by *a priori* necessity, as against mice and planets which exist contingently. And some have maintained that being such that its existence is independent of its being perceived is an essential property of a material thing. Moore's way of putting this was that we should not 'call anything a material object' whose existence was dependent on its being perceived.[36]

The point of remarking on these well-known distinctions is to call attention to the notion which all philosophers have (even those who make a point of rejecting it) that it is possible for a proposition to be *a priori* and also about things. Thus the words 'A perfect being exists by the necessity of its own nature' are understood by philosophers to make an *a priori* claim about the existence of a special object. Similarly, the words 'A material thing exists independently of its being perceived' are taken to express an *a priori* proposition about the nature of material things. And when it is realised that the sentence 'It is impossible to think of what does not exist' (and the equivalent sentence 'Whatever is thought of exists') does not state an empirical proposition, the idea that it expresses a necessary proposition about how thought and reality stand in relation to each other presents itself with irresistible force. There is no gainsaying the powerful impression the sentence creates of being about thoughts and objects, an impression so vivid that, in Kant's words, 'even the wisest of men cannot free themselves from it'. This, together with the fact that an argument is brought in to support the claim it makes, gives rise to the notion that the claim is both non-empirical, or *a priori*, and about things. The impossibility referred to by the sentence 'It is impossible to think of what does not exist' is a logical impossibility; and the necessity referred to by the corresponding sentence, 'It is necessarily the case that whatever one thinks of exists', is a logical necessity.

Many, if not all, philosophers,[37] are under the domination of the impression that logical necessity and physical necessity, and also logical impossibility and physical impossibility, are generically the same, and that they differ from each other only in degree of inflexibility. Thus Wittgenstein speaks of 'the hardness of the logical *must*'.[38] The usual view is that a logical impossibility implies a corresponding physical impossibility and a logical necessity the corresponding physical necessity, but not conversely. What is physically impossible, i.e. an impossibility in nature, cannot in fact be upset, but can be conceived of as being upset; whereas what is logically impossible can be upset either in fact or in conception. And while a physical necessity (i.e. an immutability laid down by a law of nature) cannot be overruled in fact but can in conception, a logical necessity cannot be overruled either in fact nor in conception. One of Russell's remarks illustrates this view graphically: 'Men, for example, though they form a finite class, are, practically and empirically, just as impossible to enumerate as if their number were infinite.'[39] It is, of course, logically impossible to finish counting a non-ending number of elements, as this would imply counting the last member of a series which has no last member. This fact in conjunction with Russell's remark would imply that as in the case of an astronomically huge set of elements which it is 'practically and empirically' impossible to enumerate, the elements of an infinite aggregate cannot be enumerated either empirically or in conception. The idea is that running through the elements of such an aggregate is not only logically impossible but is *also* physically impossible.

This is the picture we naturally form of the relationship between the concepts of logical and physical impossibility. Our picture changes radically, however, when we scrutinise these concepts with care. Consider the following two sentences:

It is impossible to grow a tulip which is not a flower.
It is impossible to grow a tulip from an acorn.

Russell would undoubtedly say that is is just as impossible 'empirically' to grow a tulip from an acorn as it is to grow a tulip that is not a flower. It is clear, however, that the impossibility described by 'grows a tulip which is not a flower' is an inconceivability, as against the impossibility described by 'grows a tulip from an acorn', which is conceivable. Following Spinoza, we might say that only God could make a tulip grow from an acorn, but that not even God could grow a tulip which is not a flower; furthermore, not even God could conceive of something being a tulip and not a flower. This means that God would attach no descriptive sense to the phrase 'grows a tulip that is not a flower', which is a theological way of saying that the phrase has no descriptive sense. The implication is that unlike the phrase 'grows a tulip from an acorn', the function in the language of 'grows a tulip that is not a flower' is not to describe anything. The expression which refers to what is declared to be impossible in the sentences 'It is impossible to grow a tulip from an acorn' *describes* what is declared to be impossible, while the corresponding expression in the sentence declaring a logical impossibility does not describe a circumstance that is declared impossible. This holds for the two sentences, 'It is impossible to enumerate the men in the world' and 'It is impossible to enumerate an infinite number of elements'. The referring phrase of the first sentence describes a process, while the referring phrase of the second does not. This difference between logical and physical impossibility shows that they are different in kind. It also shows that a sentence which makes a statement as to what is logically impossible is not about things. The Parmenidean sentence 'It is impossible to think of what does not exist', construed as stating a logical impossibility, says nothing about what cannot be thought. Taking the word 'impossible' to mean 'logically impossible', the phrase 'thinks of what does not exist' has no use to describe what we cannot think.

Another way of seeing that a sentence which expresses a logically necessary proposition says nothing about things is provided by considering the affirmative equivalent of 'It is impossible to grow a tulip that is not a flower', namely, 'To grow a tulip is necessarily to grow a flower', or more simply, 'A tulip necessarily is a flower'. It will be clear that the term 'flower' does not function in the sentence to distinguish, either in fact or in conception, among tulips. The adjective 'yellow' in 'A buttercup is always yellow' functions in the sentence to distinguish among conceivable buttercups. It sets apart buttercups that are yellow from other imaginable buttercups, and thus has a characterising use. The term 'flower' does not set apart tulips that are flowers from other possible tulips, and therefore does not have a characterising use in the sentence 'A tulip necessarily is a flower'. Whatever the information the sentence may be used to convey, it has no use to convey information about tulips. The point may perhaps be brought out by rewriting the two sentences in somewhat unnatural English, in the following way: 'A tulip is a tulip that is a flower', 'A buttercup is a buttercup that is yellow'. The expression 'a tulip that is a flower', unlike the expression 'a buttercup that is yellow', attributes nothing to what is referred to by its grammatical subject: the meaning of 'a tulip that is a flower' is not something in addition to the meaning of 'tulip'. Thus, with respect to what it asserts about *a property* of tulips, there is no difference between 'A tulip is a tulip that is a flower' and the factually empty tautology, 'A tulip is a tulip'. The first sentence is as empty of information about tulips as is the second. Neither sentence states anything about the nature of tulips, and we might say, therefore, that neither is *about* tulips. To make a general statement regarding sentences which express *a priori* propositions, they are all empty of information about the world. They are ontologically mute.

This general maxim is of first importance for a correct understanding of the way philosophy works. It can readily be seen to apply to the words 'Whatever thing we think of must exist', providing they express, or are advanced as expressing, an *a priori* truth. Consider the following equivalent even though awkward way of writing the sentence, 'Whatever thing we think of exists': 'It is always the case that the thought of a thing is the thought of an existing thing'. Since, by hypothesis, the sentence expresses a logically necessary proposition, the phrase 'the thought of an existing thing' does not, as does the phrase 'the thought of a buttercup', function in such a way as to set apart some thoughts from other thoughts, e.g. thoughts of buttercups from thoughts of things which are not buttercups. It does not serve to set apart thoughts of existing things from thoughts of non-existing things. This implies that the *theoretical* range of application of the two expressions, 'thought of an existing thing' and 'thought of a thing', coincide precisely. This in turn implies that the first says no more about thoughts than does the second. With respect to thoughts, they say the same. Hence, viewed as expressing a logically necessary truth, the sentence 'All thoughts of things are thoughts of existing things' is as barren of information about thoughts as is the tautology 'All thoughts of things are thoughts of things'. Wittgenstein declared that a tautology 'says nothing'.[40] Not to go into the question as to whether a tautology says nothing at all, we can say that a tautology says nothing about *things*. Whatever it is that we know in knowing a proposition to be a tautology, or more generally an *a priori* truth, we know nothing about the world.

It is relatively simple now to see why a logically necessary truth cannot imply a corresponding factual truth and why a logical impossibility cannot imply a corresponding physical impossibility. The general reason is that from a proposition which carries no information whatever about things no proposition which supplies such information is deducible. A proposition which has factual content cannot be entailed by a proposition which has none. The proposition expressed by 'It is physically impossible for a kangaroo to jump a mile' states what a kangaroo cannot as a matter of fact do. The phrase 'kangaroo which jumps a mile' describes what we can imagine happening in nature, although it never in fact happens. Hence the proposition cannot logically be inferred from any necessary proposition, any more than it can be inferred from the proposition that a kangaroo either jumps a mile or does not jump a mile. It is the same with the proposition that bread must bake at a temperature of 400° F. It is tempting to adopt the view that what is true necessarily is also true as a mere matter of fact and that what is logically impossible is also physically impossible. But taken for what it appears to be on the surface, as making a logical claim about entailments between kinds of propositions, the view is mistaken.

Perhaps the best way of making this clear is to articulate the logical point that is involved. The fact that a given proposition has its truth-value by logical necessity prevents it from being about things or from having factual content; and the fact that a given proposition is about things implies that it does not have its truth-value by logical necessity. The general point is that an *a priori* proposition cannot entail one that is contingent. A proposition whose actual truth-value is its only possible truth-value cannot entail a proposition which is in principle capable of either of two truth-values. To put the matter with the help of C. I. Lewis's symbol for logical possibility, '$\Diamond$', where we have p necessary and q possibly false, i.e.

$$\sim \Diamond \sim p, \ \Diamond q,$$

we cannot have

$$p \rightarrow q.$$

For the theoretical possibility of q having a truth-value other than the one imposed on it by its being entailed by p is ruled out by p's being necessary. The consequences of an *a priori* proposition are themselves *a priori* and thus empty of ontological content. Interpreted as denoting a logically necessary proposition, the sentence 'Whatever is thought of exists' will fail to have an associated sentence expressing a matter of fact claim about what invariably happens in nature.

Two connected questions present themselves at this point. One is the general question as to what necessary propositions are about, or better, what the subject-matter of a sentence expressing a necessary proposition is. The subject-matter of the sentence 'Percherons are draft horses' is Percherons, horses of a certain breed; but philosophers seem to wander in a fog, either Platonic or nominalistic, when they seek to identify the subject-matter of the sentence 'A Percheron is an animal'. The other question is whether the philosophical sentence 'It is impossible to think of what does not exist' (and its affirmative equivalent) does in fact express a logically necessary proposition and whether it is put forward by Parmenidean philosophers as doing so in ordinary language. There is a tendency to think that it does make a non-empirical claim, and despite disavowals philosophers cannot resist thinking that the claim is both non-empirical and also about things. Kant suggested that a proposition could have 'inner necessity' and also be a truth about phenomena. This has been taken by many philosophers as the rock upon which the metaphysical science of the world would be built. As has been seen, however, if a proposition is *a priori* it cannot carry information about phenomena, regardless of whether or not its predicate is a component of its subject. The clear implication is that if one wishes to read a book of the world, no book in the vast library of philosophy will be of the slightest use. Hume stated this point colourfully when he said that if a book contains no abstract reasoning concerning number nor any experimental evidence concerning matter of fact, 'it can contain nothing but sophistry and illusion'.[41]

It is important for the light thrown on philosophical theories to get a clear idea of what necessary propositions are about, and of the kind of information they carry. Necessary propositions, one would gather from the abundance of philosophical theories about their nature, are a baffling and elusive species. To mention several of the theories: one has it that a necessary proposition is an inductive generalisation to which a high degree of probability attaches; according to another theory, it states an unalterable relationship between abstract entities; a third maintains that it is about the use of terminology in a language. It is bewildering, to say the least, to witness three learned people reflecting on a simple proposition such as that a Percheron is an animal, or that $2 + 2 = 4$, and emerging with intractably rival conclusions: one, that the arithmetical proposition is about the terms '2 + 2' and '4'; another, that it is about abstract entities denoted by these terms; and the third, that it is an inductive proposition based on the examination of instances. There are still other theories. It would not be to the point here to venture into the maze of philosophical theories concerning the *a priori*, however inviting that may be. The question as to what necessary propositions are about, and what kind of information we obtain from them, is dealt with best and with the least amount of mystification by looking at them as before through the spectacles of the *sentences* used to express them. And the explanation will be least roundabout if we consider sample sentences which express propositions stating something to be impossible.

The sentence 'It is impossible for there to be a Percheron which is not an animal', like the sentence 'It is impossible for there to be 4 minus 5 sheep in the meadow' and 'It is impossible to grow a tulip which is not a flower', makes no statement about what is not the case. The fact that it expresses a proposition which is not open to falsification implies that the phrase which refers to what is declared by the sentence to be impossible has no use to describe an imaginable thing or occurrence or state of affairs. The phrase 'Percheron which is not an animal', like 'keeps 4 minus 5 sheep in the meadow', 'comes to the last member of an unending series' and 'grows a tulip which is not a flower', is *descriptively senseless*. Part of *understanding* the sentences 'It is impossible for there to be a Percheron which is not an animal' and 'It is impossible to keep 4 minus 5 sheep in a meadow' consists in knowing that the phrases referring to what is declared to be impossible have no descriptive content. Hence, knowing that these sentences express *a priori* propositions is equivalent to knowing that certain combinations of words in a language do not function descriptively in that language. It is this fact which leads some philosophers to the view that necessary propositions are really verbal. The objections to this view are well known and would seem to be conclusive, although knowing these objections does not deter philosophers from holding it. We may be sure that what makes the conventionalist secure in this view about the nature of *a priori* necessity in the face of the objections is that his view is *philosophical*. We have only to remind ourselves of Moore's paradox to realise this.

The subject-matter of the sentence 'It is impossible for there to be a Percheron which is not an animal' is no more verbal than it is factual. From the fact that in knowing that the sentence expresses an *a priori* truth what we know is an empirical fact about a combination of words, and furthermore that this is all there is to know, it is tempting to identify this fact of usage as the subject-matter of the sentence. But the sentence makes no declaration about the phrase occurring in it. The fact that the phrase has no descriptive content prevents the sentence from being about things, and the fact that the sentence expresses a logically necessary proposition prevents it from making an empirical declaration about usage. The consequence, however strange it may at first seem, is that the sentence, even though perfectly intelligible, has no subject-matter: it says nothing about either things or words and thus, to use Wittgenstein's expression again, says nothing.

The idea that an indicative sentence might have a literal meaning but nevertheless have no subject-matter and make no statement about anything, apparently produces discomfort in the minds of philosophers. Like an oyster which tries to remove an irritant by manufacturing a pearl, a philosopher tries to make up for what language denies him by *manufacturing* a subject of discourse for it. The result is a thicket of theories. Philosophers of the *a priori* rid themselves of a linguistic discomfort but in doing so produce a typical philosophical symptom, an irreducible number of views. Anyone who prefers fact to semantically induced fantasy will experience little trouble reconciling himself to the idea that a sentence whose meaning is an *a priori* proposition has no subject about which it makes a statement. He will have little trouble seeing that, although it says nothing about words, in knowing what it says we know only facts of usage.

This fact about sentences for *a priori* propositions is, perhaps, shown most simply and clearly by writing out the following equivalences:

(1) The fact that the sentence 'It is impossible to grow a tulip which is not a flower' expresses an *a priori* proposition
   is equivalent to
   the fact that the sentence '"grows a tulip which is not a flower" is a phrase that has no descriptive function' expresses a true verbal proposition.

(2) the fact that the sentence 'A tulip is a flower' expresses a logically necessary proposition
   is equivalent to
   the fact that the sentence, '"flower" applies by reason of usage in the language to whatever "tulip" applies to' expresses a true verbal proposition.

To hold that (1) and (2) are equivalent is not to imply that the proposition expressed by 'The phrase, "grows a tulip which is not a flower" has no use' is the same as the proposition expressed by 'It is impossible to grow a tulip which is not a flower'. Neither is it to imply that the proposition expressed by 'Usage dictates the application of the term "flower" to whatever "tulip" applies to' is the same as the proposition expressed by 'A tulip is necessarily a flower', or by 'Being a tulip *entails* being a flower'. The fact about usage expressed by the first sentence of each of the two pairs of sentences is what we know in understanding the second sentences, and we know nothing in addition to these facts in knowing the propositions expressed by the second sentences. The facts which we know are nevertheless not the subject-matter of the sentences and cannot be identified with the propositions they express.

Mathematics, which may be truly described as the systematic science of the *a priori*, has been a source of wonder and mystification to many people. Hardy represented the mathematician as gazing into an intricate system of objects less gross than those encountered in sense experience, and recording what he sees. The view we have arrived at here about the nature of the *a priori* de-Platonises mathematics, without reinstating Hilbert's form of conventionalism. To make an observation on *part* of what a mathematician's work consists in, it is the explication of rules of usage presented in a form of speech in which no terms are mentioned, i.e. in the ontological idiom.

We are now in a position to see clearly that the sentence 'It is impossible to think of what does not exist' does not, as the words entering into it are ordinarily used, express an *a priori* proposition. The supposition that it does implies that the phrase 'thinks of what does not exist' is not a descriptive combination of words, that it has no use to convey information. And the supposition that the equivalent sentence 'Whatever is thought of exists' expresses a logically necessary proposition implies that usage dictates the application of 'exists' to whatever is named as the object of thought: usage dictates the application of 'exists' to what is meant, for example, by the nouns in the expressions 'thinks of a nightingale' and 'thinks of a Gorgon'. It will be plain that anyone who has the idea that these sentences make logical claims will think that 'thinks of what does not exist' has no application to any theoretical occurrence and that 'exists' applies to whatever is referred to by terms which are intelligible values of x in 'thinks of x'. To anyone who is able to resist playing the game of philosophy, it will also be plain what the facts with regard to usage are. It is a fact that the phrase 'thinks of non-existing things' does have a correct use in the language, and it is a fact that there is no rule dictating the application of 'exists' to whatever is referred by suitable values of 'thinks of x'. To touch briefly on the term 'non-existing thing', it and the term 'existing thing' constitute a pair of antithetical terms which are semantically related. If one is deprived of its use, the other loses its use. If 'non-existing thing' did not serve to distinguish amongst describable things, 'existing thing' would not serve to set apart some describable things from others. Hence it could not function descriptively in the language. From the supposition that 'A thought of a thing is a thought of an existing thing' expresses a logically necessary proposition it follows that the sentence is tautological (empty of content), with respect to thoughts of things; and being able to show that it follows hinges on the fact that 'existing thing' and 'non-existing thing' are antithetical terms.

As is known, many important philosophers have, if we are to take them at their word, fancied that they had demonstrated contradictions in the meanings of such everyday words as 'motion', 'cause', 'space' and 'time', and some recent language-oriented thinkers have gone straight to the position that these philosophers had false beliefs about the use such words have in ordinary language.[42] A paradoxical claim like 'Motion is self-contradictory, and does not exist' is capable of presenting a linguistic face to some philosophers, just as it is capable of presenting an ontological face to others. But if we notice the talk and behaviour with which the claim is surrounded, the impression that it implies a mistaken idea about actual usage evaporates. It is not necessary to look hard in order to see that there is nothing in the behaviour of a metaphysician who says motion is self-contradictory to suggest that he actually believes people who use motion-indicating words to be suffering from a linguistic delusion, the delusion that they are conversing intelligibly while making no literal sense. Nor is it difficult to see that the metaphysician himself uses motion terminology in the ordinary conduct of life in the way everyone else does. Neither in his talk nor in his behaviour, nor even in his behaviour while pronouncing and arguing for the philosophical view that motion is unreal, does he betray having unusual thoughts about usual terminology. His view seems to be completely dissociated from his everyday use of language. This is why Bradley was able to say, 'Time, like space, has most evidently proved not to be real, but to be a contradictory appearance. I will, in the next chapter, reinforce and repeat this conclusion by some remarks on change.'[43] The reason why the inconsistency in these words went unnoticed — or if noticed soon fell under amnesia — is that there is no inconsistency. This means that a paradoxical philosophical theory (as well as a superficially non-paradoxical theory) is not a disguised statement about the correct use of an expression.

It is now generally recognised, except by the most benighted, that after being exposed as mistaken, a philosophical view returns as a claimed truth, sometimes in its original form, sometimes dressed up in a new terminology. This occurs over and over again. A philosophical 'mistake' is like the giant Antaeus who sprang back with renewed vigour every time he was sent crashing to earth by Hercules. Antaeus finally met his end, but a philosophical mistake is never laid to rest. A mistake that occurs in scientific disciplines does not behave in this way; and the realistic conclusion to draw, which fits in with the behaviour and ordinary talk of philosophers, is that a philosophical 'mistake' is not a mistake. An American general, after being removed from his command, said that old soldiers do not die, they just fade away. A philosophical mistake may for a time fade away, but it never goes out of existence and never is in want of adherents. The *déjà vu* feelings we so often experience in philosophy invariably turn out to be justified when we succeed in translating the new claim back into an old and familiar one.

A philosopher presents his theory with the air of someone who brings light and truth to his special subject, but the words he uses make no reference whatever either to things in the world or to the actual use of terminology in a language. What the nature of his theory is or, better still, what he is doing with terminology, requires an explanation which will fit in with the fact that philosophy never frees itself from its mistakes, and therefore can never look forward to the resolution of disputes which everywhere infect it. The only explanation which does this is that his theory is a disguised intro-duction of changed terminology (or sometimes a disguised counter to it). A philosopher does not use familiar language either in the way the natural scientist uses it nor in the way the mathematician uses it. His work consists of doing nothing more substantial than altering language; but he presents his verbal creations in the fact-stating form of speech and thereby conceals from all of us, including himself, what he does with terminology.

Wittgenstein perceived this and was led to remark: 'Die Menschen sind im Netz der Sprache verstrickt und wissen es nicht.'[44] A debate over a gerrymandered piece of standard terminology can go on and on without prospect of future resolution, because no sort

of *fact* is in question. It will be clear that a 'mistake' which is constituted by redistricted nomenclature is in no danger of being refuted
by fact and is capable of an indefinite number of reincarnations.
Wittgenstein said that a philosophical problem has no solution, but
only a dissolution. This is a way of saying that a philosophical
question has only be to understood aright — be linguistically
unmasked — in order to cease being a *problem*. The idea that a
philosophical theory is an ontologically presented language
innovation (or an ontologically expressed opposition to it) helps us
understand why disputes over whether it is true or false are intract-
able. They are disputes in which exotic linguistic preference, not
truth, is at issue. The fact that the disputes are endless also indicates
that no practical consequences, which normally justify the adoption
of a new notation, attach to a language change introduced in
philosophy. It is noticing this which made Wittgenstein remark that
philosophical language is 'like an engine idling, not when it is doing
work'.[45]

An idle semantic departure from actual usage when presented in
the form of speech in which statements about things are made is
capable of generating a dispute of indefinite duration. No fact, old
or new, can bring it to a final conclusion. And one thing, but not the
only one, which makes it important to philosophers and gives it
continuing life, is the appearance it has of being a dispute about
things or occurrences in the world. Even so-called linguistic
philosophers remain the dupes of this appearance. Their idea is that
in some way the investigation of linguistic usage is relevant to a
philosophical dispute about things, and in the end will settle it. The
notion behind this idea is that a false philosophical theory is a
disguised misdescription of usage, but that a true philosophical
theory is not just about words but is about the world. The implication which is imbedded in this notion is that there can be no false
philosophical theory about *things*, and thus that a true philosophical
theory is a necessary truth about things. This can be recognised as a
reincarnation of the idea that truths about things can be learned
without going to the things themselves.

It is easy to understand now what it is about such sentences as
'Motion does not really occur' and 'To be a thing, e.g. a glove, is to
be perceived', which creates the impression that they are about
reality. Quite generally, a gerrymandered piece of terminology
when presented in the fact-stating form of speech tends to create the
impression that a theory is being stated, and this impression is

strengthened to the point of becoming irremovable when the expression of a hidden idea is involved.[46] What Moore called a philosophic moment is compounded of two symbiotic ingredients: a piece of trumped-up semantics in union with a temporary suspension of the reality principle[47] in favour of an unconscious wish. A philosopher who explicitly or by implication holds that a truth about things can be obtained without investigating them, at a superficial level plays a game with language but at a deeper level uses the game to gratify the still active desire for omniscience. In the case of the Spinozistic thesis that the order and connection of things is the same as the order and connection of ideas, the unconscious wish behind his version of the Parmenidean thesis is clairvoyance. Something Freud said is particularly relevant in the present connection:

> the philosophy of today has retained some essential features of the animistic mode of thought — the overvaluation of the magic of words and the belief that the real events in the world take the course which our thinking seeks to impose on them.[48]

To return to the philosopher who claims to have demonstrated a contradiction in the meaning of the word 'motion' and who goes on to tell us that motion does not really occur. He does not say anything which is in conflict with the actual use of the word 'motion'. He has decided to contract the application of 'real' and withhold its application from whatever 'is in motion' correctly applies to. He presents his semantic decision in the language of ontology and in this way creates the appearance of making a startling assertion about the true state of the cosmos. The argument he gives for his assertion makes it look as if, by an analytical penetration into concepts or into the labyrinth of linguistic usage, he was able to arrive at a basic truth about things.

Russell's remark that everyone except a philosopher can see the difference between a post and his idea of a post would seem to apply to Berkeley, whose view, taken literally, implies that a post is no more than an idea.[49] Samuel Johnson showed that he knew the difference between a thing and an idea of the thing by kicking a stone, but his action furnished no evidence against the philosophical view that to be a thing, such as a post or a stone, is to be perceived. One philosopher stated that our senses reveal only sense data (or ideas) to us, but his inability to say what else our senses might reveal shows that he was not using language to make a statement of fact. Similarly, a Berkeleian who maintains that the existence of a thing depends upon its being perceived is unable to say what it would be like for an unperceived thing to exist, or what it would be like to encounter a thing which is not an idea. He is not using language to make a matter of fact statement about things, which is why Johnson's kicking a stone does not count as evidence against what he says. But thought of as intended to express an *a priori* proposition, the sentence 'To be a thing is to be perceived' would be equivalent to the entailment sentence 'Being a thing *entails* being perceived'. We should then have to suppose that a Berkeleian has the idea that as English is ordinarily used the phrase 'unperceived thing' is devoid of conceptual content, and also that he has the idea that usage dictates the application of 'is perceived' to whatever 'thing' correctly applies to. Berkeley's advice to speak with the vulgar but to think with the learned shows that he had no such mistaken idea about usage. The proper conclusion to come to is that his view is nothing more substantial than a deceptively presented piece of changed terminology — a vacuously stretched use of 'perceived' which makes it applicable to whatever 'thing' correctly applies to.

The words 'It is impossible to think of what does not exist', which serve to reassure some philosophers and strike others as an extravagant violation of common sense, are of a kind with 'Motion does not really exist' and 'Things such as chimneys and mountains cannot exist unperceived'. They bring before us, in a veiled and dramatised form, an idle restricting of terminology, i.e. a change in the application of an expression in dissociation from any practical intention to institute a change in its actual use. They present an academically contracted application of the expression 'thinks of what does not exist', an application whose range has been shrunk to nothing. In his special language game, 'thinks of a thief who does not exist' has been shorn of its descriptive sense. In depriving the phrase of its descriptive use the philosopher also deprives the related antithetical phrase, 'thinks of a thief who exists', of its function to describe. But this he leaves unmentioned, and for good reason: his purpose is not to introduce practical changes in language, rather it is to create certain effects.

A Parmenidean metaphysician speaks the language of the learned without giving up the language of the vulgar. He asserts that one cannot think of what does not exist and that whatever is thought of must exist, and also continues to speak, like everyone else, of things that do not exist as well as of things that do exist. Everyday language not only remains the instrument he uses to communicate factual information, it also serves as the constant backdrop in front of which he speaks his philosophical lines. The things he does with language would lose their power to bring into existence the illusion that he is expressing a theory about thoughts and things if, instead of being paraded in front of unchanged everyday language, they were *incorporated* into it. For then both expressions, 'thinks of a non-existing thing' and 'thinks of an existing thing', would lose their use in sentences about states of affairs. They would pass out of currency, and with their disappearance from language the philosophical theory would evaporate. In order to create an illusion with his altered nomenclature, ordinary, everyday language must remain intact, which is why philosophical talk has no tendency whatever to modify or change ordinary language. Wittgenstein explained what a philosopher is doing who says, 'Only my pain is real', as keeping ordinary language and putting another beside it,[50] a language in which 'his pain' has no application. Similarly, we may say that a philosopher who asserts 'It is impossible to think of things which once were and no longer are' is keeping ordinary language and putting another beside it, and that he does this for the magical effect he is able to produce.[51]

People have the idea not only that a technical philosopher advances theories about the nature and existence of things, but also that he arrives at them by some sort of controlled investigation. Freud thought that philosophy 'behaves like a science and works in part by the same methods'. And a leading contemporary philosopher has described philosophy as 'a wing of science where aspects of method are examined more deeply or in a wider perspective than elsewhere'.[52] Undoubtedly, philosophers have found reassurance and support in his words. But the idea that philosophy works like a science is as far removed from reality as is the idea that a philosophical view has theoretical content. A philosophical view is a semantic blown-egg, a bubble; and a semantic bubble is not the outcome of an investigation which employs scientific techniques or methods. If we can bring ourselves to scrutinise a philosophical argument with care, we shall find that what looks like a piece of scientific reasoning is of a kind with the theory it supports. A philosophical theory is constituted by an altered piece of language; and in general, an alteration in the range covered by an expression is bound up with similarities and differences in the functioning of related expressions occurring in the statement of the argument. The wish to highlight a likeness between certain expressions or a difference between them requires introducing changes into the language which will accentuate or minimise the likeness or difference. When these changes are presented in the ontological idiom, they take the form of an argument for a theory.

To illustrate, Heraclitus's statement, 'You cannot step into the same river twice' is a picturesque way of calling attention to the difference between the use of 'same' in 'same river' and its use in 'same street', coupled with the academic decision to discontinue applying 'same' to rivers, and the like. Highlighting the point that there is only a difference of degree, not one of kind, between rivers and streets enables a philosopher to withhold applying the word 'same' not only to rivers, but also to streets. The view that everything constantly changes, or that things are really events, is the outcome of these two moves with the word 'same'.

Moore had a poor opinion of the argument he formulated for the Bradleian–Parmenidean view; but in philosophy what is one man's poison is another man's meat, and what is a philosopher's poison at one time may well become his meat at another. Moore's formulation makes explicit a reason for holding the view. Regardless of whether it is thought bad or good it is a reason, which lends to the view the scientific air that it was arrived at by the employment of a method. Moore supposes Bradley to be arguing as follows: 'A thing cannot have a property, unless it is there to have it, and since unicorns . . . do have the property of being thought of, there certainly must be such things.' The implication of Moore's words is that a philosopher who says, 'It is impossible to think of what does not exist', believes that the phrase 'being thought of' denotes a property of things. According to this idea, to assert that the moon is being thought of is to assert that it has the property *being thought of*, just as to assert that the moon is round is to assert that it has the property *being round*. Moreover, *being thought of* is a property of such a kind that it can only be ascribed to a subject that is 'there to have it'. Wittgenstein's observation that you cannot hang a thief who does not exist but you can think of one who does not exist tells us the *sort* of property Moore takes a philosopher to understand by the expression 'being thought of': it denotes the sort of property he elsewhere calls a 'relational property'. In other words, it refers to a relation between objects — in the present context, to an action that is performed on one thing by another. Moore's formulation of the Bradleian argument carries with it the suggestion that Bradley took the words 'thinks of the moon' as describing something that is being done to the moon. It suggests that Bradley, and others, have the idea that the use in the language of 'thinks of a thief' is like the use of 'hangs a thief', 'opens the door' and 'milks a goat'.

It is hardly necessary to remark that a philosopher gives no evidence of having this idea about the *actual* use of 'thinks of a thief'. Except for his philosophical theory and his philosophical argument, he talks like everyone else. It is reasonable to suppose that instead of having a wrong idea about the use of 'thinks of' in expressions like 'thinks of a thief' and 'thinks of a unicorn' he wishes to assimilate it to transitive verbs occurring in such expressions as 'hangs a thief' and 'rides a unicorn'. When a philosopher insists that it is just as impossible to think of a unicorn that does not exist as it is to ride a unicorn that does not exist, he is not wrong about linguistic usage. Instead he is urging an artificial classification of 'thinks of' with transitive verbs denoting an action. A grammatical similarity appeals to him, and he accents it, while muting a semantic difference. The argument for the view that it is impossible to think of what does not exist is an academic grouping together of verbs which a grammatical likeness makes possible. The view itself is a vivid way of announcing this grouping.

The Parmenidean philosophical theory is a remarkable structure, one that has the substance of a cobweb and yet is as durable as the pyramids of Egypt. At the centre of the structure is a piece of unconsciously reframed grammar that is presented in the non-verbal form of speech and projected onto the language in everyday use, without being incorporated into it. The result of this game with terminology is a lively illusion that a theory about the relation between thoughts and things is being presented and supported by a line of reasoning. Behind the verbal sleight-of-hand we can detect the archaic wish for effortless knowledge which is still active in the unconscious of many thinkers. There can be hardly any doubt that the overriding strength of this wish is responsible for the blindspots philosophers have to the anomalies of their discipline. Philosophers, like Plato, Spinoza, Hegel and Bradley, subjectively picture themselves in the role of surveyor of all that there is and as composing the cosmic *Baedecker*. The reality behind this gratifying image is less appealing: the spectator of the universe deflates into a juggler who plays empty tricks with grammar.

A number of things Wittgenstein has said carry with them the implication that a philosophical theory is a kind of neurotic symptom. Thus, he wrote, 'The philosopher is the man who has to cure himself of many sicknesses of the understanding'.[53] If indeed philosophy can be correctly described as a sickness, it is a sickness of which no philosopher wishes to be cured. His 'sickness' of the understanding, on which he looks as a lofty achievement, gives him pleasure and also has a commercial value. Seeing this, it is not hard to understand why a philosopher should be reluctant to open his eyes to the insubstantiality of his subject. The most powerful forces which work against his looking with an analytical eye at his subject are hidden from him, one of which is the subjectively retained belief in the super-human reach of his thought. This belief is of utmost importance to him, as it gives him the feeling that instead of being weak and at the mercy of external agencies, he is powerful and self-sufficient. Linked with the idea of his omniscience is the belief in the causal power of thought, the power to think things into and out of existence and to have mental control over their behaviour. The world systems of philosophers are not only the epic accounts of mental journeys, they also describe worlds that have been brought into existence by the minds of philosophers. In his unconscious a philosopher's mind has omniscience and omnipotence, and it is language which enables it to possess these attributes.

A philosophical theory is a complex structure the greater part of which is hidden in the unconscious. Its importance to the philosopher is great enough to prevent him from prying into its two uppermost parts, a gerrymandered piece of language and an intellectual illusion. He is like the king in the fairy-tale whose exhibitionist needs prevented him from seeing that the cloth which the two rascally tailors wove for his garment was transparent air. If we look into the Parmenidean thesis we can discern a further subterranean idea which is related to the fairy-tale, and may be useful to allude to briefly, as it will help us understand better the need of a philosopher to be deceived by his own production. For the philosopher is both tailor and king, deceiver and deceived. There are two equivalent formulations of the Parmenidean thesis,

> Whatever is thought of exists; and
> It is impossible to think of what does not exist.

It is the second formulation which provides us with a clue as to what creates the need to be deceived. The suggestion of the words 'One cannot think of what does not exist' is that there is something whose non-existence is *too painful* to be thought of, something whose non-existence is 'unthinkable and unspeakable' and must be banished from the mind. It is not difficult to identify, with reasonable certainty, the anatomical entity that is referred to: it is not possessed by some and its loss is feared by others. In each case it is the unspeakable non-being, actual or feared. The importance to the philosopher of his sentence about the way thoughts and things are related is understandable. With it he is not only able to create an illusion which gives him narcissistic satisfaction, he is also able to fend off the invasion of anxiety.

Notes

1. W. V. Quine (1970), 'Philosophical Progress in Language Theory', *Metaphilosophy*, vol. 1, p. 2.

2. W. V. Quine (1960), *Word and Object*, New York: Wiley, p. 207.

3. A. J. Ayer (1971), *Russell and Moore: The Analytical Heritage*, Cambridge, Mass.: Harvard University Press, p. 245.

4. S. Freud (1965), *New Introductory Lectures on Psychoanalysis*, New York: W. W. Norton, trans. and ed. James Strachey. (Standard edition of the *Complete Psychological Works*, vol. 22, p. 16; 1st edn 1933.)

5. *Scientific Thought* (1927), New York: Harcourt Brace, p. 19.

6. Ibid.

7. Ibid., p. 18.

8. Ibid.

9. *Tractatus Logico-Philosophicus*, 4.112, trans. Pears and McGuinness.

10. 'Philosophy and "Common Sense"', in *G. E. Moore. Essays in Retrospect* (1970), London: Allen & Unwin, ed. Alice Ambrose and Morris Lazerowitz, p. 203.

11. 'A Defence of Common Sense' (1959), in *Philosophical Papers* London: Allen & Unwin (first published in *Contemporary British Philosophy* (1925), 2nd series, London: Allen & Unwin, ed. J. H. Muirhead, p. 41).

12. James Strachey's literal translation is: 'With his nightcaps and the tatters of his dressing-gown he patches up the gaps in the structure of the universe.'

13. *New Introductory Lectures on Psychoanalysis*, p. 160–1.

14. *Free Associations: Memories of a Psycho-Analyst* (1959), New York: Basic Books, p. 60.

15. Ibid., p. 165.

16. Ibid., p. 15.

17. Ibid., p. 16.

18. This difference is dismissed by so-called conventionalists, but is developed into a theory about abstract objects by Platonists.

19. 'A Reply to My Critics', in *The Philosophy of G. E. Moore*, The Library of Living Philosophers, vol.. IV, ed. P. A. Schilpp, p. 675–6.

20. A. J. Ayer, *Russell and Moore: The Analytical Heritage*, p. 180.

21. This is developed in detail in my *Philosophy and Illusion* (1968), London: Allen & Unwin, pp. 119–40.

22. A. N. Prior (1971), *Objects of Thought*, reviewed in *The Times Literary Supplement*.

23. John Burnet, *Greek Philosophy, Part I, Thales to Plato* (1928), London: Macmillan, p. 67.

24. *The Blue Book*, p. 31.

25. *The Principles of Mathematics* (1938), New York: W. W. Norton, p. 450, 2nd edn.

26. Ibid., p. 451.

27. Ibid., pp. 450–61.

28. Ibid., p. 451.

29. pp. 379–80.

30. p. 381.

31 *Philosophical Studies* (1922), London: Routledge & Kegan Paul, p. 215.

32. Ibid., p. 216.

33. Benjamin Farrington (1944), *Greek Science, Its Meaning for Us*, London: Penguin Books, p. 50.

34. For an extended discussion of Moore's disconcerting observation that philosophers hold views incompatible with what they know to be true, see 'Moore's Paradox' in my *The Structure of Metaphysics* (1955), London: Routledge & Kegan Paul.

35. For a discussion whether this is an actual or only a semantically contrived distinction, see my *Studies in Metaphilosophy* (1964), London: Routledge & Kegan Paul, p. 6.

36. *Some Main Problems of Philosophy* (1953), London: Allen & Unwin, Ch. 1, p. 9.

37. It is safe to say *all* philosophers: scratch the semantic veneer of the so-called linguistic philosopher and you will find the metaphysician underneath.

38. *Remarks on the Foundations of Mathematics*, p. 37.

39. *The Principles of Mathematics*, Introduction, p. vii.

40. *Tractatus Logico-Philosophicus*, 4.461, trans. Ogden.

41. *An Enquiry Concerning Human Understanding* (1902), Oxford: Clarendon, ed. L. A. Selby-Bigge, Sec. XII, Part III.

42. For an exposition of this thesis, see Norman Malcolm, 'Moore and Ordinary Language' in *The Philosophy of G. E. Moore*, The Library of Living Philosophers, vol. IV, ed. P. A. Schilpp.

43. *Appearance and Reality*, p. 43.

44. *Philosophische Grammatik* (1969), Frankfurt-am-Main: Suhrkamp, Schriften 4, ed. Rush Rhees, p. 462.

45. *Philosophical Investigations*, p. 51.

46. Wittgenstein has made the penetrating observation that 'Behind our thoughts, true or false, there is always to be found a dark background, which we are only later able to bring into the light and express as a thought'. *Notebooks, 1914–16* (1969), Oxford: Basil Blackwell, p. 36e. There can be no doubt that the dark background contains unconscious material.

47. One thing which indicates a weakened sense of reality with respect to his discipline is the philosopher's unconcern about the total absence of stable results in it. Occasionally in its busy history, now covering a period of 25 centuries, a philosopher has awakened to the ubiquitous chaos that reigns in his subject, but his return to peaceful slumber has always been prompt.

48. *New Introductory Lectures on Psycho-Analysis*, Ch. XXXV, 'The Question of a Weltanschauung', p. 166, standard edn.

49. More accurately, a system of ideas in the mind of God. Phenomenalism, which comes from this view, is that a physical object is a system of actual and *possible* sense data.

50. The Yellow Book (notes taken by Alice Ambrose and Margaret Masterman in the intervals between dictation of *The Blue Book*).

51. I do not wish to imply that Wittgenstein would go on to this sort of conclusion.

52. W. V. Quine, 'Philosophical Progress in Language Theory', *Metaphilosophy*, vol. 1, no. 1, p. 2.

53. *Remarks on the Foundations of Mathematics*, p. 157. He described his own treatment of a philosophical question as being 'like the treatment of an illness' (*Philosophical Investigations*, p. 91). It is interesting to realise that despite his rejecting psychoanalysis (after first having admired Freud's ideas) Wittgenstein at times took, in external respects, a psychoanalytical approach to philosophy. What might be called a displaced return of the rejected appears to have taken place in him.

It is well known that Wittgenstein compared a philosophical problem with a mental cramp, a comparison which suggests that a philosophical problem was in some way an irritant from which he wished to free himself. In one place he wrote: 'The real discovery is the one which makes me capable of stopping doing philosophy when I want to — the one that gives philosophy peace, so that it is no longer tormented by questions which bring *itself* in question.'[1] The impression these words create is that philosophy, into which he had unusual penetration, was something of a torment to him, perhaps because his perceptions made him uneasy about the *nature* of philosophy, about what its claims really came to and what the work of its demonstration, actually is. This is a possibility that needs looking into.

Stopping doing philosophy plainly does not have the effect of making philosophy disappear, any more than giving up mathematics makes mathematics disappear. Wittgenstein wanted more than the ability to put the problems of philosophy out of mind. His aim, it seems, was to make them go out of existence. In his words: 'the clarity we are aiming at is indeed *complete* clarity. But this simply means that philosophical problems should *completely* disappear.'[2] His stated task has the air of a magical feat: it makes one think of the magician who, with a wave of his hand, makes the lady disappear.

It is not certain what Wittgenstein means by 'complete clarity'. He has said that what the philosopher needs is to 'command a clear view of the use of our words'.[3] Consulting lexicographers, grammarians, etc. no doubt would improve our use of words and give us a clearer view of the workings of language, but no philosophical problem would be made to go out of existence by any such procedure. What is the clarity about the use of words which may be expected to remove philosophical problems? It would seem that the special philosophical use of words, which in some subtle way differs from their ordinary use, is what needs to be clarified. We know how to proceed in ordinary circumstances which require clearing up verbal misunderstandings. The latter, he asserts, 'are not the cases we have to do with'.[4] What is called for is not a reform of language, but insight into the fact that the philosophical use of language is 'like an engine idling'.[5] To attain this end he says 'there is not a philosophical method, though there are indeed methods, like different therapies'. One such method involves his use of simple language-games, 'set up as *objects of comparison* which are meant to throw light on the facts of our language by way not only of similarities but also of dissimilarities'.[6] This is one of the procedures employed in 'constantly giving prominence to distinctions which our ordinary forms of language easily make us overlook'.[7] In general, whatever the means employed, the intention is to call attention to differences among forms of expression used by philosophers that are similar to those in everyday language. One similarity is obvious: the fact-stating indicative form of speech in which philosophers advance their claims with the air of stating 'facts recognised by any reasonable human being'.[8] Wittgenstein holds that the philosopher 'is not aware that he is objecting to a convention',[9] and that he is confused into supposing he is rejecting a proposition as false when he is merely rejecting a form of expression'.[10] Hence the first rule of procedure is 'to destroy the outward similarity between a metaphysical proposition and an experiential one'.[11]

In the present essay we shall concentrate on one means of effecting this, which he stated during the period between the *Tractatus* and the *Investigations*, roughly coinciding with the *Blue* and *Yellow Books*. Some things that Wittgenstein remarked on provide a procedure for making philosophical problems disappear. This procedure involves explaining what philosophers do with antithetical terms to create the appearance that a theory about things is being put forward. Wittgenstein did not expressly connect the examination of philosophers' use of antithetical terms with the aim of making a philosophical problem disappear. A connection does nevertheless exist. Here, the attempt will be made to do two things: first, to explicate by means of examples how the use of terms in what he called 'a typically metaphysical way — without their antitheses'[12] creates the effect of a fact-claiming pronouncement; second, to show how bringing back these terms 'to their original home'[13] in everyday speech makes the problems presented by their occurrence in the formulation of views disappear.

Before proceeding to an illustration, something should be said about the semantic relationship between antithetical terms. Terms like 'tall' and 'short' used to describe, say, adult human beings, exemplify an ordinary use, each term having a possible application. Even if all adults were as tall as Watusi, the term 'short' would nevertheless retain its use in the language to refer to adults. Observation establishes the application of terms such as 'tall' and 'short'; and where induction from observation establishes the universal application of a term, the antithesis of the term would, like 'dinosaur', apply to nothing. But observation would not eliminate its having a possible range of application. What might be called empirically descriptive terms function to distinguish between two classes of things even though one class is in fact empty. The fact that one term is never used as a modifying term, e.g. 'griffin', does not affect the possibility of its having more than zero denotation.

An important point about antithetical terms is that they are, so to speak, semantic Siamese twins; one cannot function without the other. Thus, *being tall* implies *not being short*. We cannot have the idea of a tall person without also having the idea of a short person. If in virtue of the fact that one of a pair of antithetical terms had universal application while its semantic twin had none, our language were to change in such a way that the latter term (and its synonyms) lost its place in the language, then its antithesis would cease to function. Both terms equally would pass out of currency — e.g. if 'short' lost its use without restitution being made by the introduction of another term functioning as it does, then 'tall' would also lose its present use. The adjective 'tall' would no longer serve to distinguish between persons, and the denotation of 'tall person' would necessarily be identical with the denotation of 'person'. The sentence 'All adults are tall adults' would reduce to the uninformative tautology 'All adults are adults' instead of to 'All adults are non-short adults'.

Consider the pre-Pythagorean arithmetic, which would normally be described as an arithmetic of rational numbers. *We* could say that all numbers of that system are rational, since in our arithmetic both 'rational' and 'irrational' have an application. But if we, like the pre-Pythagoreans, had ideas only of such sequences as $1, \frac{1}{2}, \frac{1}{4}, \frac{1}{8}, \ldots$ and $1, \frac{1}{2}, 2, \frac{1}{3}, 3, \frac{1}{4}, \frac{2}{3}, \frac{3}{2}, 4, \frac{1}{5}, \ldots$, there would be no term 'irrational' to refer to numbers, and neither would there be the term 'rational'. Neither word would have a use to refer to a property of a number. In these circumstances, anyone who was asked to cite a rational number would not understand the request, as the word 'rational' would have no place in his notation. He would be in the same situation as a citizen of Emerald City who was asked to fetch a green thing.

In the present paper our concern will be with pairs of antithetical terms of a special kind, of which one member is declared to be self-contradictory. The attempt will be made to show that certain philosophical theories are brought into existence by considerations professing to establish that one of a pair of antithetical terms implies a contradiction. It perhaps does not need to be argued that an inconsistent expression such as 'round square' (i.e. one which stands for an inconsistent concept), has no conceivable denotation. Unlike an expression which lacks denotation as a matter of empirical fact, (e.g. 'dinosaur') its having no denotation is by logical necessity: the term 'round square' has no use in the language of geometry to refer to a figure; it is not the name of a defining property of a class and therefore cannot have even zero denotation. An *a priori* true general proposition such as *All prime numbers > 2 are odd* implies the universal application of *odd* to primes > 2; and its equivalent, *There is no even prime > 2*, implies that *even prime > 2* has no theoretical denotation. The effect of these facts on the mathematician's language is to deny to the expression 'even prime > 2' any use to refer to a prime. And the descriptive force of the expression 'odd prime > 2' is no more than 'prime > 2'. In general, it may be said that the outcome of a *reductio ad absurdum* proof is the perception of a fact about the use of an expression in the language, namely, that it does not function descriptively. Anyone who follows the proof accepts this outcome.

Although philosophical theories have the appearance of being statements about things, arguments brought in support of them resemble in some respects *reductio ad absurdum* proofs of mathematics. To cite a paradigm example, Zeno's 'proof' that motion is impossible consists in arguing that the concept *motion* implies a contradiction. Disregarding the question whether this philosophical statement is about the world — as indeed it seems to be — we have to conclude that the argument appears to relegate the antithesis of *in motion*, namely, *stationary*, to the status of *odd prime > 2*. Its intent is to demonstrate that *stationary* applies to all bodies, just as *odd* applies to all primes > 2, and that *moving*, like *even prime > 2*, has no possible application.

Other attempts to establish philosophical contradictions in concepts are well known. Berkeley's argument against 'the absolute existence of unthinking things',[14] Bradley's argument that all relations are internal, Hobbes' argument that all desires are selfish, and the more recent claim by some logical positivists that nothing but mathematical propositions and basic propositions can be certain. Consider Berkeley's view that there can be no such thing as an unthinking substance existing independently of perception. 'Objects perceived by the senses', he says, 'are . . . nothing but combinations of [sensible] qualities',[15] and he urges us to 'look into [our] thoughts, and so trying whether we can conceive it possible for a sound, or figure, or motion, or colour to exist without the mind or unperceived.'[16] Various reasons led to the conclusion that what Locke contended for 'is a downright contradiction'.[17] The least inquiry into our thoughts, he says, makes it evident that '*the absolute existence of sensible objects in themselves*, or *without the mind* . . . mark out either a direct contradiction, or else nothing at all',[18] 'the very existence of an *unthinking being* consists in *being perceived*'.[19]

It is plain from Berkeley's words that he is maintaining that the antithesis of 'unperceived sensible object', namely, 'perceived sensible object', has universal application to objects such as chairs and tables. 'Things perceived by sense may be termed *external*, he says, 'with regard to their origin, in that they are not generated from within by the mind itself, but imprinted by a Spirit'.[20] Thus everything, 'all the choir of heaven and furniture of the earth . . . [have subsistence only in] a mind'.[21] Now, if Berkeley's claim were analogous to the conclusion of a mathematical *reductio ad absurdum* proof, 'unperceived sensible object' would cease to have a use to refer to anything. And 'perceived sensible object', since it denotes every conceivable object, would contract into 'sensible object'. Nevertheless, anyone who use the term 'unperceived thing', or more specific terms such as 'star in another galaxy', knows that in our language these terms are contradiction-free — Berkeley included, as he acknowledged in allowing that it is 'more proper and conformable to custom'[22] that objects in nature 'be called *things* rather than *ideas*'.[23] Had he demonstrated an inconsistency in the concept *unperceived sensible object*, then scientists who communicate to each other the discovery of hitherto unknown natural objects would be in the position of conveying information by means of terms having no use to refer to things. It is only in the special philosophical language of Berkeley that 'unperceived sensible object' denotes a contradiction. But, as he himself makes clear, he does not expect, or intend, any modification of 'the speech of the vulgar', in which 'perceived object' and 'unperceived object' behave like a pair of antithetical terms such as 'tall' and 'short'.

It has already been indicated that if either of two antithetical terms which behave like 'tall' and 'short' had as a matter of fact no denotation, this fact would be established by observation. In the case of antithetical terms such as 'odd prime > 2' and 'even prime > 2', empirical observation is irrelevant to deciding whether they have an application.[24] Berkeley's view appears to state a matter of fact about things, but if indeed it does, it would have support in empirical evidence. Instead of evidence, however, Berkeley produces an argument. (Parenthetically, it might be said that a philosophical claim about what there is has its support in what is naturally taken to be a demonstration.) Berkeley seems to be demonstrating the same sort of thing about *unperceived sensible object* that can be demonstrated about *even prime > 2*, which is that it 'marks out a direct contradiction'. Nevertheless, there is an important difference between *All primes > 2 are odd* and *All sensible objects depend for their existence on being perceived*: the fact that there is an entailment between *being a prime > 2* and *being odd* is paralleled by the fact about usage that 'even prime > 2' has no use to refer to anything, whereas the *purported* entailment between *being a sensible object* and *being perceived* is associated with no fact of usage. Berkeley's explicit claim implies that 'unperceived sensible object' has no descriptive use.

It is important in the present context to keep in mind that this consequence is coupled with the fact that both antithetical terms retain their function in ordinary discourse. Taken jointly they imply that the contradiction Berkeley 'uncovers' in 'unperceived sensible object' does not exist. Therefore, either Berkeley is mistaken in thinking a term of ordinary language is self-contradictory or else he has *imported* a contrived contradiction into it. We cannot think that he has a mistaken idea about actual usage,[25] since while 'thinking with the learned' at the same time he speaks with the vulgar and shows his knowledge of the language of the vulgar by his advice to speak with the vulgar as they speak. The language of the learned cannot therefore be constituted of mistaken claims about ordinary language. It can only be supposed that a verbal game is being played. To hold that 'sensible object existing unperceived' is a contradiction comes to a holiday[26] suppression of phrases like 'the ink in my fountain pen' and 'the pound note in my wallet'. Only a contrived, holiday contradiction can coexist with actual use.

Furthermore, the antithesis of 'unperceived sensible object' has an anomalous position in Berkeley's language game. If an entailment between *being a sensible object* and *being perceived* had been demonstrated, then 'perceived sensible object' would have been shown to mean the same as 'sensible object', and 'perceived' would have no use to distinguish among sensible objects. Despite this, Berkeley retains the word as if it functioned like 'tall' in the sentence 'All adults are tall'. The sentence, 'A sensible object is a perceived object' masquerades as the pronouncement of a theory about things. The use of the phrase 'perceived object' occurring in Berkeley's claim is as contrived as the contradictoriness of its antithesis: its application is stretched by semantic fiat to apply to all things. By rejecting one antithetical term and retaining the other, Berkeley creates the impression that a theory about things is being advanced. The linguistic mechanics by which his 'theory' is made to spring into existence is the combination, in the philosophical language of the subjective idealist, of a manufactured contradiction in one term and the artificial retention of the other. The result of this manoeuvring with language is the illusion that a theory is being presented.

The way to dispel the illusion of there being a theory can now be readily seen. Where antithetical terms are involved, Wittgenstein's recommendation to 'destroy the outward similarity between a metaphysical proposition and an experiential one' will consist in 'bringing words back from their metaphysical to their ordinary usage', that is, reinstating an academically banished term. All that is required is to call attention to the fact that this term has a use in the language, which implies that it is not self-contradictory. In consequence the artificially stretched antithesis is restored to its actual range of denotation. To return to our example, if 'unperceived object' is brought back 'to its original home', where it has a possible application, its antithesis 'perceived object' will be restored to its use, and both terms equally will have a use to distinguish between objects. When this is done, the philosophical theory disappears, and with it the controversies surrounding it.

Notes

1. *Philosophical Investigations*, p. 51.
2. Ibid.
3. Ibid., p. 49
4. Ibid., p. 51.
5. Ibid.
6. Ibid., p. 50.
7. Ibid., p. 51.
8. Ibid., p. 122.
9. *The Blue Book*, p. 57.

10. *Wittgenstein's Lectures, Cambridge 1932–1935*, from the notes of Alice Ambrose and Margaret Macdonald, ed. Alice Ambrose, p. 69.

11. *The Blue Book*, p. 55.

12. Ibid., p. 46.

13. *Philosophical Investigations*, p. 48.

14. *The Principles of Human Knowledge* (1929), in *Berkeley. Essays, Principles, Dialogues,* ed. Mary Whiton Calkins, New York: Scribners, p. 137.

15. Ibid., p. 175.

16. Ibid., p. 135.

17. Ibid., p. 136.

18. Ibid., p. 137.

19. Ibid., p. 173.

20. Ibid., pp. 174–5.

21. Ibid., p. 127.

22. Ibid., p. 144.

23. Ibid.

24. For a different (philosophical) position, see C. I. Lewis, *An Analysis of Knowledge and Valuation*, pp. 91–3.

25. Samuel Johnson, in kicking the stone, implied that he took Berkeley to be following ordinary linguistic conventions and expressing a false belief about things.

26. Wittgenstein said that 'philosophical problems arise when language goes on holiday', *Philosophical Investigations*, p. 19.

PUBLICATIONS

Alice Ambrose

'Finitism in Mathematics', *Mind*, 44 (1935), 186–203, 317–40

'The Nature of The Question, Are There Three Consecutive 7's in the Development of π?', *Michigan Academy of Science, Arts and Letters* (1936), pp. 505–13

'Finitism and the Limits of Empiricism', *Mind*, 46 (1937), 379–85; and in her *Essays in Analysis* (1966)

'Moore's "Proof of an External World"', in P. A. Schilpp (ed.) *The Philosophy of G. E. Moore*, ('The Library of Living Philosophers', vol. IV, 1942), 395–419; and in her *Essays in Analysis* (1966)

'Self-contradictory Suppositions', *Mind*, 53 (1944); and in her *Essays in Analysis* (1966)

'The Problem of Justifying Inductive Inference', *Jour. of Philosophy* 44 (1947), 253–72; and in her *Essays in Analysis* (1966)

'Everett J. Nelson on "The Relation of Logic to Metaphysics"', *Philosophical Review*, 58 (1949), 12–15

'The Problem of Linguistic Inadequacy', in Max Black (ed.) *Philosophical Analysis*, 1950, 15–38; and in her *Essays in Analysis (1966)*

'Linguistic Approaches to Philosophical Problems', *Jour. of Philosophy* 49 (1952), 289–301; and in her *Essays in Analysis* (1966)

'On Entailment and Logical Necessity', *Proc. of Aristotelian Soc*, 56 (1956), 241–58; and in her *Essays in Analysis* (1966)

'Wittgenstein on Some Questions in Foundations of Mathematics', *Jour. of Philosophy*, 52 (1955), 197–213; and in K. T. Fann (ed.) *Wittgenstein. The Man and His Philosophy: An Anthology* (1967), 265–83; and in her *Essays in Analysis* (1966); and in S. G. Shanker (ed.) *Ludwig Wittgenstein: Critical Assessments*, vol. III (1985).

'Proof and the Theorem Proved', *Mind*, 68 (1959), 435–45; and in her *Essays in Analysis* (1966)

'Three Aspects of Moore's Philosophy', *Jour. of Philosophy*, 57 (1960), 516–24; and in A. Ambrose and M. Lazerowitz (eds) *G. E. Moore. Essays in Retrospect* (1970); and in her *Essays in Analysis* (1966)

'Philosophical Doubts', *Massachusetts Review*, 1 (1960), 270–90

'Austin's *Philosophical Papers*', *Philosophy*, 38 (1963), 201–17

Essays in Analysis (George Allen & Unwin, London; Humanities Press, New York, 1966), 263

'Invention and Discovery', in her *Essays in Analysis* (1966), 66–87; and in S. G. Shanker (ed.) *Necessity and Language* (1985)

'Wittgenstein on Universals', in W. E. Kennick and M. Lazerowitz (eds) *Metaphysics. Readings and Reappraisals* (1966), 80–91; and in A. Ambrose, *Essays in Analysis* (1966); and in K. T. Fann (ed.) *Wittgenstein. The Man and His Philosophy: An Anthology* (1967)

'Unknowables and Logical Atomism', in her *Essays in Analysis* (1966), 122–42; and as 'Incognosseibles y Atomismo logico', *Dianoia* sección segunda (1966), pp 183–200.

'Factual, Mathematical and Metaphysical Inventories', in *Essays in Analysis* (1966), 233–57, and in S. G. Shanker (ed.) *Necessity and Language* (1985)

'Metamorphoses of the Principle of Verifiability', in F. C. Dommeyer (ed.) *Current Philosophical Issues, Essays in Honor of Curt John Ducasse* (Springfield, Illinois, Charles C. Thomas, 1966), 54–79

'Internal Relations', *Philosophical Review*, 21 (1967), 256–61

'On Criteria of Literal Significance', *Crítica*, 1 (1967), 49–72

'The Revolution in Philosophy', *Massachusetts Review*, 9 (1968), 551–65

'The Changing Face of Philosophy', (The Katherine Asher Engel Lecture, Smith College), (1968), 3–27

'Philosophy, Language and Illusion' in Charles Hanly and M. Lazerowitz (eds) *Psychoanalysis and Philosophy* (International Universities Press, New York, 1970), 14–34

'Mathematical Generality', in A. Ambrose and M. Lazerowitz (eds) *Ludwig Wittgenstein. Philosophy and Language* (1972), 287–318; and in S. G. Shanker (ed.) *Necessity and Language* (1985)

'Believing Necessary Propositions', *Mind*, 83 (1974), 286–90

'Commanding a Clear View of Philosophy', Presidential Address to American Philosophical Assoc. (1975), 63–78; and in M. Lazerowitz and A. Ambrose *Essays in the Unknown Wittgenstein* (Prometheus Books, Buffalo, New York, 1984)

'The Yellow Book Notes in Relation to *The Blue Book*', *Crítica*, 9 (1977), 3–23; and in M. Lazerowitz and A. Ambrose *Essays in the Unknown Wittgenstein* (1984)

'The Defense of Common Sense', *Philosophical Investigations*, 1 (1978), 1–13

'Is Philosophy "an Idleness in Mathematics"?', in George W. Roberts (ed.) *Bertrand Russell Memorial Volume* (1979), 105–28; and in M. Lazerowitz and A. Ambrose *Essays in the Unknown Wittgenstein* (1984)

'Wittgenstein on Mathematical Proof', *Mind*, 91 (1982), 264–72; and in M. Lazerowitz and A. Ambrose *Essays in the Unknown Wittgenstein*

(ed.) *Wittgenstein's Lectures. Cambridge, 1932–35*. From the Notes of Alice Ambrose and Margaret Macdonald (Rowman & Littlefield, Totowa, New Jersey; and Basil Blackwell, Oxford, 1979; and University of Chicago Press, 1982), 226

Morris Lazerowitz

'Tautologies and the Matrix Method', *Mind*, 46 (1937), 191–205

'The Principle of Verifiability', *Mind*, 46 (1937), 372–8

'"Penumbral" Functions', *Mind*, 47 (1938), 58–60

'The Null Class of Premises', *Mind*, 47 (1938), 357–60

'Meaninglessness and Conventional Use', *Analysis* (1938)

'Strong and Weak Verification', *Mind*, 48 (1939), 202–13

'Self-contradictory Propositions', *Philosophy of Science*, 7 (1940), 229–40

'Moore's Paradox', in P. A. Schilpp (ed.) *The Philosophy of G. E. Moore*, ('The Library of Living Philosophers', vol. IV, 1942), 369–95

'The Existence of Universals', *Mind*, 55 (1946), 1–25

'The Positivistic Use of "Nonsense"', *Mind*, 55 (1946), 247–55

'Are Self-contradictory Expressions Meaningless?', *Philosophical Review* 58 (1949)

'Strong and Weak Verification II', *Mind*, 59 (1950)

'Substratum', in Max Black (ed.) *Philosophical Analysis* (1950), 176–94

'The Paradoxes of Motion', *Proc. of Aristotelian Soc.*, 51 (1951–52), 261–80

'Negative Terms', *Analysis*, 12 (1952), 51–66; and in Margaret Macdonald (ed.) *Philosophy and Analysis* (1954), 70–87

'Moore and Philosophical Analysis', *Philosophy*, 33 (1958), 193–221

'On Universals. A Review of a Symposium', *Philosophical Review* 67 (1958), 421–4; and in his *Philosophy and Illusion* (1968)

'The Relevance of Psychoanalysis to Philosophy', in Sidney Hook (ed.) *Psychoanalysis, Scientific Method and Philosophy. A Symposium* (New York Univ. Press, 1959), 133– 56; and in his *Studies in Metaphilosophy* (1964)

The Structure of Metaphysics (Routledge & Kegan Paul, London, 1955), 280

'The Hidden Structure of Philosophical Theories', *Massachusetts Review*, 1 (1960), 723–48; and in his *Studies in Metaphilosophy* (1964)

'Philosophy and Psychoanalysis', Japanese Journal (name untranslated) (1963)

'Austin's *Sense and Sensibilia*', *Philosophy*, 38 (1963), 227–43; and in his *Philosophy and Illusion* (1968)

'Moore's *Commonplace Book*', *Philosophy*, 39 (1964), 165–74; and in his *Philosophy and Illusion* (1968)

'Understanding Philosophy', in F. C. Dommeyer (ed.) *Current Philosophical Issues. Essays in Honor of Curt John Ducasse* (Charles C. Thomas, Springfield, Illinois, 1966), 27–54; and in his *Philosophy and Illusion* (1968)

Studies in Metaphilosophy (London, Routledge & Kegan Paul, 1964), 264

'The Metaphysical Concept of Space', in his *Studies in Metaphilosophy* (1964); and in S. G. Shanker (ed.) *Necessity and Language* seccion segunda (1985) 200–15

'Wittgenstein. Post-*Tractatus*', *Dianoia* (1966)

'Philosophy and Illusion', *Crítica*, 1 (1967), 55–77; and in his *Philosophy and Illusion* (1968)

'Time and Temporal Terminology', in his *Philosophy and Illusion* (1968) 141–66; and as 'Tiempo y Terminologie Temporal', *Dialogos* (1968)

Philosophy and Illusion (George Allen & Unwin, London: and Humanities Press, New York, 1968), 262

'Paradoxes', in W. E. Kennick and M. Lazerowitz (eds) *Metaphysics. Readings and Reappraisals* (1966), 366–87; and in his *Philosophy and Illusion* (1968)

'Moore and Linguistic Philosophy', *Yearbook of Japanese Jour. of Philosophy of Science* (1969); and in his *The Language of Philosophy* (1977), 108–26

'Metaphilosophy', *Crítica*, 5 (1971), 3–23; and in his *The Language of Philosophy* (1977)

'Moore's Ontological Program', *Ratio*, 14 (1972), 45–58; and in his *The Language of Philosophy* (1977)

'Necessity and Probability', *Mind*, 83 (1974), 282–5

'A Note on "Metaphilosophy"', *Metaphilosophy*, 1, (1970), 91

'Necessity and Language', in A. Ambrose and M. Lazerowitz (eds) *Ludwig Wittgenstein. Philosophy and Language* (1972), 233–70; and in S. G. Shanker (ed.) *Necessity and Language* (1985)

'The Infinite', in his *The Language of Philosophy* (1977), 141–63; and in George W. Roberts (ed.) *Bertrand Russell Memorial Volume* (George Allen & Unwin, 1979); and in S. G. Shanker (ed.) *Necessity and Language* (1985)

The Language of Philosophy. Freud and Wittgenstein (Reidel, Dordrecht, 1977), 209

'On Talking About Philosophy', *Metaphilosophy*, 8 (1977), 253–6

'The Passing of an Illusion', in his *The Language of Philosophy* (1977) 163–202; and in S. G. Shanker (ed.) *Necessity and Language* (1985)

'The Philosopher and Daydreaming', *Philosophical Investigations*; and rev. version in *Essays in the Unknown Wittgenstein* (1984), 225–33

'Parmenidean Semantics', with William D. Anderson, *Crítica*, 13 (1981), 3–22

'The Flybottle; Wittgenstein and Bouwsma', *Rep. Phil. Pol.*, 5 (1981), 31–42; and in M. Lazerowitz and A. Ambrose (eds) *Essays in the Unknown Wittgenstein* (1984)

'On a Property of a Perfect Being', *Mind*, 92 (1983), 257–63; and in M. Lazerowitz and A. Ambrose (eds) *Essays in the Unknown Wittgenstein* (1984)

'Philosophical Semantics', in Alwyn van der Merwe (ed.) *Old and New Questions in Physics, Cosmology, Philosophy, and Theoretical Biology. Essays in Honor of Wolfgang Yourgrau* (1983) Plenum Publishing Corp., New York

'Cassandra in Philosophy' (Katherine Asher Engel Lecture, Smith College, 1983), 5–18

'The Problem of Justifying Induction', in Charles Hanly and M. Lazerowitz (eds) *Psychoanalysis and Philosophy*, (International Universities Press, New York, 1970), 210–56

Morris Lazerowitz and Alice Ambrose in S. G. Shanker (ed.) *Necessity and Language* (Croom Helm, London, 1985)

Joint Publications

Fundamentals of Symbolic Logic (Holt, Rinehart & Winston, New York, 1948; rev. ed., 1962), 328; and as *Fundamentos de Lógica Symbólica* (Instituto de Investigaciones Filosóficas, Universidad Nacional Autónoma de México, 1968), traduccíor de Francisco Gonzalez Avamburo, ed. José Antonio Robles

Logic: The Theory of Formal Inference (Holt, Rinehart & Winston, New York, 1961; rev. ed., *Scientia*, Aalen, Germany, 1972), 78

'Ludwig Wittgenstein. Philosophy, Experiment and Proof', in C. A. Mace (ed.) *British Philosophy in the Mid-Century* (2nd ed., 1966), 155–201; Part I by M. Lazerowitz 'Wittgenstein on the Nature of Philosophy', reprinted in K. T. Fann (ed.) *Wittgenstein: The Man and his Philosophy* (1967); and in his *Philosophy and Illusion* (1968)

'Assuming the Logically Impossible', *Metaphilosophy*, 15 (1984), 91–100; and in S. G. Shanker (ed.) *Necessity and Language* (1985)

Philosophical Theories, (Mouton, Paris, The Hague, 1976), 304

Essays in the Unknown Wittgenstein (Prometheus Books, Buffalo, New York, 1984), 233

'Fiction and the Square of Opposition', *Yearbook of Japanese Jour. of Philosophy of Science* (1969), 145–61

'*A Priori* Truths and Empirical Confirmation', *Crítica*, vol. 15, no. 44 (1983), 43–51; and in S. G. Shanker (ed.) *Necessity and Language* (1985)

Joint Editors

G. E. Moore. Essays in Retrospect (George Allen & Unwin, London, 1970), 376

Ludwig Wittgenstein. Philosophy and Language (George Allen & Unwin, London, 1972), 325

INDEX OF NAMES